WILLIAMS-SONOMA

Vegetarian

The Best of Williams-Sonoma Kitchen Library

Vegetarian

GENERAL EDITOR
CHUCK WILLIAMS

RECIPE PHOTOGRAPHY
ALLAN ROSENBERG

Contents

Introduction

Today, many lovers of good food think of themselves at least sometimes as vegetarian. Perhaps, like growing numbers of people, you eat a vegetarian diet full-time out of ethical beliefs or health concerns. But you might also consider yourself a vegetarian just once or twice a week when you make a meatless main course or when dining out at a vegetarian restaurant. Or perhaps you are so dazzled by the fresh produce in farmers' markets and well-stocked food stores, and so aware of their nutritional benefits, that you sometimes do not even think of adding meat, poultry, or seafood to the menu, or use them just sparingly.

In short, it is easier than ever to think of yourself as a vegetarian, a fact celebrated by this book. For full-time and part-time vegetarians alike, the following pages provide a guide to selecting and cooking with vegetables, beans, legumes, grains, pastas, eggs, and cheeses, along with a generous collection of 197 international recipes from which you can build countless vegetarian meals or simply enhance your diet with more delicious vegetarian recipes. You will find Italian favorites such as Bruschetta Primavera and Spaghetti with Marinara Sauce. French-inspired dishes include Spiced Lentils and a Classic Cheese Soufflé. There are lively tastes of American regional cooking such as Roasted Cajun Potatoes and Farmers' Market Corn Custard. Familiar specialties abound from other parts of the world, too, including Asia (Sesame Treasure Vegetables, Noodles with Spicy Peanut Sauce, Tofu-Vegetable Fried Rice), the Middle East (Hummus, Tabbouleh, Falafel Burgers with Tahini Mayonnaise), and Latin America (Mexican Layered Tortillas and Pinto Beans, Chili with Cornmeal Dumplings, Tostada Salad with Tomatillo Salsa).

A GARDENFUL OF CHOICES

The good earth yields a true cornucopia of vegetables. Leaves, from lettuces to spinach to hearty dark greens such as kale and Swiss chard. The cabbage family, embracing white, purple, and green cabbages, juicy-crisp napa cabbage, cauliflower, broccoli, and Brussels sprouts. Stalks, shoots, and buds such as celery, asparagus, and artichokes. Root vegetables including carrots, turnips, parsnips, and beets, and the starchy tubers comprising potatoes and sweet potatoes. Mushrooms, from familiar white buttons to Asian specialties such as shiitake and oyster mushrooms to wild varieties such as chanterelles and morels. Pungent onions, shallots, and garlic. And a whole category of vegetable fruits, so named because, though eaten as vegetables they are botanically classified as fruits, including tomatoes, eggplants, mild bell peppers, hot chiles, soft-skinned and hard-shelled squashes.

The nutritional benefits of vegetables are just as varied and generous. They abound in vitamins and minerals, including vitamins A and C, potassium, folate, and even calcium, present in dark leafy greens. Vegetables are rich sources of dietary fiber, too, while being low in fat and calories.

There are many cooking methods suited to vegetables. Boiling and steaming present them at their most pristine, as in Poached Asparagus, and also serve as a preliminary step before puréeing for dishes like Olive Oil Mashed Potatoes. Gentle braising or stewing is often used to mingle flavors, as in North African Vegetable Stew or Braised Fennel. Sautéing and stir-frying yield vibrant, tender-crisp results as diverse as Stir-fried Swiss Chard with Feta Cheese and Sautéed Potatoes with and Mushrooms with Goat Cheese. Roasting and baking intensify flavors while producing tenderness; try using dense vegetables such as tubers and roots (Baked Beets with Orange) and winter squashes (Baked Acorn Squash with Chutney). Grilling adds delicious smoky charring while bringing tenderness to vegetables from onions to peppers to asparagus, all of which join forces in Mixed Vegetable Grill.

Whatever the method, success begins with buying the best produce that you can find. Nowadays, most vegetables can be shipped to markets from just about everywhere but shopping at your local farmers' market or a well-stocked food store will ensure the best quality. When choosing vegetables, you will always get the best value if you buy whatever is in season and grown locally. And, of course, many vegetable lovers grow delicious vegetables in their home gardens too.

LEGUMES: STAPLES FROM THE POD

Beans, peas, and lentils, also known as pulses or legumes, are all plump seeds that form inside pods and are specifically grown and harvested to be dried, shelled, and stored for future cooking. (Some are also eaten fresh.) The category presents a colorful array of shapes, sizes, and colors, as well as a range of earthy to almost sweet flavors and robust, satisfying textures. Familiar dried peas include split green and yellow peas and large, tan chickpeas. Lentils range from green to yellow, red to brown to black. Another bean of note is the protein-rich soybean, which is most often commercially processed to make the custardy vegetarian staple called tofu.

All these dried seeds are outstanding sources of protein, fiber, complex carbohydrates, vitamins, and minerals. Being easy to store for up to a year in dried form, they have become dietary staples of cultures around the world, a fact well evidenced in such recipes as Lentil Salad with Red Pepper, Mint, and Feta; Three-Bean Vegetarian Chili; and Spiced Black-eyed Peas with Yogurt and Ginger.

Today's heightened awareness of healthy eating has made beans, peas, and lentils more widely available than ever before. Seek a source that has a good, regular turnover of product, whether the legumes are sold in bulk or in plastic bags, because older beans tend to be drier and take longer to cook. Inspect the product, rejecting any that are shriveled or show signs of mold, an indication of improper drying. Buy only as much as you plan to cook within a few months, and store in airtight, labeled, and dated containers in your pantry.

Always allow sufficient time before cooking dried beans to presoak them as directed in the recipe, an essential rehydration step. Dried peas (except for chickpeas) and lentils, being smaller and less dense, with thinner skins, require no presoaking. Virtually all bean, dried pea, and lentil dishes freeze well for up to a year; after cooking, let them cool thoroughly before packing in airtight, freezer-safe containers.

FROM THE GRANARY

Grains, the edible seeds of cultivated grasses, form the cornerstone of many vegetarian meals. This broad category includes all kinds of rice, from long, slender basmati grains to the short, plump Arborio variety to unmilled brown rice with its chewy hull intact; and corn, which when dried and ground becomes versatile cornmeal, also known by the Italian term polenta. Wheat, of course, is also a grain, and apart from its role in baked goods is probably most popular when its flour is transformed into pasta and other noodles.

Grains may be steamed to make fluffy pilafs such as Basmati Rice with Dried Fruits and Nuts. Simmer and stir grains and you get smooth, creamy-textured dishes like Risotto with Mozzarella and Sun-Dried Tomatoes or Polenta with Vegetable Ragout. Of course, all you have to do is boil pasta and it is ready to top with a sauce, as in Fettuccine with Cranberry Beans and Pesto; or to layer and bake in a casserole, such as Green and White Lasagne.

Well-stocked food stores offer an assortment of grains. When shopping for rice, select the right variety for the recipe. With pasta, pick the type called for or substitute one of similar size and shape to best complement the sauce or topping. Grains or pasta can be stored in airtight containers at room temperature for up to a year.

KEY PROTEIN SOURCES:
EGGS AND CHEESE

For many vegetarians, eggs and cheese are key sources of nutrients. Eggs supply protein, vitamins A, D, and E, and such minerals as phosphorous, manganese, iron, calcium, and zinc.

Of course, the primary appeal of these two popular ingredients lies in their taste and versatility. Eggs can be cooked on their own by boiling, poaching, scrambling, frying, or baking. Whip egg whites until foamy, fold in a sauce enriched with cheese, bake in the oven, and an airy soufflé miraculously rises.

Buy eggs that are labeled AA, an indication of the highest quality and of freshness at the time that they are packed. Grade A, the next level, are also fine. As for size, large eggs are used in the development of most recipes unless otherwise specified. Always check inside the carton to make sure the shells are uncracked and clean; look at the sell-by date, too, so you will buy the freshest eggs available. Refrigerated unbroken eggs will stay fresh as long as 5 weeks past their sell-by date.

A good cheese shop, delicatessen, or food store with a rapid turnover of product is the best place to buy cheeses. Whenever possible, ask for cheeses freshly cut from a larger wheel or block, and avoid those that

lack uniform color or veining or are cracked or discolored near their rinds. Refrigerate cheeses, wrapped in waxed paper to hold in their moisture and then tightly sealed in plastic wrap, for up to 1 1/2 weeks for softer varieties like Brie, jack, or creamy goat cheese; 2 to 4 weeks for harder varieties such as Cheddar or Swiss; and up to 10 months for very hard aged cheeses such as Parmesan.

PUTTING IT ALL TOGETHER

There you have it: a wide and appetizing array of every category of recipe that could be considered vegetarian. In addition, this book concludes with a chapter of the basics you may need, including a flavorful Vegetable Stock; sauces and salsas including Pesto Sauce, Tomato Sauce, and Tomato Salsa; a basic, versatile salad dressing; such condiments as Red Pepper Aioli and Tahini Mayonnaise; and a few other essential recipes such as Classic Risotto and Steamed White Rice.

Let this collection be your fundamental guide if you have devoted yourself to a vegetarian lifestyle, planning daily and weekly menus from a wide assortment of recipes for a well-balanced diet. If you are happy being a part-time vegetarian, please let this book provide a constant source of inspiration as you add new, delicious vegetable, bean, grain, egg, or cheese dishes to your repertoire. How you use it is entirely, and delightfully, up to you.

Starters & Salads

Guacamole

This classic dip is simply made from ripe avocados, onion, chiles, tomatoes, and cilantro. To reduce the hotness of the dish, seed the chile peppers before chopping. Accompany the guacamole with tortilla chips or raw vegetables for dipping.

2 large ripe avocados

1 tablespoon finely chopped onion

1 or 2 fresh serrano chile peppers, finely chopped

2 fresh cilantro (fresh coriander) sprigs, finely chopped

Fresh lime juice

Salt

Cut each avocado in half, remove the pits and scoop out the pulp into a bowl. Mash lightly with a fork.

Add the onion, chiles, tomato, and cilantro and stir with a fork until well mixed. Season to taste with lime juice and salt.

Serve immediately, as guacamole gradually darkens when exposed to the air.

Makes about 2 cups (1 lb/500 g); Serves 6

Roasted Eggplant with Pita

If you make this low-fat dish ahead of time, wait until just before serving to fold in the mint and almonds. The recipe can easily be halved to serve 6; use 2 medium eggplants instead of 3 large ones.

3 large eggplants (aubergines)

2/3 cup (3 oz/90 g) almonds

1 cup (8 oz/250 g) plain nonfat yogurt

2 tablespoons lemon juice, or to taste

1 tablespoon minced garlic

1 teaspoon minced jalapeño chile, or more to taste

2 teaspoons ground cumin

Salt and ground pepper to taste

1/4 cup (1/3 oz/10 g) chopped fresh mint

4 pita bread rounds, each cut into 6 wedges

Preheat an oven to 400°F (200°C). Place the eggplants on a baking sheet and prick all over with a fork. Roast, tuning occasionally for even cooking, until the eggplants are soft and tender, about 1 hour. Remove from the oven and let sit until cool enough to handle. Using a vegetable peeler, peel the eggplants and place the pulp in a colander to drain for about 30 minutes.

Reduce the oven temperature to 350°F (180°C). Spread the almonds on a baking sheet and toast until lightly colored and fragrant, 5–7 minutes. Remove from the oven, let cool, and chop; set aside.

Place the eggplant pulp in a food processor or blender and pulse to purée. Add the yogurt, lemon juice, garlic, chile, and cumin. Pulse briefly to mix. Add the salt and pepper to taste.

Transfer the purée to a serving bowl. (If desired, cover and refrigerate for up to 6 hours.) Stir in the chopped almonds and mint. Serve with the pita wedges.

Serves 12

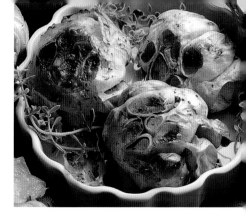

Grill Roasted Garlic

Slow cooking turns a head of garlic mellow, with each clove becoming soft and creamy. To eat, squeeze the whole cloves free of their skins and onto crackers or thinly sliced French bread.

Prepare a fire for indirect-heat cooking in a covered grill (page 310). Position the grill rack 4–6 inches (10—15 cm) above the fire.

Using a sharp knife, slice off the top $^{1}/_{4}$–$^{1}/_{2}$ inch (6–12 mm) from each garlic head. Rub off some of the loose papery skin covering each head, taking care to keep the heads intact. In a small bowl, combine the garlic heads, olive oil, thyme, $^{1}/_{2}$ teaspoon salt, and $^{1}/_{2}$ teaspoon pepper. Toss to combine and coat the garlic evenly.

Place the garlic heads on the center of the rack, cover the grill, and open the vents halfway. Cook, turning the garlic heads three or four times, until the cloves feel very soft when squeezed gently with tongs or your fingers, 35–40 minutes. Don't worry if the skin chars in spots.

Remove from the grill and serve warm onto thinly sliced French bread or crackers.

Serves 4

4 heads garlic

2 tablespoons olive oil

1 tablespoon chopped fresh thyme or $^{1}/_{2}$ teaspoon dried thyme

Salt and freshly ground pepper

1 loaf thinly sliced French bread or crackers

Bruschetta Primavera

Use a long, slender baguette-type loaf for the bread and cut the slices on the diagonal. The brief grilling this recipe requires can easily be done at the last minute over an existing fire or in a grilling pan placed on the stove.

Prepare a fire for direct-heat cooking in a grill (page 309). Position the grill rack 4–6 inches (10–15 cm) above the fire.

In a small bowl, stir together the tomatoes, parsley, basil, minced garlic, $^1/_2$ teaspoon salt, and $^1/_4$ teaspoon pepper. Set aside.

Arrange the bread slices on the rack. Grill, turning two or three times, until the bread is golden brown on both sides, about 3 minutes total.

Remove from the grill and immediately rub one side of each slice with a cut garlic clove, pressing the garlic into the surface of the bread. Discard the garlic clove. Brush or drizzle the olive oil over the same side of the bread. Top each slice with about 1 tablespoon of the tomato mixture and place on a platter. Serve as soon as possible. If left to stand, the bread will gradually soften, although it will still taste good.

Serves 4–6

2 large tomatoes, peeled and seeded (page 313), then diced

$^1/_4$ cup ($^1/_3$ oz/10 g) chopped fresh flat-leaf (Italian) parsley

2 tablespoons chopped fresh basil or 1 teaspoon dried basil

1 large clove garlic, minced, plus 4–6 garlic cloves, halved

Salt and freshly ground pepper

12 slices crusty bread, each about $^1/_2$ inch (12 mm) thick (see note)

$^1/_3$–$^1/_2$ cup (3–4 fl oz/80–125 ml) olive oil

Hummus

A flavorful purée made from chickpeas and tahini (toasted sesame seed paste), hummus is a popular first course in eastern Mediterranean countries. Serve with Parmesan Pita Toasts (page 21).

1 cup (7 oz/220 g) dried chickpeas (garbanzo beans)

Juice of 2–3 lemons

1/2 cup (4 oz/125 g) tahini

3 tablespoons extra-virgin olive oil, plus extra for drizzling

6 cloves garlic, minced

1/4 teaspoon ground cumin

Salt

Paprika, minced fresh flat-leaf (Italian) parsley, black pepper, black olives, and lemon wedges for garnish

Pick over the chickpeas and discard any damaged chickpeas or stones. Rinse the chickpeas. Place in a bowl, add plenty of water to cover, and soak for about 3 hours.

Drain the chickpeas and place in a saucepan with water to cover by 2 inches (5 cm).

Bring to a boil, reduce the heat to low, and simmer, uncovered, until the skins begin to crack and the chickpeas are tender, 45–60 minutes. Drain, reserving the cooking liquid. Set aside a few chickpeas to use as garnish.

In a food processor fitted with the metal blade or in a blender, combine the cooked chickpeas, juice of 2 lemons, tahini, 2 tablespoons of the reserved cooking liquid, the 3 tablespoons olive oil, garlic, cumin, and 3/4 teaspoon salt. Process until a soft, creamy paste forms, adding a little more cooking liquid if needed. Taste and add more lemon juice and salt as needed.

To serve, spread the hummus on a serving plate or place in a bowl. Garnish with paprika, minced parsley, pepper, olives, lemon wedges, and the reserved chickpeas. Drizzle with olive oil. Serve with warmed pita bread for dipping.

Serves 6

Parmesan Pita Toasts

Quick to grill over the still-glowing coals of an existing fire, these easy-to-assemble toasts can be placed on the rack after you've removed the main course. They can also be placed under the broiler for a few minutes.

Prepare a fire for direct-heat cooking in a grill (page 309). Position the grill rack 4–6 inches (10–15 cm) above the fire.

Cut the pita breads in half and gently open the pita "pockets." Sprinkle 1 tablespoon of the Parmesan cheese inside each pocket, then press down firmly on the bread with your hand. Brush both sides of each half with olive oil and sprinkle with salt.

Arrange the pita halves on the rack. Grill, turning two or three times, until the bread is lightly browned and the cheese has melted slightly, 4–5 minutes total.

To serve, cut each half into wedges and arrange on a serving dish. Serve hot.

Serves 4–6

4 pita breads, each about
6 inches (15 cm) in diameter

1/2 cup (2 oz/60 g) grated
Parmesan cheese

Olive oil for brushing

Salt

Asian Turnovers

1 tablespoon Asian sesame oil

1 tablespoon peanut oil

1/2 lb (250 g) napa or savoy cabbage leaves, cut into 1/2-inch (12-mm) pieces

1/2 lb (250 g) sugar snap peas, trimmed and halved on the diagonal

1/2 lb (250 g) fresh mushrooms, brushed clean

6 green (spring) onions

2 tablespoons peeled and minced fresh ginger

1 tablespoon *each* soy sauce and dry sherry

Salt and freshly ground pepper

All-purpose (plain) flour for dusting

1 box (17 1/4 oz/535 g) frozen puff pastry (2 sheets), thawed

2 egg yolks beaten with 2 tablespoons water

FOR THE DIPPING SAUCE:

1/2 cup (4 fl oz/125 ml) soy sauce

1/4 cup (2 fl oz/60 ml) rice wine vinegar

1/2 teaspoon hot-pepper sauce

1/2 teaspoon sugar

1/2 cup (3/4 oz/20 g) chopped fresh cilantro (fresh coriander)

In a large frying pan or wok over medium-high heat, warm the sesame and peanut oils. When the oils are hot, add the cabbage and snap peas and cook, stirring constantly, until the cabbage wilts, 3–4 minutes.

Thinly slice the mushrooms and green onions. Increase the heat to high and add the mushrooms, green onions, ginger, soy sauce, and sherry. Cook, stirring constantly, until the mushrooms are soft and the mixture is dry, about 5 minutes. Transfer to a bowl and season to taste with salt and pepper. Let cool completely.

Preheat the oven to 400°F (200°C).

To assemble the turnovers, on a well-floured surface and using a floured rolling pin, roll out 1 puff pastry sheet about 1/8 inch (3 mm) thick. Using a round cutter 4 inches (10 cm) in diameter, cut out 8 rounds from the dough. Place about 2 tablespoons of the filling on one-half of a round. Brush the edges of the opposite half lightly with the egg-water mixture. Fold the round in half to enclose the filling; press the edges together firmly to seal. Repeat with the remaining rounds.

Place the turnovers on an ungreased baking sheet, spacing them about 2 inches (5 cm) apart. Repeat with the remaining pastry sheet and filling. Brush the top side of each turnover with the remaining egg mixture.

Bake until golden, about 15 minutes.

Meanwhile, make the dipping sauce: In a bowl, stir together the soy sauce, vinegar, hot-pepper sauce, sugar, and cilantro until the sugar dissolves and the ingredients are well mixed. Divide evenly among small individual sauce bowls.

Serve the turnovers hot from the oven, accompanied with the dipping sauce.

Makes 16 turnovers; serves 4–6

Zucchini Fritters with Red Pepper Relish

These fritters make a wonderful side dish and work equally well as a first course. Serve them alone or with Garlic Mayonnaise (page 302), Tahini Mayonnaise (page 303), or Tomatillo Salsa (page 303).

Using the large holes on a handheld shredder or a food processor fitted with the shredding blade, shred the zucchini. Place in a colander set over a bowl and sprinkle with $1/2$ teaspoon salt to draw out the moisture. Let stand for 1 hour.

In a bowl, combine the bell peppers, tomato, garlic, cumin, cayenne, olive oil, 1 tablespoon of the lemon juice, and the parsley. Stir to mix well. Season the relish to taste with salt and pepper and additional lemon juice, if needed. Set aside.

Remove the zucchini from the colander and pat dry with paper towels. In a bowl, lightly beat the egg. Sift the flour over the egg and stir to mix well. Stir the zucchini into the egg mixture. Season to taste with pepper and mix well.

In a deep, heavy saucepan, pour in canola oil to a depth of 1 inch (2.5 cm). Heat to 375°F (190°C) on a deep-frying thermometer, or until a small drop of the zucchini mixture sizzles immediately upon contact with the oil. When the oil is hot, drop in the zucchini mixture by tablespoonfuls, a few at a time; do not crowd the pan. Fry, turning once, until golden brown on both sides, 1–2 minutes total. Using a slotted spoon, transfer fritters to a paper towel–lined plate and keep warm until all are cooked. Repeat with the remaining batter.

Transfer the fritters to a warmed platter or individual plates and serve immediately. Pass the pepper relish at the table.

Makes about 24 fritters; serves 6

6 small zucchini (courgettes), $1^{1}/_{4}$ lb (625 g) total weight, trimmed

Salt and freshly ground pepper

2 red bell peppers (capsicums), roasted and peeled (page 308), then finely diced

1 tomato, peeled and seeded (page 313), then finely chopped

1 clove garlic, minced

$1/2$ teaspoon ground cumin

Large pinch of cayenne pepper

1 tablespoon olive oil

$1–1^{1}/_{2}$ tablespoons fresh lemon juice

2 tablespoons chopped fresh flat-leaf (Italian) parsley

1 egg

$2/_{3}$ cup (3 oz/90 g) all-purpose (plain) flour

Canola oil for deep-frying

Baked Potato Crisps

These light, crisp chips take only a little time to prepare. Use olive oil cooking spray to moisten the potatoes lightly. Add a dusting of cayenne pepper and paprika or Parmesan cheese with the herbs, if you like.

2 russet baking potatoes, 1/2–3/4 lb (250–375 g) each, unpeeled and well scrubbed

1 tablespoon olive oil

Salt and freshly ground pepper

1 teaspoon chopped fresh flat-leaf (Italian) parsley (optional)

1 teaspoon minced fresh chives

Preheat the oven to 400°F (200°C).

Grease 2 nonstick baking sheets with olive oil.

Cut the potatoes into slices 1/8 inch (3 mm) thick. Place the potatoes in a bowl and toss with the olive oil to coat evenly. Season to taste with salt and pepper.

Place on the prepared baking sheets. Bake until crisp and browned, 20–25 minutes.

Transfer to a serving dish and toss with the parsley and chives, if desired. Taste and adjust the seasonings. Serve immediately.

Serves 2–4

Pesto Baked Potato Wedges

These tasty wedges make excellent hors d'oeuvres for a cocktail party. Serve them bubbling hot right from the oven. They are also delicious served with Garlic Mayonnaise (page 302) or Red Pepper Aioli (page 303) on the side.

Preheat the oven to 425°F (220°C).

Prick the skin in a few places with a fork. Rub each potato with 1 teaspoon of the oil to coat evenly. Place the potatoes on an ungreased baking sheet in the middle of the oven. Bake until tender when pierced with a knife or skewer, about 1 hour. The potatoes should be cooked through and slightly crisp on the outside. Remove from the oven and set aside until cool enough to handle.

Preheat the broiler (grill).

Cut each potato in half lengthwise and then in half again, to create 4 wedges. Spread the cut sides of each wedge evenly with some of the pesto and place the wedges on an ungreased baking sheet, pesto side up.

Place under the broiler and broil (grill) until bubbling, about 3 minutes. Place on a serving platter and serve immediately.

Serves 2–4

2 medium-sized baking potatoes such as Russet, scrubbed thoroughly to remove dirt and dried with a kitchen towel

3 tablespoons Pesto Sauce (page 301)

Avocado, Grapefruit, and Endive Salad

Serve this simple, refreshing salad as part of a weekend brunch or light, warm-weather dinner. Shop for the avocados a few days in advance to ensure they ripen in time.

FOR THE VINAIGRETTE:

¼ cup (⅓ oz/10 g) lightly packed chopped fresh mint

¼ cup (2 fl oz/60 ml) lemon juice

½ cup (4 fl oz/125 ml) grapefruit juice

1 cup (8 fl oz/250 ml) olive oil

3 tablespoons honey

1 tablespoon grated grapefruit zest

Salt and freshly ground pepper to taste

FOR THE SALAD:

3 pink grapefruits

4 small heads Belgian endive (chicory/witloof), separated into leaves and thinly sliced lengthwise

1 cup (1 oz/30 g) fresh mint leaves, plus ¼ cup (⅓ oz/10 g) chopped fresh mint

3 ripe avocados, halved, pitted, peeled, and thinly sliced lengthwise

To make the vinaigrette, in a small saucepan, combine the chopped mint and lemon juice and bring to a boil. Remove from the heat and let steep for 10 minutes. Strain into a bowl. Add the grapefruit juice, olive oil, honey, and grapefruit zest and whisk together until blended. Season with salt and pepper, then taste and adjust the sweet-tart ration if necessary.

Cut off the top and bottom of each grapefruit. Working with 1 grapefruit at a time, place one of the cut sides down on a work surface. Starting at the top and following the contour of the grapefruit, cut off the skin, including all of the white pith. Holding the grapefruit over a small bowl and using a sharp knife, cut between the grapefruit sections, freeing the sections and dropping them into the bowl. Repeat with the remaining grapefruits. Set aside.

To make the salad, combine the endive leaves and whole mint leaves in a salad bowl. Drizzle with half of the vinaigrette and toss to coat. Place on a serving platter or divide among 6 individual places. Alternate the grapefruit segments and avocado slices atop the greens. Drizzle with the remaining vinaigrette and top with the chopped mint. Serve immediately.

Serves 6

Pineapple Salad with Radicchio and Sprouts

Use alfalfa, sunflower, or soybean sprouts for this delicate, light, and healthful salad. Green leaf lettuce can replace the radicchio. The pineapple may be from a can, but drain it well before adding to the salad.

Line a salad bowl with the radicchio leaves. In another bowl, mix together the pineapple and pine nuts. In a small bowl, stir together the lemon juice, vinegar, sugar, and salt and pepper to taste until well mixed. Add the oil and stir vigorously until well blended.

Pour half of the dressing over the pineapple mixture and mix well. Toss the sprouts with the remaining dressing. Spoon the pineapple mixture atop the radicchio. Garnish with the sprouts and serve.

Serves 4

1 head radicchio (red chicory), separated into leaves

8 slices pineapple, cut into small cubes

1 handful of pine nuts

1 teaspoon fresh lemon juice

1 tablespoon balsamic vinegar

1/2 teaspoon sugar

Salt and freshly ground pepper

1/4 cup (2 fl oz/60 ml) extra-virgin olive oil

1/4 lb (120 g) sprouts (see note)

Warm Spinach Salad
with Artichokes and Gruyère

If pressed for time, skip the artichoke preparation below and use 1 jar (12 oz/375 g) artichoke hearts in brine, drained and quartered. Fresh Parmesan cheese can be substituted for the Gruyère.

2 lemons

12 small artichokes

6 fresh thyme sprigs

6 fresh parsley sprigs

2 bay leaves

10 cloves garlic

1/2 cup (4 fl oz/125 ml) olive oil

Salt and freshly ground pepper

3/4 lb (375 g) baby spinach leaves, carefully washed and well dried

Balsamic and Red Wine Vinegar Dressing (page 302)

3 hard-boiled eggs, peeled and coarsely chopped

2 oz (60 g) Gruyère cheese, shaved into paper-thin strips with a vegetable peeler

Using a vegetable peeler, remove the lemon zest from both lemons and place in a saucepan. Cut the lemons into halves and squeeze the juice into the same pan.

Working with 1 artichoke at a time, pull off the tough outer leaves until you reach the pale green leaves at the center. Cut off the top one-third of the artichoke and trim the stem even with the base. Add the artichoke to the saucepan. Toss gently to coat with the juice. Repeat with the remaining artichokes.

Add the thyme and parsley sprigs, bay leaves, garlic, olive oil, and salt and pepper to taste to the saucepan. Add water just to cover the artichokes. Place a round piece of parchment paper the diameter of the pan directly on top of the artichokes to prevent them from browning. Bring the water to a boil over high heat. Reduce the heat to medium-low and simmer the artichokes until they begin to soften, about 5 minutes. Remove from the heat and let cool.

Meanwhile, place the spinach in a large bowl.

When the artichokes have cooled, drain and cut them lengthwise into quarters. In a frying pan over medium heat, combine the artichokes and dressing and heat, stirring occasionally, until the artichokes are warm, about 2 minutes. Remove from the heat and season to taste with salt and pepper.

Add the artichokes and dressing to the spinach and toss to mix. Immediately transfer to a large serving bowl or individual plates. Garnish with the chopped egg and Gruyère. Serve at once.

Serves 6

Waldorf Salad
with Mustard Dressing

Waldorf salad was created at the original Waldorf Astoria Hotel in New York City. The salad may be assembled, except for the dressing, about 2 hours before the meal, covered and stored in the refrigerator.

3/4 cup (3 oz/90 g) walnut or pecan halves

4 crisp, firm apples, such as pippin, McIntosh, or Rome

Juice of 1 lemon

1 cup (5 oz/155 g) finely diced celery

1/2 cup (3 oz/90 g) diced red bell pepper (capsicum)

3 green (spring) onions, including part of tender green tops, finely chopped

3/4 cup (6 fl oz/180 ml) sour cream

1 tablespoon Dijon mustard

1 1/2 tablespoons honey

1 teaspoon minced fresh mint

Salt and freshly ground pepper

1–2 heads Bibb lettuce

Preheat an oven to 200°F (95°C). Spread the nut halves on a baking sheet and lightly toast in the oven, 6–7 minutes; they should not brown. Chop coarsely and set aside.

Peel, quarter, and core the apples. Cut into 1/2-inch (12-mm) dice and toss with the lemon juice in a bowl. Add the celery, bell pepper, green onions, and nuts. Set aside.

In a separate bowl, combine the sour cream, mustard, honey, and mint. Whisk together until well blended. Season to taste with salt and pepper. (More mustard, honey, or mint may be added, if desired.)

Add the dressing to the apple mixture and mix well.

Separate the lettuce leaves and use only the crisp inner leaves; reserve the larger leaves for another use. Arrange around the rim of a serving plate. Spoon the salad into the center of the plate. Serve immediately.

Serves 8–10

Fennel, Pear, and Frisée Salad

The fennel and greens can be assembled up to 30 minutes ahead of time, but slice the pears and dress the salad just before serving. Use pears such as Comice or Bartlett.

To make the vinaigrette, in a small bowl, stir together the vinegar and grated ginger. Let stand for 5 minutes, then whisk in the sugar and the oil. Season with salt and pepper. Set aside.

To make the salad, trim the tough stems from the frisée or watercress and toss to coat. Divide among 4 plates. Arrange the fennel and pear slices over the greens and drizzle the rest of the vinaigrette over the top. Serve immediately.

Serves 4

FOR THE VINAIGRETTE:

6 tablespoons (3 fl oz/90 ml) white wine vinegar

1 tablespoon peeled and grated fresh ginger

3/4 teaspoon sugar

3/4 cup (6 fl oz/180 ml) olive oil

Salt and ground pepper to taste

FOR THE SALAD:

1 medium head frisée or 2 bunches watercress

2 small fennel bulbs

2 firm but ripe pears

Baked Goat Cheese with Salad Greens

For this salad, select a mixture of salad greens that include red leaf lettuce, radicchio, butter (Boston) lettuce, mustard greens, frisée, mizuna, arugula (rocket), and/or oakleaf lettuce, in any combination.

Preheat the oven to 400°F (200°C).

Cut each cheese round in half horizontally to make 6 rounds in all. Place on a plate and drizzle with the olive oil, turning once to lightly coat both sides. Set aside.

In a small bowl, whisk together the dressing, garlic, and salt and pepper to taste. Set aside.

Spread the bread crumbs on a plate. Coat the rounds of goat cheese on both sides with the crumbs and then place well spaced on a baking sheet. Bake until the cheese rounds are slightly bubbling around the edges, 4–6 minutes.

Place the greens in a bowl and drizzle with the dressing. Toss well and divide the greens among 6 salad plates. Place a hot cheese round in the center of each mound of greens. Serve immediately.

Serves 6

3 small rounds fresh goat cheese, each about $1/4$ lb (125 g), $2^1/2$ inches (6 cm) in diameter, and 1 inch (2.5 cm) thick

2 tablespoons extra-virgin olive oil

Balsamic and Red Wine Vinegar Dressing (page 302)

1 clove garlic, minced

Salt and freshly ground pepper

$1^1/2$ cups (6 oz/185 g) fine dried bread crumbs

4 large handfuls mesclun or mixed salad greens, torn into large bite-sized pieces, carefully washed and well dried

Endive, Fennel, and Walnut Salad

Offer this sophisticated salad as a first course for dinner or as the main course for lunch. Toasted pecans or hazelnuts (filberts) can be used in place of the walnuts.

2 small fennel bulbs with stalks and feathery fronds attached

3 heads Belgian endive (chicory/witloof), cored and cut crosswise into 1-inch (2.5-cm) pieces

1 large head radicchio, cored and thinly sliced

1/2 cup (3 oz/90 g) slivered pitted Kalamata olives

2 tablespoons balsamic vinegar

1 tablespoon plus 1 teaspoon Dijon mustard

1/4 cup (2 fl oz/60 ml) olive oil

Salt and freshly ground pepper

3/4 cup (3 oz/90 g) walnuts, toasted (page 311) and coarsely chopped

8–10 tablespoons (2–1/2 oz/60–75 g) coarsely grated Parmesan cheese

Cut off the stalks and feathery fronds from the fennel bulbs. Reserve the fronds and discard the stalks or reserve for another use. Remove any bruised outer leaves from each bulb and thinly slice the bulbs crosswise. Chop enough of the fronds to measure $^1\!/_4$ cup ($^1\!/_3$ oz/10 g).

In a large bowl, combine the sliced fennel, fennel fronds, endive, radicchio, and olives. Toss to mix.

In a small bowl, whisk together the vinegar and mustard. Gradually whisk in the oil. Add to the salad and toss to coat. Season to taste with salt and pepper and mix in the walnuts.

Divide the salad evenly among individual plates. Sprinkle each serving with 1 tablespoon Parmesan cheese and serve.

Serves 8–10

Green Salad with Mustard-Shallot Vinaigrette

This full-flavored vinaigrette coats the salad greens and adds a little zip to the crunchy cucumbers. You can make the vinaigrette early in the day and toast the walnuts and wash and crisp the greens a few hours ahead.

Preheat an oven to 350° F (180° C). Spread the walnuts on a baking sheet and toast until lightly colored and fragrant, 5–7 minutes. Remove from the oven and let cool.

In a salad bowl, combine the salad greens, cucumbers, walnuts, and dill, if using.

To make the vinaigrette, in a small bowl, whisk together the mustard and vinegar. Gradually whisk in the olive oil until well blended. Stir in the shallots and season with salt and pepper.

Drizzle the vinaigrette over the salad, toss well, and serve.

Serve 6

$1^{1}/_{2}$ cups (6 oz/185 g) walnuts

9 cups (9 oz/280 g) mixed torn salad greens, including romaine (cos) and butter lettuces and watercress

2 cucumbers, peeled, seeded, and diced

3 tablespoons chopped fresh dill (optional)

FOR THE MUSTARD–SHALLOT VINAIGRETTE:

2 tablespoons Dijon mustard

3 tablespoons red wine vinegar

$^{1}/_{2}$ (4 fl oz/125 ml) mild olive oil

$^{1}/_{4}$ ($1^{1}/_{4}$ oz/37 g) minced shallots

Salt and freshly ground pepper to taste

Mixed Bean Salad with Balsamic Dressing

Bursting with colors and flavors, this nutritious salad is made from a medley of beans. Slices of toasted or grilled bread rubbed with garlic and drizzled with olive oil can be served on the side. Serve this salad at room temperature or chilled.

½ cup (3½ oz/105 g) dried black beans

½ cup (3½ oz/105 g) dried black-eyed peas

½ cup (3½ oz/105 g) dried adzuki beans

¼ cup (2 fl oz/60 ml) balsamic vinegar

2 teaspoons Dijon mustard

½ cup (4 fl oz/125 ml) extra-virgin olive oil

Salt and freshly ground pepper

½ lb (250 g) green beans, trimmed and cut into 1-inch (2.5-cm) lengths

1 small red onion, chopped

3 tablespoons chopped fresh flat-leaf (Italian) parsley

Pick over the beans and discard any damaged beans or stones. Rinse the dried beans separately. Place the beans in separate bowls, add plenty of water to cover, and soak for about 3 hours.

Drain the beans and place in separate saucepans with water to cover by 2 inches (5 cm). Bring to a boil, reduce the heat to low, and simmer, uncovered, until the skins begin to crack and the beans are tender, about 1 hour for the black beans, 45 minutes for the black-eyed peas, and 30 minutes for the adzuki beans. Drain and combine in a large bowl.

Meanwhile, in a small bowl, whisk together the vinegar, mustard, olive oil, and salt and pepper to taste. Add to the warm beans, toss well, and let cool.

Bring a saucepan three-fourths full of water to a boil. Add salt to taste and the green beans and boil until tender, 4–5 minutes. Drain and let cool.

Add the green beans, onion, and parsley to the cooled mixed beans. Toss well and serve at room temperature or chilled.

Serves 6

Chickpea Salad with Olives, Green Onions, and Herbs

Adapted from a dish native to the south of France, this recipe can also be made with small white (navy) beans, pinto beans, black beans, cranberry (borlotti) beans, or red or white kidney beans.

Pick over the chickpeas and discard any damaged chickpeas or stones. Rinse the chickpeas. Place in a bowl, add plenty of water to cover, and soak for about 3 hours.

Drain the chickpeas and place in a saucepan with water to cover by 2 inches (5 cm). Bring to a boil, reduce the heat to low, and simmer, uncovered, until tender, 45–60 minutes. Drain and let cool.

In a large bowl, whisk together the vinegar, olive oil, garlic, all the herbs, and salt and pepper to taste. Add the cooled beans, black and green olives, and green onions, and mix until well blended.

Transfer to a serving bowl and serve at room temperature.

Serves 6–8

1 cup (7 oz/220 g) dried chickpeas (garbanzo beans)

1/4 cup (2 fl oz/60 ml) red wine vinegar

6 tablespoons (3 fl oz/90 ml) extra-virgin olive oil

4 cloves garlic, minced

1 tablespoon minced fresh mint

1 tablespoon minced fresh basil

1 teaspoon minced fresh thyme

1 teaspoon minced fresh rosemary

1 teaspoon minced fresh oregano

Salt and freshly ground pepper

1/4 cup (1 oz/30 g) Niçoise or Kalamata olives, pitted and coarsely chopped

1/4 cup (1 oz/30 g) green olives, pitted and coarsely chopped

1 small bunch green (spring) onions, including tender green tops, thinly sliced

Tostada Salad with Tomatillo Salsa

Garnish this Mexican-style salad with sour cream, chopped green (spring) onions, sliced avocados, lime wedges, and cilantro sprigs. Other cheeses, such as Cheddar or mozzarella, can be used in place of the jack cheese.

1 cup (7 oz/220 g) dried black beans

1 cup (8 fl oz/250 ml) corn oil

6 corn tortillas, each 6 inches (15 cm) in diameter

2 cups (8 oz/250 g) coarsely shredded Monterey jack cheese

1 small head romaine (cos) lettuce, carefully washed, well dried, and thinly sliced crosswise

Tomatillo Salsa (page 303) for serving

Pick over the beans and discard any damaged beans or stones. Rinse the beans and drain. Place in a bowl, add plenty of water to cover, and let soak for about 3 hours.

Drain the beans and place in a saucepan with water to cover by 2 inches (5 cm). Bring to a boil, reduce the heat to low, and simmer, uncovered, until the beans are tender, about 1 hour. Remove from the heat and drain. Set aside.

In a frying pan over medium-high heat, warm the corn oil. When it is hot, slip a tortilla into the oil and cook until golden and almost crisp, 1–2 minutes. Using tongs, transfer to paper towels to drain. Repeat with the remaining tortillas.

To serve, place each tortilla on a plate. Distribute the beans, cheese, lettuce, and salsa evenly over the tortillas.

Serves 6

Black Bean Salad
with Bell Peppers and Corn

This striking dish is perfect for summer entertaining and travels well for a picnic. It can be made several hours ahead of time and is an excellent accompaniment to soups. Serve with tortilla chips, if you like.

Pick over the beans and discard any damaged beans or stones. Rinse the beans. Place in a bowl, add plenty of water to cover, and soak for about 3 hours.

Drain the beans and place in a saucepan with water to cover by 2 inches (5 cm). Bring to a boil, reduce the heat to low, and simmer, uncovered, until the skins begin to crack and the beans are tender, 1–1 1/4 hours. Drain and let cool.

Bring a saucepan three-fourths full of lightly salted water to a boil. Add the corn kernels and cook for 1 minute. Drain and let cool.

Cut all of the bell peppers and the red onion into 1/4-inch (6-mm) dice. In a salad bowl, combine the bell peppers, onion, corn, garlic, and parsley and toss to mix. Add the olive oil, vinegar, and salt and pepper to taste and toss again. Add the beans, toss well, and serve.

Serves 6–8

1 cup (7 oz/220 g) dried black beans

Kernels from 1 ear of fresh corn

1/2 red bell pepper (capsicum), seeded and deribbed

1 green bell pepper (capsicum), seeded and deribbed

1 yellow bell pepper (capsicum), seeded and deribbed

1 small red onion

1 clove garlic, minced

3 tablespoons chopped fresh flat-leaf (Italian) parsley

1/2 cup (4 fl oz/125 ml) olive oil

4–5 tablespoons red wine vinegar

Salt and freshly ground pepper

Tabbouleh

For a light, healthful lunch, serve this popular Middle Eastern salad alongside a bowl of Spring Vegetable Soup with Pesto (page 60) or Butternut Squash-Carrot Soup (page 64) and wedges of Parmesan Pita Toasts (page 21).

1 cup (6 oz/185 g) medium-fine bulgur

2/3 cup (5 fl oz/160 ml) extra-virgin olive oil

1 cup (8 fl oz/250 ml) fresh lemon juice, plus more to taste

5 cloves garlic, minced

Salt and freshly ground pepper

6 green (spring) onions, including tender green tops, cut into slices 1/4 inch (6 mm) thick

2 large bunches fresh flat-leaf (Italian) parsley, stemmed and chopped

1/3 cup (1/2 oz/15 g) chopped fresh mint

5 large tomatoes, cut into 1/4-inch (6-mm) dice

2 cucumbers, peeled, halved lengthwise, seeded, and cut into 1/4-inch (6-mm) dice

Warmed pita breads, cut into wedges, or romaine (cos) lettuce leaves for serving

Place the bulgur in the bottom of a large salad bowl. In a small bowl, whisk together the olive oil, the 1 cup (8 fl oz/250 ml) lemon juice, the garlic, and 1 teaspoon salt. Pour over the bulgur and toss well. Layer on top of the bulgur, in the following order, the green onions, parsley, mint, tomatoes, and cucumbers. Season the cucumbers well with salt and pepper and cover the bowl with plastic wrap.

Refrigerate for at least 24 hours or for up to 48 hours.

Bring the salad to room temperature. Toss the ingredients together, then taste and adjust the seasoning with additional salt, pepper, and lemon juice, if necessary.

Serve with warmed pita bread or romaine lettuce leaves for scooping up bitefuls of the salad.

Serves 6–8

Lentil Salad with Red Pepper, Mint, and Feta

Lentils, like most legumes, are a terrific source of protein. Look for green lentils in well-stocked food stores with a high turnover. Fresh goat cheese can be substituted for the feta.

1 cup (7 oz/220 g) dried green lentils

6 tablespoons (2½ fl oz/75 ml) extra-virgin olive oil

5 tablespoons (3 fl oz/80 ml) red wine vinegar, plus more to taste

2 cloves garlic, minced

½ teaspoon ground cumin

Salt and freshly ground pepper

1 small red onion, diced

1 red bell pepper (capsicum), seeded, deribbed, and finely diced

¼ cup (⅓ oz/10 g) chopped fresh mint, plus whole sprigs for garnish

6 oz (185 g) feta cheese, crumbled

Pick over the lentils and discard any damaged lentils or stones. Rinse the lentils and drain. Place in a saucepan and add water to cover by 2 inches (5 cm). Bring to a boil, reduce the heat to medium-low, and simmer, uncovered, until the lentils are tender, 15–20 minutes. Drain immediately and set aside in a large bowl.

In a small bowl, whisk together the olive oil, the 5 tablespoons (3 fl oz/80 ml) vinegar, garlic, cumin, and salt and pepper to taste. Add to the warm lentils and toss together to coat evenly. Add the onion and bell pepper and toss gently. Let stand for 20 minutes at room temperature.

Season to taste with more salt, pepper, and vinegar, if necessary. Add the mint and toss to mix well. Transfer the salad to a platter or individual plates. Sprinkle with the feta, garnish with mint sprigs, and serve.

Serves 6

Couscous Salad with Cucumbers, Peppers, and Tomatoes

This zesty salad is a delicious meal on its own, but it can also be tucked into pita bread with lettuce to serve as a sandwich. It can be made up to 2 hours in advance; cover and refrigerate until ready to serve.

In a saucepan, bring 1 cup (8 fl oz/250 ml) water to a boil. Remove from the heat and add the couscous and $^1/_2$ teaspoon salt. Stir well, cover, and let stand for 10 minutes. Uncover and transfer the couscous to a large, shallow baking dish, fluffing with a fork and spreading it evenly. Let cool completely.

Transfer the couscous to a large bowl. Scatter the bell peppers, tomatoes, cucumber, chile, and cilantro over the top.

In a small bowl, whisk together the olive oil, lemon juice, cumin, paprika, and garlic. Season to taste with salt and pepper. Add to the couscous and toss together well. Before serving, taste and adjust the seasoning, if necessary.

Serves 6

1 cup (6 oz/185 g) couscous

Salt and freshly ground pepper

2 green bell peppers (capsicums), roasted (page 308), and cut into $^1/_2$-inch (12-mm) squares

$^1/_2$ lb (250 g) cherry tomatoes, halved

1 cucumber, peeled, halved lengthwise, seeded, and cut into $^1/_2$-inch (12-mm) dice

1 small fresh red or green jalapeño or serrano chile, seeded and minced

$^1/_3$ cup ($^1/_2$ oz/15 g) chopped fresh cilantro (fresh coriander)

6 tablespoons (3 fl oz/90 ml) extra-virgin olive oil

5 tablespoons ($2^1/_2$ fl oz/ 75 ml) fresh lemon juice

$1^1/_2$ teaspoons ground cumin

$^1/_2$ teaspoon paprika

3 cloves garlic, minced

Spring Rice Salad with Lemon-Dill Dressing

This light and colorful salad is a terrific first course. If any of the vegetables are unavailable in the market, you can substitute green beans, zucchini (courgettes), broccoli, or even fresh peas with equally delicious results.

1 cup (7 oz/220 g) long-grain white rice or basmati rice

2¹/₂ cups (20 fl oz/625 ml) Vegetable Stock (page 300) or water

Salt and freshly ground pepper

1 large fennel bulb, trimmed and cut lengthwise into slices ¹/₄ inch (6 mm) thick

¹/₂ lb (250 g) sugar snap peas or snow peas (mangetouts), trimmed

¹/₂ lb (250 g) asparagus, trimmed and cut into 1-inch (2.5-cm) lengths

3–4 tablespoons fresh lemon juice

3–4 tablespoons chopped fresh dill

1 clove garlic, minced

¹/₂ cup (4 fl oz/125 ml) extra-virgin olive oil

Lemon wedges for garnish

Fresh dill sprigs for garnish

If using basmati rice, rinse well and drain.

In a heavy saucepan, combine the stock and ¹/₂ teaspoon salt and bring to a boil. Slowly add the rice, reduce the heat to low, cover, and cook, without stirring, for 20 minutes; do not remove the cover. After 20 minutes, uncover and check to see if the rice is tender and the water is absorbed. If not, re-cover and cook for a few minutes longer until the rice is done. Remove from the heat, fluff the grains with a fork, and transfer to a bowl to cool.

Bring a saucepan three-fourths full of water to a boil. Add salt to taste, the fennel, and the peas and blanch for 2 minutes. Using a slotted spoon, transfer the vegetables to a bowl and let cool. Add the asparagus to the same water and simmer just until tender, 3–4 minutes. Drain and let cool with the other vegetables.

In a large bowl, whisk together the lemon juice, dill, garlic, olive oil, and salt and pepper to taste. Add the cooled rice and vegetables and toss together.

Place the salad on a large serving platter or in a bowl. Garnish with lemon wedges and dill sprigs.

Serves 6–8

Wild Rice Salad with Walnuts and Oranges

You can serve this rich and nutty salad as a first course or as a side dish. If you like, garnish the salad with sliced green (spring) onions or arugula (rocket), flat-leaf (Italian) parsley, or watercress leaves.

Rinse the rice well and drain. Place in a heavy saucepan and add the boiling water and 1 teaspoon salt. Bring to a boil, reduce the heat to low, cover, and cook, without stirring, until the rice is tender and all of the water is absorbed, about 40 minutes. Remove from the heat, transfer to a large bowl, and let cool completely.

Meanwhile, preheat the oven to 350°F (180°C). Spread the walnuts on a baking sheet and toast until fragrant and lightly golden, 5–8 minutes. Remove from the oven, let cool, and chop coarsely. Set aside.

Cut off the top and bottom of each orange. Working with 1 orange at a time, place one of the cut sides down on a work surface. Starting at the top and following the contour of the orange, cut off the skin, including all of the white pith. Holding the orange over a small bowl and using a sharp knife, cut between the orange sections, freeing the sections and dropping them into the bowl. Repeat with the remaining oranges. Set aside.

In another small bowl, whisk together the vinegar, orange juice, orange zest, olive oil, nut oil, and salt and pepper to taste.

Add the walnuts and parsley to the cooled rice. Pour the dressing over the top and toss gently to mix. Add the orange wedges to the salad and toss well, or transfer the salad to a serving platter and arrange the wedges along the edges.

Serves 6

1 cup (6 oz/185 g) wild rice

2 3/4 cups (22 fl oz/680 ml) boiling water

Salt and freshly ground pepper

3/4 cup (3 oz/90 g) walnuts

2 large seedless oranges

2 tablespoons red wine vinegar

1/4 cup (2 fl oz/60 ml) fresh orange juice

1 teaspoon grated orange zest

3 tablespoons extra-virgin olive oil

1 tablespoon hazelnut, pecan, or walnut oil

2 tablespoons chopped fresh flat-leaf (Italian) parsley

Soups & Stews

Chilled Curried Potato-Leek Soup

Creamy puréed potatoes give this light, refreshing soup extra body. Herbed croutons can be used as a garnish in addition to the chopped chives. This soup is best served chilled and is quite nice on a hot summer day.

2 tablespoons unsalted butter

2 yellow onions, chopped

3 leeks, white part and 1 inch (2.5 cm) of the green, halved lengthwise, carefully washed (page 310), and sliced cross-wise

1 clove garlic, minced

1 tablespoon curry powder

3 cups (24 fl oz/750 ml) Vegetable Stock (page 300) or water

4 red potatoes, about 1 lb (500 g) total weight, peeled and thinly sliced

Salt and freshly ground pepper

3 cups (24 fl oz/750 ml) milk, or as needed

2 tablespoons finely chopped fresh chives

In a 4-qt (4-l) soup pot over medium-low heat, melt the butter. Add the onions and leeks and sauté, stirring, until the vegetables begin to soften, about 5 minutes. Add the garlic and curry powder and sauté, stirring occasionally, until the onions and leeks are soft, about 10 minutes. Add the stock, potatoes, and 1 teaspoon salt. Cover and cook until the potatoes are soft when pierced with a fork, about 20 minutes.

Pour in the 3 cups (24 fl oz/750 ml) milk and stir to mix well. Working with 2 cups (16 fl oz/500 ml) of soup at a time, place in a blender and purée on high speed until very smooth and light, about 3 minutes. As each batch is puréed, transfer it to a large bowl. If the soup is too thick, add more milk and stir until the soup is the consistency of heavy (double) cream. Cover and chill for 2 hours.

Season to taste with salt and pepper. Ladle into chilled bowls and garnish with the chives. Serve immediately.

Serves 6

Cold Cucumber Soup

This soup can also be garnished with chopped toasted walnuts, pine nuts, or almonds. Prepare the soup the day before serving and chill well. Adjust the seasonings at serving time.

In a saucepan over medium heat, melt the butter. Add the onion and sauté until tender and translucent, 8–10 minutes. Add 3 cups (24 fl oz/750 ml) of the stock and the potato, raise the heat to high, and bring to a boil. Reduce the heat to medium and simmer, uncovered, for 10 minutes. Add the cucumbers and continue to simmer until the cucumbers are soft, about 10 minutes longer.

Working in batches, transfer to a food processor or a blender and purée until smooth. If the purée is too thick, add as much of the remaining 1 cup (8 fl oz/250 ml) stock or broth as needed to thin to a soup consistency. Transfer to a bowl, let cool slightly, and then whisk in the cream. Cover and refrigerate the soup until well chilled, at least 3 hours or as long as overnight.

Season to taste with salt and pepper. Ladle into chilled bowls and garnish with cucumber slices and the herb of choice and serve.

Serves 6

2 tablespoons unsalted butter

1 yellow onion, diced

3–4 cups (24–32 oz/750 ml–1 l) Vegetable Stock (page 300)

1 small potato, about 4 oz (125 g), peeled and diced

3 cucumbers, peeled, seeded and diced

1 cup (8 oz/250 ml) plain yogurt or 1/2 cup (4 fl oz/125 ml) heavy (double) cream

Salt and freshly ground pepper

1 cucumber, thinly sliced for garnish (optional)

3 tablespoons chopped fresh dill, mint, or basil for garnish (optional)

Spring Vegetable Soup with Pesto

Pesto brings out the fresh character of this soup. You can top each bowl with a spoonful of pesto before serving as directed, or pass the pesto separately in a small bowl at the table for guests to help themselves.

½ cup (3½ oz/105 g) dried small white (navy) beans

2 tablespoon olive oil

1 yellow onion, chopped

2 carrots, peeled and cut into ½-inch (12-mm) dice

2 celery stalks, cut into ½-inch (12-mm) dice

2 cups (12 oz/375 g) fresh plum (Roma) tomatoes, peeled and seeded (page 313), then chopped, or canned plum (Roma) tomatoes, seeded, drained, and chopped

1 tablespoon tomato paste

8 cups (64 fl oz/2 l) Vegetable Stock (page 300) or water

½ lb (250 g) green beans, trimmed and cut into 1-inch (2.5-cm) lengths

¼ lb (125 g) dried penne or small elbow macaroni

1 bunch Swiss chard, carefully washed, leaves and stems cut into 1-inch (2.5-cm) pieces

Salt and freshly ground pepper

Pesto (page 301) for serving

Pick over the white beans and discard any damaged beans or stones. Rinse the beans and drain. Place in a bowl, add plenty of water to cover, and let soak for about 3 hours.

Drain the beans and place them in a saucepan with water to cover by 2 inches (5 cm). Bring to a boil over high heat. Reduce the heat to medium-low and simmer, uncovered, until almost tender, 30–40 minutes. Drain and set aside.

In a 4-qt (4-l) soup pot over medium-low heat, warm the olive oil. Add the onion, carrots, and celery and sauté, stirring, until the vegetables are soft, about 25 minutes. Add the tomatoes, tomato paste, stock, and cooked white beans and simmer, uncovered, for 25 minutes.

Add the green beans and pasta, cover, and simmer until the pasta is tender, about 15 minutes. Add the Swiss chard and simmer until it wilts, about 5 minutes. Season to taste with salt and pepper.

Ladle the soup into warmed bowls and place a large spoonful of pesto on top of each serving. Serve at once.

Serves 6

Spiced Squash and Apple Soup

Golden in color and fragrant in spice, this soup is the perfect start to an autumn or winter holiday dinner. Butternut squash is similar to pumpkin in taste and texture but is easier to peel and dice.

In a large pot over medium heat, melt the butter. Add the onions and apples and cook, stirring often, until tender, about 10 minutes. Stir in the nutmeg, allspice, and cinnamon and cook for about 1 minute. Then add the squash and the stock, raise the heat to medium-high, and bring to a boil. Reduce the heat to low and simmer, uncovered, until the squash is very tender 20-30 minutes.

Remove from the heat and let cool slightly. Working with 2 cups (16 fl oz/500 ml) of soup at a time, place in a blender and purée on high speed until smooth. As each batch is puréed, transfer to a large saucepan. Add enough of the remaining liquid to make a medium-thick soup. Season with salt and pepper, then taste and adjust the spices. If not serving right away, reserve any leftover liquid, as the soup may thicken on standing. (This soup may be made up to 1 day ahead refrigerated uncovered until cold, and then covered.)

Place the soup over medium-low heat and heat almost to a boil. Ladle into warmed bowls and top with thin apple slices. Serve immediately.

Serves 10-12

1/4 cup (2 oz/60 g) unsalted butter or extra-virgin olive oil

1/4 cup (2 fl oz/60 ml) olive oil

2 large green apples, peeled, cored, and diced, plus thin slices for garnish

2 teaspoon ground nutmeg

1/2 teaspoon ground allspice

1/2 teaspoon ground cinnamon

10 cups (5 lbs/2.5 kg) peeled, seeded, and diced butternut squash (about 4 squashes)

3 qt (3 l) Vegetable Stock (page 300)

Salt and freshly ground pepper

Greens and Farfalle Soup

Small elbow macaroni, penne, orzo, or fusilli can replace the farfalle in this hearty soup. And, if you like, you can also substitute greens such as spinach, turnip greens, beet greens, or kale for the escarole and Swiss chard.

In a 4-qt (4-l) soup pot over medium-low heat, warm the olive oil. Add the garlic and red pepper flakes and cook, stirring constantly, until the garlic is soft but not golden, about 2 minutes. Add the stock and bring to a boil over high heat. Add the pasta, reduce the heat to medium, and simmer, uncovered, until the pasta is cooked, 12–15 minutes.

Add the escarole and Swiss chard, stir well, and continue to simmer just until the greens wilt but are still bright green, about 3 minutes. Remove from the heat and add the lemon juice. Season to taste with salt and pepper.

Ladle into warmed bowls and serve immediately. Pass the Parmesan at the table.

Serves 6

2 tablespoons extra-virgin olive oil

3 cloves garlic, finely chopped

Small pinch of red pepper flakes

8 cups (64 fl oz/2 l) Vegetable Stock (page 300)

1/4 lb (125 g) dried farfalle

1/4 lb (125 g) escarole (Batavian endive), carefully washed and cut into 1-inch (2.5-cm) pieces

1/4 lb (125 g) Swiss chard, carefully washed and cut into 1-inch (2.5-cm) pieces

2 teaspoons fresh lemon juice

Salt and freshly ground pepper

3/4 cup (3 oz/90 g) grated Parmesan cheese

Butternut Squash–Carrot Soup

This exotic soup bursts with complex sweet and hot flavors. If you like, garnish each serving with a few paper–thin lime slices and whole fresh cilantro (fresh coriander) leaves in place of the yogurt.

2 tablespoons olive oil

1 large yellow onion, chopped

1 butternut squash, about 1¼ lb (625 g), peeled, halved, seeded, and coarsely chopped

3 large carrots, peeled and coarsely chopped

½ teaspoon sugar

1 teaspoon paprika

1¼ teaspoons ground cumin

¾ teaspoon ground turmeric

¾ teaspoon ground coriander

6 cups (48 fl oz/1.5 l) Vegetable Stock (page 300) or water

Salt and freshly ground pepper

½ cup (4 fl oz/125 ml) plain yogurt

⅓ cup (½ oz/15 g) chopped fresh cilantro (fresh coriander), including stems

1 tablespoon fresh lime juice

In a 4-qt (4-l) soup pot over medium-low heat, warm the olive oil. Add the onion and sauté, stirring occasionally, until soft, about 10 minutes. Add the squash, carrots, and sugar and sauté, stirring, for 10 minutes. Add the paprika, cumin, turmeric, and coriander and continue to sauté, stirring occasionally, for 10 minutes longer. Add the stock and bring to a boil over high heat. Reduce the heat to low and simmer, uncovered, until the squash and carrots are soft, 30–40 minutes. Remove from the heat and let cool slightly.

Working with 2 cups (16 fl oz/500 ml) of soup at a time, place in a blender and purée on high speed until very smooth and light, about 3 minutes. As each batch is puréed, transfer it to a large saucepan. If the soup is too thick, thin with a little water until it is the consistency of heavy (double) cream.

Place the soup over medium-high heat and warm to serving temperature. Season to taste with salt and pepper.

Meanwhile, in a small bowl, whisk 1 teaspoon water into the yogurt until smooth. Season to taste with salt and pepper.

To serve, stir the cilantro and lime juice into the soup, mixing well. Ladle the soup into warmed bowls and drizzle with the yogurt. Serve at once.

Serves 6

Cream of Squash Soup

This soup can be prepared up to the point where the cream is added, then covered and refrigerated for up to 24 hours, then finish just before serving. Green (spring) onion makes an extra-festive garnish.

Preheat an oven to 375°F (190°C).

Stick 1 or 2 whole cloves in the flesh of each squash piece. Place the pieces flesh-side down in a baking pan or ovenproof dish. Pour in the boiling water. Place in the oven and bake until tender when the flesh is pierced with a fork, about 1 hour, adding additional boiling water if the pan begins to dry. Remove from the oven and leave the squash in the pan until cool, 20–25 minutes. Discard the cloves and scoop out the flesh; you should have about 5 cups (2 1/2 lb/1.25 kg). Set aside.

In a large saucepan over low heat, melt the butter. Add the onion and marjoram, cover, and cook over very low heat until translucent and tender, 15–20 minutes. Remove from the heat.

Working with 2 cups (16 fl oz/500 ml) of soup at a time, place in a blender and purée on high speed until very smooth and light, about 3 minutes. As each batch is puréed, transfer it to a saucepan. Stir in the stock and lemon juice to the saucepan.

Place the soup over medium-low heat, stirring frequently, to blend the flavors, 8–10 minutes. Do not allow to scorch. Season to taste with salt and pepper.

Just before serving, stir the cream into the soup and heat almost to a boil. Ladle into warmed soup bowls and top with a dollop of sour cream and a grating of nutmeg or a sprinkling of parsley or mint. Serve at once.

Serves 6–8 with leftovers

1 piece banana, Hubbard, or pumpkin squash, 3 1/2–4 lb (1.5–2 kg), cut into quarters and any seeds and strings removed

4–8 whole cloves

1 cup (5 oz/155 g) chopped yellow onion

1/2 teaspoon crushed dried marjoram

4 cups (32 fl oz/1 l) Vegetable Stock (page 300)

1 teaspoon fresh lemon juice

Salt and freshly ground pepper

1 cup (8 fl oz/250 ml) heavy (double) cream

Sour cream

Freshly grated nutmeg or chopped fresh parsley or mint

Lentil Soup

This soup can be prepared the day before and reheated, but wilt and stir in the greens just before serving. A dollop of yogurt or crème fraîche adds a sharpness that cuts the richness of the lentils.

2 tablespoon olive oil

1 large yellow onion, diced

1 teaspoon ground cumin

1 large or 2 small carrots, peeled and diced

2 cups (14 oz/440 g) green lentils

5–6 cups (40–48 fl oz/ 1.25–1.5 l) Vegetable Stock (page 300)

2 cups (4 oz/125 g) coarsely Chopped spinach, swiss chard, or watercress carefully washed

Salt and freshly ground pepper to taste

Plain yogurt or crème fraîche (page 309) for garnish (optional)

In a saucepan over medium heat, warm the olive oil. Add the onion and sauté until tender and translucent, about 8 minutes. Add the cumin, carrots, lentils, and stock or broth. The amount of liquid will vary depending upon how dry the lentils are; older dryer lentils will require the larger amount. Reduce the heat to low, cover, and simmer until the lentils are soft; begin testing for doneness after 20 minutes.

Meanwhile, in a large sauté pan over medium heat, place the spinach with just the rinsing water clinging to the leaves. Cook, turning occasionally, just until wilted, about 2 minutes. Transfer to a fine-mesh sieve and drain well, pressing out the excess liquid.

Stir the wilted greens into the lentils. Season with salt and pepper to taste. Serve at once in warmed bowls; top each serving with yogurt or crème fraîche, if desired.

Serves 6

Yellow Split Pea Soup with Spiced Yogurt

This mildly gingery soup is best when served hot, but it is also good chilled. The distinctive yogurt topping is similar to Indian *raita*, a blend of yogurt and various spices.

1¹⁄₂ cups (10¹⁄₂ oz/330 g) yellow split peas

3 tablespoons unsalted butter

1 yellow onion, chopped

1 carrot, peeled and cut into ¹⁄₄-inch (6-mm) dice

2 teaspoons peeled and grated fresh ginger

7 cups (56 fl oz/1.75 l) Vegetable Stock (page 300) or water

Salt and freshly ground pepper

FOR THE GARNISH:

¹⁄₂ cup (4 oz/125 g) plain yogurt

¹⁄₈ teaspoon ground turmeric

¹⁄₈ teaspoon ground cumin

¹⁄₈ teaspoon ground coriander

Salt and freshly ground pepper

3 tablespoons chopped fresh cilantro (fresh coriander)

Pick over the split peas and discard any damaged peas or stones. Rinse the peas thoroughly and drain.

In a soup pot over medium heat, melt the butter. Add the onion and carrot and sauté, stirring, until the vegetables are soft, about 10 minutes. Add the ginger and stock. Bring to a boil, reduce the heat to low, and simmer gently until the peas are completely soft, 45–60 minutes.

Remove from the heat and let cool slightly. Working in batches, place in a food processor fitted with the metal blade or in a blender. Purée until smooth. Thin with water or additional stock to achieve the desired consistency. Return the purée to a clean pot and reheat to serving temperature. Season to taste with salt and pepper.

Meanwhile make the garnish: In a small bowl, whisk together the yogurt, turmeric, cumin, ground coriander, and salt and pepper to taste.

Ladle the soup into individual bowls. Drizzle with the spiced yogurt, sprinkle with the cilantro, and serve immediately.

Serves 6

Tomato-Rice Soup with Garlic and Herbs

Make this light and flavorful soup at the height of summer, when tomatoes are a brilliant red and herbs bountiful. Garnish it with a touch of parsley, if you like. Serve with a red wine such as Côtes du Rhône.

In a heavy saucepan over very low heat, warm the olive oil. Add the garlic and onion and sauté, stirring, until soft, about 15 minutes. Add the tomatoes, stock, and 1 cup (8 fl oz/250 ml) water and simmer, uncovered, for 10 minutes.

Add the rice and herbs and continue to simmer, uncovered, until the rice is just cooked, 15–20 minutes longer.

Add the vinegar, red wine, and salt and pepper to taste. Simmer for 2 minutes. Ladle into individual bowls and serve immediately.

Serves 6

3 tablespoons olive oil

1/2 cup (2 1/2 oz/75 g) garlic cloves, halved

1 small yellow onion, minced

2 1/2 cups (15 oz/470 g) fresh tomatoes, peeled and seeded (page 313), then chopped, or canned tomatoes, seeded, drained, and chopped

3 cups (24 fl oz/750 ml) Vegetable Stock (page 300)

1/3 cup (2 oz/60 g) long-grain white rice

3 tablespoons mixed chopped fresh flat-leaf (Italian) parsley and chives

1 tablespoon mixed chopped fresh oregano, thyme, and/or summer savory

1 tablespoon red wine vinegar

1/4 cup (2 fl oz/60 ml) fruity red wine such as Côtes du Rhône or Zinfandel

Salt and freshly ground pepper

Wild Rice and Mushroom Soup

This hearty soup can be served as a meal alone on a cold winter's day. Serve with fresh country bread and garnish with fresh chopped parsley sprigs, if you like. For a lighter version, replace the heavy cream with milk.

Rinse the rice well and drain. Place in a saucepan and add the boiling water and ¹/₂ teaspoon salt. Bring to a boil, reduce the heat to medium-low, cover, and cook, without stirring, until the rice is tender and the water is absorbed, about 40 minutes. Remove from the heat and set aside to cool completely.

Meanwhile, in a soup pot over medium heat, melt the butter. Add the onion and celery and sauté, stirring, until the vegetables are soft, about 10 minutes. Add the wine and reduce over high heat until only 1–2 tablespoons remain, about 3 minutes. Add the mushrooms and sauté, stirring, until very soft, about 15 minutes.

Add the stock, bring to a boil, reduce the heat to low, and simmer, uncovered, for 20 minutes to blend the flavors. Add the wild rice and cream and simmer for 5 minutes longer (do not boil). Season to taste with salt and pepper.

Ladle into individual bowls and garnish with the parsley. Serve immediately.

Serves 6

¹/₂ cup (3 oz/90 g) wild rice

2 cups (16 fl oz/500 ml) boiling water

Salt and freshly ground pepper

2 tablespoons unsalted butter

1 yellow onion, finely chopped

1 celery stalk, finely chopped

¹/₂ cup (4 fl oz/125 ml) dry white wine

³/₄ lb (375 g) fresh button mushrooms, brushed clean and sliced

4 cups (32 fl oz/1 l) Vegetable Stock (page 300) or water

¹/₂ cup (4 fl oz/125 ml) heavy (double) cream

1 tablespoon chopped fresh flat-leaf (Italian) parsley

Black Bean Soup with Tomato Salsa

One of the great all-American soups, this Southwestern specialty can be garnished with a wide variety of choices: grated Cheddar cheese, chopped fresh cilantro, a dollop of sour cream, diced red onions, or a simple squeeze of fresh lime juice.

1¼ cups (9 oz/280 g) dried black beans

¼ cup (2 fl oz/60 ml) olive oil

1 large yellow onion, minced

3 cloves garlic, minced

1 teaspoon ground cumin

2 teaspoons chili powder

Tomato Salsa (page 303)

Pick over the beans and discard any damaged beans or stones. Rinse the beans. Place in a bowl, add plenty of water to cover, and soak for about 3 hours.

Drain the beans. In a large saucepan over medium heat, warm the olive oil. Add the yellow onion and sauté until soft, about 10 minutes. Add the garlic, cumin, chili powder, drained beans, and 8 cups (64 fl oz/2 l) water. Bring to a boil, reduce the heat to low, and simmer gently, uncovered, until the beans are very tender and begin to fall apart, 2–3 hours.

When the soup is ready, season to taste with salt and pepper. Ladle into individual bowls and garnish each serving with a spoonful of the salsa. Serve immediately.

Serves 6

Cauliflower and Cheddar Cheese Soup

This soup is also delicious made with fresh corn kernels, broccoli, butternut squash, acorn squash, or pumpkin in place of the cauliflower. Gruyère can be used as a garnish instead of Cheddar.

Trim the cauliflowers, removing the green leaves and green stems. Cut 1 of the cauliflower heads into 1/2-inch (12-mm) florets. Bring a saucepan three-fourths full of lightly salted water to a boil. Add the florets, reduce the heat to medium-low, and simmer until tender when pierced with a fork, 10–12 minutes. Drain well; set aside. Cut the remaining cauliflower head into 2-inch (5-cm) pieces; set aside.

In a 4-qt (4-l) soup pot over medium-low heat, melt the butter. Add the yellow onion and sauté, stirring, until soft, about 10 minutes. Add the garlic and sauté, stirring, for 2 minutes longer.

Add the stock, reserved raw cauliflower pieces, mustard, and nutmeg and bring to a boil. Reduce the heat to low and simmer, uncovered, until the cauliflower is soft, about 30 minutes. Remove from the heat and cool slightly.

Working with 2 cups (16 fl oz/500 ml) of soup at a time, place in a blender and blend at high speed until very smooth and light, about 3 minutes. As each batch is puréed, transfer it to a clean, large saucepan. Place the soup over medium-low heat, pour in the milk, and stir well. Bring the soup to a simmer and add the cooked florets and 1 1/2 cups (6 oz/185 g) of the cheese. Stir well until the cheese melts and the soup is hot, about 5 minutes. Season to taste with salt and pepper.

Ladle the soup into warmed bowls. Sprinkle evenly with the remaining 1/2 cup (2 oz/65 g) cheese and the green onions. Serve immediately.

Serves 6

2 small heads cauliflower, 2 1/2 lb (1.25 kg) total weight

2 tablespoons unsalted butter

1 large yellow onion, chopped

1 clove garlic, minced

4 cups (32 fl oz/1 l) Vegetable Stock (page 300) or water

1 teaspoon dry mustard

Pinch of freshly grated nutmeg

1 1/2 cups (12 fl oz/375 ml) milk

2 cups (8 oz/250 g) coarsely shredded sharp white Cheddar cheese

Salt and freshly ground pepper

2 tablespoons sliced green (spring) onions

Corn, Bell Pepper, and Potato Chowder

For a heartier soup, add 3 more small bell peppers (capsicums). Cut into halves, remove the seeds and ribs, then cut into ½-inch (12-mm) squares and sauté in 1 tablespoon olive oil until soft.

2 tablespoons unsalted butter

2 yellow onions, coarsely chopped

1 small carrot, peeled and coarsely chopped

2 yellow bell peppers (capsicums), seeded, deribbed (page 308), and coarsely chopped

¼ teaspoon fresh thyme leaves

6 cups (48 fl oz/1.5 l) Vegetable Stock (page 300) or water

Kernels from 6 ears of fresh corn, or 4–5 cups (about 1½ lb/750 g) frozen corn kernels

½ lb (250 g) russet potatoes, peeled and cut into ½-inch (12-mm) dice

1 cup (8 fl oz/250 ml) milk

Salt and freshly ground pepper

2 tablespoons finely chopped fresh chives or green (spring) onions

In a 4-qt (4-l) soup pot over medium-low heat, melt the butter. Add the yellow onions, carrot, bell peppers, and thyme and sauté, stirring occasionally, until the vegetables are soft, about 15 minutes.

Add the stock and half of the corn and bring to a boil over medium-high heat. Reduce the heat to low, and simmer, uncovered, until the vegetables are very soft, about 20 minutes. Remove from the heat and let cool slightly. Working with 2 cups (16 fl oz/500 ml) of soup at a time, place in a blender and purée on high speed until very smooth and light, about 3 minutes. As each batch is puréed, transfer it to a large saucepan.

Place the soup over medium heat and bring to a simmer. Add the potatoes and the remaining corn and simmer, uncovered, until the potatoes are soft when pierced with a fork, about 15 minutes. Pour in the milk, stir well, and return to a simmer. Season to taste with salt and pepper.

Ladle into warmed bowls and garnish with the chives or green onions. Serve immediately.

Serves 6

Okra with Tomatoes

Okra is dearly loved by those who are familiar with it. Here, the fresh tomato sauce gives it a zesty taste. This stew is good served over Steamed White Rice (page 304).

In a frying pan over medium heat, warm the olive oil. Add the onion and sauté until soft, about 2 minutes. Add the garlic and cook until soft, about 1 minute longer. Add the rosemary and okra and stir until coated thoroughly with the oil.

Stir in the tomato sauce. Add the tomatoes, bay leaf, and red pepper flakes. Simmer, uncovered, over medium heat until the okra is tender, 10–15 minutes.

Season to taste with salt and pepper. Discard the bay leaf and garlic halves. Serve hot or warm, garnished with the parsley.

Serves 4–6

3 tablespoons olive oil

1 yellow onion, chopped

1 clove garlic, cut in half

1 teaspoon dried rosemary

1 lb (500 g) okra, stemmed and thinly sliced crosswise (about 3 cups)

1 cup (8 fl oz/250 ml) Tomato Sauce (page 302)

4 tomatoes, coarsely chopped

1 bay leaf

1/4 teaspoon red pepper flakes

Salt and freshly ground pepper

2 tablespoons chopped fresh flat-leaf (Italian) parsley

Summer Ratatouille

This classic French dish of fresh summer vegetables is cooked slowly in fragrant olive oil. If possible, make it a day in advance of serving to allow the flavors to meld. Serve at room temperature as a salad, or warm as an appetizer.

1 small globe eggplant (aubergine), about 1 lb (500 g)

Salt and freshly ground pepper

¹/₄ cup (2 fl oz/l60 ml) olive oil

1 red onion, thinly sliced

1 yellow or red bell pepper (capsicum), seeded, deribbed, and sliced lengthwise

2 cloves garlic, cut in half

2 large ripe tomatoes, sliced

1 teaspoon dried thyme

1 teaspoon dried oregano

¹/₄ cup (2 fl oz/60 ml) Vegetable Stock (page 300)

2 tablespoons chopped fresh flat-leaf (Italian) parsley or basil

Cut the unpeeled eggplant lengthwise into quarters, then cut each quarter into long, thin strips. Place in a colander, sprinkle with salt, and allow to drain for about 30 minutes.

In a large frying pan over medium heat, heat the olive oil. Add the onion and sauté until soft, about 5 minutes. Add the bell pepper, garlic, and tomatoes and stir well. Stir in the thyme and oregano.

Meanwhile, rinse the eggplant under cold water and dry well with paper towels. Add to the pan, along with the stock. Cover and simmer over low heat, stirring occasionally to prevent sticking, until the vegetables are tender, 20–30 minutes.

Discard the garlic halves. Season to taste with salt and pepper. Transfer to a warmed serving platter, and sprinkle with the parsley or basil. Serve hot, warm, or at room temperature.

Serves 4

Autumn Vegetable Stew

This wholesome stew made with a variety of fresh vegetables is wonderful over brown rice or bulgur, and leftovers are good cold, drizzled with a few drops of olive oil and vinegar. Serve with fresh country bread.

Using a vegetable peeler, peel the squash. Halve it lengthwise, scrape out the seeds, and then cut into 1-inch (2.5 cm) cubes. Cut the unpeeled potatoes into pieces about the same size. Halve the pepper through the stem end and remove the stem, ribs, and seeds. Cut into 1-inch (2.5-cm) squares. Set the vegetables aside.

In a large saucepan or a Dutch oven over medium-low heat, warm the olive oil. When the oil is hot, add the onion and garlic and cook, stirring, until the onion has softened, about 5 minutes. Add the squash, potatoes, stock, tomatoes, corn, sage, 1 teaspoon salt, and 1/4 teaspoon pepper and stir to combine. Bring to a boil over medium-high heat, reduce the heat to low, cover, and simmer for 10 minutes to cook the potatoes and squash partially.

Stir in the bell pepper, raise the heat to medium, and return to a boil. Cover, reduce the heat to low, and simmer until the vegetables are tender but still firm when pierced with a knife, 10–15 minutes longer.

Ladle into warmed shallow bowls and serve at once.

Serves 4

1 small butternut squash, about 1 1/2 lb (750 g)

4 red potatoes, about 1 lb (500 g) total weight

1 green or red bell pepper (capsicum)

2 tablespoons olive oil

1 large yellow onion, thinly sliced

2 cloves garlic, minced

2 cups (16 fl oz/500 ml) Vegetable Stock (page 300)

1 1/2 cups (9 oz/280 g) tomatoes, peeled and seeded (page 313), then chopped

1 1/2 cups (9 oz/280 g) corn kernels

1 teaspoon dried sage or 1 tablespoon chopped fresh sage

Salt and freshly ground pepper

Couscous with Winter Vegetable Stew

To make the sauce for this fragrant stew, look for harissa, a spicy red pepper condiment from North Africa sold in specialty-food stores. Garnish with chopped fresh cilantro and parsley, if you like.

2 tablespoons unsalted butter

1 teaspoon *each* saffron threads and ground cumin

2 cinnamon sticks

1/2 teaspoon ground turmeric

3 yellow onions, quartered

2 cloves garlic, chopped

1/2 jalapeño chile, seeded

1 small bunch fresh cilantro (fresh coriander), tied together, plus 1 tablespoon chopped

3 tomatoes, peeled and seeded (page 313), then quartered

6 cups (48 fl oz/1.5 l) Vegetable Stock (page 300)

3 small zucchini (courgettes)

1 lb (500 g) butternut squash, peeled, halved, and seeded

3 carrots, peeled and cut into 1-inch (2.5-cm) lengths

3 small turnips, peeled and quartered

Salt and freshly ground pepper

1 3/4 cups (10 1/2 oz/330 g) couscous

Harissa Sauce (page 301)

In a large soup pot over medium heat, melt the butter. Add the saffron, cumin, cinnamon sticks, turmeric, onions, garlic, jalapeño, cilantro bundle, and tomatoes. Stir until well mixed. Cover and simmer for 5 minutes. Add the stock, re-cover, and continue to simmer until the vegetables are tender when pierced with a fork, about 30 minutes longer.

Trim the zucchini. Cut the zucchini and butternut squash into 1-inch (2.5-cm) chunks and add them to the stew, along with the carrots and turnips. Cover and simmer until tender when pierced with a fork, about 20 minutes. Season to taste with 1/2 teaspoon salt and pinch of pepper. Discard the cinnamon sticks, jalapeño, and cilantro bundle. Measure out 1 cup (8 fl oz/250 ml) of broth from the stew and set aside for the Harissa Sauce.

About 10 minutes before the stew is ready, in a large saucepan, bring 1 3/4 cups (14 fl oz/440 ml) water to a boil. Remove from the heat and stir in the couscous and 1/2 teaspoon salt. Cover and let stand for 10 minutes.

Uncover the couscous and fluff with a fork. Spread the couscous on a platter and make a well in the center. Using a slotted spoon, place the vegetables in the well. Moisten the couscous with a few spoonfuls of the broth left in the pot. Serve with the harissa sauce and the remaining broth in separate bowls on the side.

Serves 6–8

Mushroom-Barley Stew with Biscuit Crust

Pick over the chickpeas and discard any damaged chickpeas or stones. Rinse the chickpeas and drain. Place in a large bowl, add plenty of water to cover, and let soak for about 3 hours.

Drain the chickpeas and place in a saucepan with water to cover by 2 inches (5 cm). Bring to a boil, reduce the heat to medium-low, and simmer, uncovered, until the chickpeas are tender, 45–60 minutes. Drain and set aside.

In a soup pot over medium heat, warm the olive oil. Add the cooked chickpeas, pearl onions, carrots, and celery and stir briefly. Sift the 2 tablespoons flour over the vegetables. Cook, stirring, for 2 minutes; do not brown. Add the stock, herbes de Provence, garlic, and barley and bring to a boil. Reduce the heat to low and simmer, uncovered, until the vegetables are tender when pierced with a fork, about 30 minutes. Add the potatoes, cover, and cook over medium heat until tender, about 30 minutes.

Brush the mushrooms clean and cut in half. Add the snap peas and mushrooms to the pot and cook for 5 minutes. Season to taste with salt and pepper. Transfer to a round 3-qt (3-l) baking dish 7–8 inches (18–20 cm) in diameter.

Preheat the oven to 400°F (200°C). In a large bowl, sift together the $2^{1}/_{2}$ cups ($12^{1}/_{2}$ oz/390 g) flour, 1 teaspoon salt, and the baking powder. Using your fingers, rub the butter into the flour until it resembles coarse meal. Add the buttermilk and stir until the mixture forms a dough. Gather into a ball and transfer to a well-floured work surface. Roll out into a round about $3/_4$ inch (2 cm) thick. Fold in half and roll out again. Fold one more time and roll out about $1/_2$ inch (12 mm) thick. Using a round cutter 2 inches (5 cm) in diameter, cut out 12 biscuits. Arrange them evenly on top of the stew.

Bake until the biscuits are golden, 20–25 minutes. Serve immediately.

Serves 6

3/4 cup (5 oz/155 g) dried chickpeas (garbanzo beans)

2 tablespoons olive oil

18 pearl onions, peeled

4 carrots, peeled and cut into 1½-inch (4-cm) lengths

2 celery stalks, cut into 1½-inch (4-cm) lengths

2 tablespoons all-purpose (plain) flour, plus 2½ cups (12½ oz/390 g)

6 cups (48 fl oz/1.5 l) Vegetable Stock (page 300)

1 teaspoon dried herbes de Provence

3 cloves garlic, minced

1/3 cup (2½ oz/75 g) pearl barley

3/4 lb (375 g) red potatoes, quartered

3/4 lb (375 g) fresh white mushrooms

1 cup (3 oz/90 g) sugar snap peas, trimmed

Salt and freshly ground pepper

1 tablespoon baking powder

1/2 cup (4 oz/125 g) unsalted butter at room temperature, cut into pieces

1 cup (8 fl oz/250 ml) buttermilk, at room temperature

North African Vegetable Stew

Juice of 1 large lemon

6 medium artichokes

5 tablespoons (2¹/₂ oz/75 ml) olive oil

Salt and freshly ground pepper

2 *each* (10 oz/315 g) carrots and zucchini (courgettes)

1¹/₂ cups (6 oz/185 g) cut-up green beans (1¹/₂-inch/4-cm lengths)

²/₃ cup (4 oz/125 g) raisins

1 large yellow onion, chopped

3 cloves garlic, minced

1 tablespoon ground coriander

2 teaspoons *each* ground cumin and paprika

1 teaspoon ground ginger

¹/₂ teaspoon cayenne pepper

2 cups (12 oz/375 g) peeled, seeded (page 313), and diced tomatoes

4 tablespoons (¹/₃ oz/10 g) *each* chopped cilantro (fresh coriander) and chopped flat-leaf (Italian) parsley

2 tablespoons finely grated lemon zest

1 cup (8 fl oz/250 ml) Vegetable Stock (page 300)

1¹/₂ cups (10¹/₂ oz/330 g) drained canned chickpeas (garbanzo beans)

Fill a large bowl three-fourths full of water and add half of the lemon juice. Trim the artichokes as directed on page 308. Cut each artichoke lengthwise into sixths and drop into the lemon water. In a sauté pan over medium heat, warm 2 tablespoons of the olive oil. Drain the artichokes and add to the pan along with 1 cup (8 fl oz/ 250 ml) water and the remaining lemon juice. Cook, stirring, until the artichokes are tender and the liquid has been absorbed, 6–8 minutes. Season to taste with salt and pepper. Set aside.

Peel and cut the carrots and zucchini into 1-inch (2.5 cm) chunks. Set aside.

Bring a large saucepan three-fourths full of lightly salted water to a boil. Add the green beans and cook until tender-crisp, about 5 minutes. Transfer to a bowl of cold water to halt the cooking. Drain. Repeat with the carrots and zucchini. The carrots should cook in 8–10 minutes, the zucchini in 3–5 minutes.

Soak the raisins for in hot water for 10 minutes. Drain and set aside.

In a large sauté pan over medium heat, warm the remaining 3 tablespoons olive oil. Add the onion and sauté, stirring occasionally, until tender, 8–10 minutes. Add the garlic, coriander, cumin, paprika, ginger, cayenne, and 2 teaspoons of black pepper and cook for 2 minutes. Add the tomatoes, 2 tablespoons *each* of the cilantro and parsley, the lemon zest, and the 1 cup (8 fl oz/250 ml) stock. Simmer until the flavors are blended, about 5 minutes. Add the chickpeas, artichokes, green beans, carrots, zucchini, and raisins. Simmer until heated through, adding more stock or some water if the mixture seems too dry. Season to taste with salt and pepper. Transfer to a serving dish and garnish with the remaining cilantro and parsley.

Serves 6

Sautéed & Stir-Fried Vegetables

Sautéed Carrots, Parsnips, and Onions

Tender-crisp fall vegetables make a savory side dish. Use a very large, heavy frying pan or a heavy pot for this quick sauté. You can substitute 1¹/₂ cups (6 oz/185 g) sliced shallots or 1¹/₂ cups (4¹/₂ oz/140 g) sliced leeks for the onion.

¹/₄ cup (2 fl oz/60 ml) olive oil

1 yellow onion

2 tablespoons chopped fresh rosemary or 2 teaspoons dried rosemary

6 large carrots, peeled and sliced on the diagonal ¹/₄ inch (6 mm) thick

6 parsnips, peeled and sliced on the diagonal ¹/₄ inch (6 mm) thick

Salt and freshly ground pepper

In a large, heavy frying pan over medium heat, warm the oil. When hot, add the onion and rosemary and sauté, stirring frequently, until the onion begins to soften, about 5 minutes. Add the carrots and parsnips and sauté, stirring occasionally, until tender-crisp and starting to brown, about 15 minutes. Season with salt and pepper.

Transfer to a warmed serving dish and serve at once.

Serves 8–10

Braised Fennel

Fennel has a sweet aniselike flavor and can be prepared several ways. This easy dish makes a light first course for a luncheon served with crusty bread. Alternatively, serve it as a side dish for dinner.

2 fennel bulbs

¼ cup (2 oz/60 g) unsalted butter

Juice of 1 lemon

1 cup (8 fl oz/250 ml) Vegetable Stock (page 300)

Salt and freshly ground white pepper

1 tablespoon finely chopped fresh flat-leaf (Italian) parsley, (optional)

Trim off any discolored areas of the fennel bulbs. Remove the tough stalks and feathery tops. Cut the bulbs into quarters lengthwise.

In a large sauté pan or frying pan over medium heat, melt the butter. Add the fennel in a single layer and sauté until golden on both sides, 6–7 minutes.

Add the lemon juice and then stir in ¹/₂ cup (4 fl oz/125 ml) of the warm stock. Using a spoon, baste the fennel with the pan juices. Season to taste with salt and white pepper. Reduce the heat to low, cover partially, and simmer until tender but not mushy, 20–25 minutes. During cooking, turn the fennel occasionally and add the remaining stock, 2 tablespoons at a time, as needed; the sauce should be syrupy at the end of cooking.

Sprinkle with the parsley, if desired, and serve hot.

Serves 4

Garlic Mushrooms

Serve this appetizing mushroom mixture as a first course with crusty bread; as a topping for Polenta Triangles with Saffron Tomato Sauce (page 248); or as a pasta sauce.

If desired, trim off and discard the tough stems of the mushrooms, then slice them $^{1}/_{4}$ inch (6 mm) thick.

In a large sauté pan over medium heat, melt the butter with the olive oil. Add the shallots and garlic and sauté, stirring, until softened, about 3 minutes. Next, add the mushrooms and sauté, stirring, until glossy and golden, about 8 minutes.

Add the parsley and stock, stir well, and cook for 2 minutes longer. Season to taste with salt and pepper and serve immediately.

Serves 4

1 lb (500 g) fresh mushrooms such as cremini, portobello, or shiitake, in any combination, brushed clean

$^{1}/_{4}$ cup (2 oz/60 g) unsalted butter

2 tablespoons olive oil

2 tablespoons minced shallots

1 tablespoon minced garlic

2 tablespoons minced fresh flat-leaf (Italian) parsley

$^{1}/_{2}$ cup (4 fl oz/125 ml) Vegetable Stock (page 300)

Salt and freshly ground pepper

Sautéed Corn with Chipotle Chiles and Thyme

Chipotle chiles are ripe jalapeño chiles that have been smoked. They are often canned in a sauce, adobo, which consists of tomatoes, vinegar, onions, and herbs. Here they lend a spicy, smoky nuance to the sweet corn.

In a large, heavy frying pan over medium heat, melt the butter. When hot, add the shallots and sauté, stirring until tender, about 2 minutes. Add the chiles and stir for 30 seconds longer.

Add the corn and chopped or dried thyme and cook, stirring frequently, until tender, about 5 minutes. Season to taste with salt and pepper and transfer to a warmed serving dish. Garnish with thyme sprigs, if desired, and serve at once.

Serves 8–10

½ cup (4 oz/125 g) butter

3 shallots, chopped

1 tablespoon finely chopped canned chipotle chiles (see note)

3 packages (1 lb/500 g each) frozen petite white corn kernels, thawed and well drained

2 tablespoons chopped fresh thyme or 2 teaspoons dried thyme

Salt and freshly ground pepper

Fresh thyme sprigs, optional

Sweet-and-Sour Cabbage

The sweet-and-sour flavors of this dish should be carefully balanced. Before chopping the cabbage, cut it into quarters, discard the tough outer leaves, and cut out the hard central core.

3 tablespoons unsalted butter

1 yellow onion, chopped

1 large tart green apple such as Granny Smith, cored and chopped

3 tablespoons red wine vinegar

Salt and freshly ground pepper

4 cups (³/₄ lb/375 g) chopped red or green cabbage, or a mixture

¹/₄ cup (2 fl oz/60 ml) Vegetable Stock (page 300)

2 tablespoons red currant jelly

In a large saucepan over medium heat, melt the butter. Add the onion and cook, stirring, for 2 minutes. Add the apple and vinegar, and season with salt and pepper. Add the cabbage and stir to mix. Cover and cook over medium heat for 10 minutes.

In a small bowl, mix together the stock and jelly and stir until the jelly dissolves completely. Stir the mixture into the cabbage. Re-cover and cook until the cabbage is tender, about 10 minutes.

Taste and add more salt, pepper, jelly, and/or vinegar as needed for a good sweet-sour balance. Serve immediately.

Serves 4

Sautéed Potatoes and Mushrooms with Goat Cheese

Bits of creamy goat cheese are added to a savory side dish of potatoes and mushrooms just before it is brought to the table. Prepare this dish close to serving time, so the potatoes are at their crispest.

2 lb (1 kg) red or white potatoes, peeled and cut into 1-inch (2.5-cm) pieces

3 tablespoons unsalted butter

2 tablespoons olive oil

1 lb (500 g) fresh button mushrooms, quartered

2 cloves garlic, minced

Salt and freshly ground pepper

½ cup (2 oz/60 g) crumbled fresh goat cheese

1 tablespoon finely chopped fresh basil

1 tablespoon finely chopped fresh chives

Bring a large pot three-fourths full of lightly salted water to a boil. Add the potatoes and cook for 5 minutes. Drain well in a colander and set aside.

In a large nonstick frying pan over medium-high heat, melt 1 tablespoon of the butter with 1 tablespoon of the olive oil. Add the mushrooms and sauté until lightly browned, about 5 minutes. Add the garlic and cook for 30 seconds. Transfer to a bowl and cover to keep warm.

Add the remaining 2 tablespoons butter and 1 tablespoon olive oil to the same pan over medium-high heat. Add the potatoes and sauté, turning occasionally until browned on all sides, 10–15 minutes. If the potatoes seem too dry, add a bit more butter or oil to the pan.

When the potatoes are browned, add the mushroom mixture, being careful to leave behind any excess liquid that has drained to the bottom of the bowl. Mix briefly and transfer to a serving bowl. Season to taste with salt and pepper and then toss in the goat cheese, basil, and chives. Serve immediately.

Serves 4–6

Potatoes O'Brien

Jack's, a restaurant in New York famous in the early 1900s for after-theater dining, originated these potatoes. You can vary the recipe by adding yellow and orange peppers if you like.

In a large frying pan over medium-high heat, melt $^{1}/_{2}$ tablespoon of the butter with $^{1}/_{2}$ tablespoon of the olive oil. Add the onion and sauté, stirring frequently, until golden brown and just beginning to caramelize, 5–7 minutes. Add the red and green bell pepper and sauté for 3–5 minutes longer. Transfer to a serving bowl.

Add $^{1}/_{2}$ tablespoon each of the remaining butter and olive oil to the same frying pan. Add half of the potatoes and cook, turning to brown on all sides, 5–7 minutes. If the potatoes are too dry, add a bit more butter or oil. Transfer to the bowl with the onion mixture. Add the remaining $^{1}/_{2}$ tablespoon each butter and olive oil and brown the remaining potatoes on all sides in the same manner.

Return the mixture to the pan. Raise the heat so the mixture quickly warms throughout. Remove from the heat and season to taste with salt and pepper. Add the parsley and mix to combine. Taste and adjust the seasoning. Transfer to a serving bowl and serve immediately.

Serves 4–6

1½ tablespoons unsalted butter

1½ tablespoons olive oil

1 large yellow onion, finely chopped

½ small red bell pepper (capsicum), seeded, deribbed, and finely diced

½ small green bell pepper (capsicum), seeded, deribbed, and finely diced

2 lb (1 kg) small white or red potatoes, peeled and cut into ½-inch (12-mm) dice

Salt and freshly ground pepper

2 tablespoons finely chopped fresh flat-leaf (Italian) parsley

Straw Potato–Leek Cake

If you like, turn the cooked pancake out onto a flameproof platter, sprinkle with a few tablespoons grated Gruyère cheese, and slip under a preheated broiler (grill) for a minute or so to melt the cheese.

Place the potatoes in a large bowl, add water to cover, and let stand for 5 minutes to remove excess starch, changing the water once when it becomes cloudy. Drain in a colander.

In a food processor fitted with the shredding disk, shred the potatoes. Alternatively, use a mandoline or handheld grater. The thicker you shred them, the crispier the cake will be. Place in a clean kitchen towel and wring tightly to remove all moisture. Transfer to a bowl and set aside.

In a frying pan over medium heat, melt 1 tablespoon of the butter with 1 tablespoon of the olive oil. Add the leeks and sauté until softened, about 5 minutes. Stir in 1 teaspoon salt and $1/2$ teaspoon pepper. Add the leeks to the potatoes and stir well.

In a large, nonstick frying pan over medium-high heat, warm the remaining 2 tablespoons butter and 2 tablespoons oil. Add the potato mixture and flatten firmly in the pan with a spatula. Cover and cook over medium-high heat until browned on the underside, 3–5 minutes. Invert a plate over the pan and, holding the plate firmly in place, invert the pan. Slide the pancake back into the pan, browned side up. Flatten firmly again, cover, and cook until browned and crisp on the second side, 3–5 minutes longer. Invert a warmed round serving platter on the pan and invert as directed above. Cut into wedges and serve hot.

Serves 4–6

2 lb (1 kg) white potatoes, peeled

3 tablespoons unsalted butter

3 tablespoons olive oil

2 leeks, including tender green tops, trimmed, carefully washed (page 310), and finely chopped

Salt and freshly ground pepper

One-Step Potato-Zucchini Pancakes

Here is a colorful alternative to plain potato pancakes. Serve as a side dish alongside a frittata for brunch. Applesauce or Tomato Salsa (page 303) makes a nice accompaniment.

1 yellow onion, quartered

2 eggs

1 russet potato, about ½ lb (250 g), peeled and cut into chunks

2 small zucchini (courgettes), cut into chunks

Salt and freshly ground pepper

2 tablespoons all-purpose (plain) flour

Vegetable oil for frying

In a food processor fitted with the metal blade, combine the onion and eggs and purée until smooth and fluffy. Add the potato and zucchini, using on-off pulses to process the mixture until finely chopped and still retaining some texture. Add ¹/₂ teaspoon salt, a pinch of pepper, and the flour and process briefly to combine; do not overprocess. Pour the batter into a bowl.

Preheat the oven to 300°F (150°C). Line a baking sheet with a double layer of paper towels. Pour oil to a depth of ¹/₂ inch (12 mm) into a large, nonstick frying pan and heat over medium-high heat. Spoon 1 tablespoon of the batter into the pan to test the oil; the batter should hold together and begin to brown. When the oil is hot enough, working in batches, form pancakes by spooning tablespoons of batter into the pan; make sure the pancakes do not touch. Flatten the pancakes with a spatula; they should be about 3 inches (7.5 cm) in diameter. Use the spatula to round and smooth the sides, if necessary. Fry until golden brown on the first side, 3–4 minutes. Flip and fry on the second side until golden brown, 3–4 minutes longer.

Transfer the pancakes to the paper towel–lined baking sheet to drain and place in the oven until all are cooked. Arrange on a warmed platter and serve immediately.

Makes 12–14 pancakes; serves 4–6

Parsnip and Carrot Fritters

Savory fritters make a wonderful accompaniment to a fresh green salad. The vegetables may be puréed a day in advance and refrigerated, then shaped just before cooking.

Place the parsnips and carrots in a saucepan, add water to cover, and place over high heat. Bring to a boil, reduce the heat to medium, and simmer, uncovered, until the vegetables are tender, 20–25 minutes. Drain well.

Transfer the parsnips and carrots to a food processor fitted with the metal blade and process to a smooth purée. Add the egg yolks and process for a few seconds, then add the $^1/_4$ cup (1 oz/30 g) flour, the baking powder, and salt and white pepper to taste. Process until well mixed. The batter should be fairly stiff; if it is too thin, add 1–2 tablespoons flour.

Using a tablespoon, form the mixture into ovals; you will have about 15 ovals in all. Tuck a pecan half into the center of each oval.

In a frying pan over medium heat, melt 1 tablespoon of the butter. When the butter foams, add one-third of the fritters and cook until golden brown, about 2 minutes on each side. Transfer to a warmed serving dish and keep warm. Add 1 tablespoon of the remaining butter to the pan and cook another one-third of the fritters in the same manner. Repeat with the remaining 1 tablespoon butter and fritters.

Garnish with the parsley sprigs and serve hot.

Serves 4–6

3 parsnips, about $^3/_4$ lb (375 g) total weight, peeled and cut into 2-inch (5-cm) pieces

3 carrots, about $^3/_4$ lb (375 g) total weight, peeled and cut into 2-inch (5-cm) pieces

2 egg yolks

$^1/_4$ cup (1 oz/30 g) all-purpose (plain) flour, plus more if needed

1 teaspoon baking powder

Salt and freshly ground white pepper

About 15 pecan halves

3 tablespoons unsalted butter

6 fresh flat-leaf (Italian) parsley sprigs

Corn-and-Jalapeño Pancakes with Tomato Salsa

Studded with corn and embellished with chiles and bell pepper, these zesty pancakes are as delicious as they are colorful. Serve them as a light meal at any time of the day—from breakfast to dinner.

2 cups (12 oz/375 g) fresh corn kernels (cut from about 3 ears) or frozen

5 fresh jalapeño chili peppers, seeded and minced

2 cloves garlic, finely chopped

1 red bell pepper (capsicum), seeded, deribbed, and finely diced

6 green (spring) onions, including tender green tops, thinly sliced

2 eggs

1¼ cups (6½ oz/200 g) all-purpose (plain) flour

½ cup (2½ oz/75 g) cornmeal

1 teaspoon baking powder

Salt and freshly ground pepper

2 tablespoons fresh lime juice

1½ cups (12 fl oz/375 ml) milk

About ⅓ cup (3 fl oz/80 ml) vegetable oil

1¼ cups (10 fl oz/315 ml) sour cream

Tomato Salsa (page 303) for serving

Bring a saucepan three-fourths full of lightly salted water to a boil. Add the corn kernels and cook for 1 minute. Drain, place in a large bowl, and let cool. Add the jalapeños, garlic, bell pepper, and green onions and mix well. Set aside.

In a food processor fitted with the metal blade, combine the eggs, flour, cornmeal, baking powder, 1 teaspoon salt, and the lime juice. Pulse a few times to mix. Add the milk and pulse a few more times to form a smooth batter. Add to the corn mixture and stir to mix. Season to taste with more salt, if needed, and pepper. Let stand at room temperature for 30 minutes.

In a large frying pan over medium heat, warm 2 tablespoons of the oil. Working in batches, spoon the batter into the pan to form pancakes about 3 inches (7.5 cm) in diameter; do not crowd the pan. Cook, turning once, until golden brown on both sides, 5–6 minutes total. Using a slotted spatula, transfer to paper towels to drain. Repeat with the remaining batter, adding oil as needed to prevent sticking.

Place the pancakes on a platter or individual plates and top with the sour cream and salsa. Serve at once.

Makes about 24 pancakes; serves 6

Eggplant in Spicy Chile Sauce

Serve this spicy eggplant dish with Noodles with Spicy Peanut Sauce (page 302) and Fragrant Rainbow Vegetable Platter (page 122). If you want a spicier dish, add more chile paste to taste. Serve this dish hot or cold.

To make the sauce, in a small bowl, stir together the chile paste, sherry, soy sauce, sugar, vinegar, and stock. Set aside.

In a wok or frying pan over high heat, warm the oil, swirling to coat the bottom and sides of the pan. When the oil is very hot but not quite smoking, add the eggplant and stir and toss every 15–20 seconds until lightly browned, 2–3 minutes. Add the garlic, ginger, and green onions and stir and toss for 1 minute longer. Quickly stir the chile sauce and add to the pan. Stir and toss every 15–20 seconds until the vegetables are mixed with the other ingredients, 3 minutes. Reduce the heat, cover, and simmer until the eggplant is tender, 10–12 minutes.

Uncover and season to taste with salt. Drizzle with the sesame oil and serve.

Serves 4

FOR THE CHILE SAUCE:

1 tablespoon chile paste with garlic

2 tablespoons dry sherry

2 tablespoons soy sauce

$1/2$ teaspoon sugar

2 teaspoons cider vinegar

$1/2$ cup (4 fl oz/125 ml) Vegetable Stock (page 300)

3 tablespoons peanut or vegetable oil

1 globe eggplant (aubergine), about 1 lb (500 g), or 4 Asian eggplants (slender aubergines), unpeeled, cut into 1-inch (2.5-cm) chunks

3 cloves garlic, minced

2 tablespoons peeled and finely chopped fresh ginger

4 green (spring) onions, including tender green tops, finely chopped

Salt

2 teaspoons Asian sesame oil

Stir-Fried Tofu, Green Beans, and Cashews

Tofu, the popular Asian curd made from soybeans, is beneficial to any diet, as it is low in calories and high in protein. Water-packed blocks of tofu can be found in the refrigerator case of most well-stocked markets.

1/4 cup (2 fl oz/60 ml) soy sauce

3 tablespoons dry sherry

2 teaspoons cornstarch (cornflour)

1 package (14 oz/440 g) firm tofu, well drained and cut into 1/2-inch (12-mm) dice

1/2 cup (2 1/2 oz/75 g) raw cashews

1 lb (500 g) green beans, trimmed and halved on the diagonal

3 tablespoons vegetable oil

6 unpeeled fresh ginger slices (1/4 inch/6 mm thick)

2 red onions, cut into 1/2-inch (12-mm) dice

1 cup (8 fl oz/250 ml) Vegetable Stock (page 300)

1/2 teaspoon Chile Oil (page 302)

Preheat the oven to 350°F (180°C). In a large bowl, whisk together the soy sauce, sherry, and cornstarch until the cornstarch is dissolved. Add the tofu and stir gently to coat. Set aside.

Spread the cashews on a baking sheet and bake until golden, 12–15 minutes. Remove from the oven and set aside.

Bring a large saucepan three-fourths full of lightly salted water to a boil. Add the green beans and cook until almost tender, about 3 minutes. Drain and set aside.

In a wok or large, deep frying pan over high heat, warm 2 tablespoons of the vegetable oil. When the oil is hot, add the ginger and stir and toss until fragrant, about 1 minute. Remove the ginger and discard.

Using a slotted spoon, remove the tofu from the marinade, reserving the marinade. Add the tofu to the pan. Stir and toss over high heat until the tofu is hot and golden on the outside, about 3 minutes. Transfer the tofu to a clean bowl and set aside.

Reduce the heat to medium. Add the remaining 1 tablespoon vegetable oil to the pan. Add the onions and stir and toss until they begin to soften, 5–7 minutes. Raise the heat to high and return the tofu to the pan, along with the green beans, reserved marinade, stock, and chile oil. Bring the mixture to a boil, stirring constantly, until the mixture thickens, about 30 seconds.

Remove from the heat and stir in the cashews. Transfer to a serving dish and serve immediately.

Serves 6

Green Beans with Garlic and Basil

Stir-frying parboiled green beans in olive oil gives the beans a rich golden-green color, and mixing them with garlic and fresh basil brings out their inherent sweetness. For the best results, look for tender, medium-sized beans.

Bring a large saucepan three-fourths full of water to a boil. Add the beans and boil until barely tender and still slightly resistant to the bite, 5–7 minutes. Drain, immerse the beans in cold water to stop the cooking, and drain well again.

In a wok or frying pan over medium-high heat, warm the olive oil, swirling to coat the bottom and sides of the pan. When the oil is very hot but not quite smoking, add the beans and stir and toss every 15–20 seconds until they just begin to brown, about 3 minutes. Add the garlic and basil and stir and toss for 30 seconds longer.

Remove from the heat, add salt and pepper to taste, and toss to combine. Taste and adjust the seasonings. Serve immediately.

Serves 4–6

1½ lb (750 g) tender green beans, trimmed if desired

2 tablespoons olive oil

1 clove garlic, minced

2 tablespoons finely chopped fresh basil

Salt and freshly ground pepper

Celery, Zucchini, and Carrots with Red Onion

This is a versatile side dish that can be adapted to whatever vegetables are fresh and in season. Other types of summer squash can replace the zucchini, and green beans or jicama can stand in for the celery or carrots.

¼ cup (2 fl oz/60 ml) peanut or vegetable oil

1 small red onion, thinly sliced

3 carrots, peeled and cut into strips 2 inches (5 cm) long, ¾ inch (2 cm) wide, and ¼ inch (6 mm) thick

3 celery stalks, cut into strips 2 inches (5 cm) long, ¾ inch (2 cm) wide, and ¼ inch (6 mm) thick

3 small zucchini (courgettes), cut into strips 2 inches (5 cm) long, ¾ inch (2 cm) wide, and ¼ inch (6 mm) thick

2 cloves garlic, minced

1 tablespoon soy sauce

Freshly ground pepper

1 tablespoon finely chopped fresh cilantro (fresh coriander)

In a wok or frying pan over high heat, warm the oil, swirling to coat the bottom and sides of the pan. When the oil is very hot but not quite smoking, add the onion and stir and toss every 15–20 seconds until slightly softened, 2–3 minutes. Push the onion to the side of the pan, then add the carrots and celery and stir and toss every 15–20 seconds until the vegetables are tender-crisp, 2–3 minutes. Add the zucchini and garlic and stir and toss all the vegetables together until the zucchini are tender, 2–3 minutes longer.

Add the soy sauce, ⅛ teaspoon pepper, and the cilantro to the pan and stir and toss just until the vegetables are well mixed with the other ingredients.

Taste and adjust the seasoning. Serve immediately.

Serves 4

Sweet-and-Sour Turnips
and Carrots with Sesame Seeds

Humble winter vegetables are lightly blanketed in a savory glaze finished with a sprinkling of toasted sesame seeds in this simple but excellent dish. Serve with Steamed White Rice (page 304).

FOR THE GLAZE:

3/4 cup (6 fl oz/180 ml) Vegetable Stock (page 300)

2 tablespoons natural rice vinegar

2 tablespoons sugar

1 tablespoon soy sauce

2 teaspoons sesame seeds

3 tablespoons peanut or vegetable oil

4 carrots, peeled, halved lengthwise, and cut into 3/4-inch (2-cm) chunks

4 turnips, peeled, quartered, and cut into 3/4-inch (2-cm) chunks

2 teaspoons cornstarch dissolved in 3 tablespoons water

Salt and freshly ground pepper

1 tablespoon finely chopped fresh flat-leaf (Italian) parsley

To make the glaze, combine the stock, vinegar, sugar, and soy sauce in a small bowl. Set aside.

In a dry wok or frying pan over medium heat, toast the sesame seeds, stirring constantly, until lightly browned, about 1 minute. Watch carefully so they don't burn. Transfer to a dish and set aside.

In the same pan over high heat, warm the oil, swirling to evenly coat the bottom and sides of the pan. When the oil is very hot but not quite smoking, add the carrots and turnips and stir and toss the vegetables together every 15–20 seconds until they just begin to brown, 5–6 minutes.

Quickly stir the glaze mixture and add it to the pan. Reduce the heat to low so that the mixture simmers gently, cover, and cook until the vegetables are just tender, 10–12 minutes. Uncover and raise the heat to high for 1 minute to reduce the pan juices. Stir and toss the vegetables with the other ingredients until well mixed.

Quickly stir in the cornstarch mixture and add it to the pan along with 1/4 teaspoon salt and 1/8 teaspoon pepper. Simmer over high heat, tossing to coat the vegetables, just until the sauce thickens, about 1 minute. Taste and adjust the seasoning.

Transfer to a warmed serving bowl and sprinkle with the parsley and toasted sesame seeds. Serve immediately.

Serves 4–6

Cabbage and Carrots with Garlic Chile Paste and Pine Nuts

This Asian-style stir-fry is crunchy and colorful and makes an excellent side dish. Mix in the toasted pine nuts, or transfer to a warmed serving dish and sprinkle the pine nuts on top.

In a dry wok or frying pan over medium heat, toast the pine nuts, stirring constantly, until lightly browned, 1–2 minutes. Watch carefully so they do not burn. Transfer to a dish and set aside.

In a small bowl, stir together the chile paste, soy sauce, sherry, and salt and pepper to taste. Set aside.

In the same pan over medium-high heat, warm the oil, swirling to coat the bottom and sides of the pan. When the oil is very hot but not quite smoking, add the leek, carrots, and bell pepper and stir and toss the vegetables together every 15–20 seconds until they are just beginning to soften, about 3 minutes. Add the cabbage and stir and toss every 15–20 seconds until just softened, about 3 minutes longer.

Quickly stir the chile paste mixture, add to the pan, and stir to combine. Bring to a boil over high heat and cook for 1 minute longer, stirring once or twice, until the vegetables are well mixed with the other ingredients. Taste and adjust the seasoning. Stir in the toasted pine nuts, or transfer to a warmed serving dish and sprinkle with the pine nuts. Serve immediately.

Serves 4–6

2 tablespoons pine nuts

1 teaspoon garlic chile paste

2 tablespoons soy sauce

1/4 cup (2 fl oz/60 ml) dry sherry

Salt and freshly ground pepper

3 tablespoons peanut or vegetable oil

1 leek, including tender green top, carefully washed (page 310) and finely chopped

2 carrots, peeled and cut into thin strips 2 inches (5 cm) long and 3/4 inch (2 cm) wide

1/2 red bell pepper (capsicum), seeded, deribbed, and cut into thin strips 2 inches (5 cm) long and 3/4 inch (2 cm) wide

1 head green cabbage, about 1 lb (500 g), cored and finely shredded

Stir-fried Swiss Chard with Feta Cheese

If you can't find Swiss chard, substitute fresh spinach. The feta cheese melts and adds a delightful savory–salty counterpoint to the chard. Serve as a side dish alongside Spaghetti with Marinara Sauce (page 233).

In a dry wok or medium frying pan over medium heat, toast the pine nuts, stirring constantly, until lightly browned, 1–2 minutes. Watch carefully so they do not burn. Transfer to a dish and set aside.

In the same pan over medium-high heat, warm the oil, swirling to coat the bottom and sides of the pan. When the oil is very hot but not quite smoking, carefully add the shallots and stir and toss every 10–15 seconds until they just begin to brown, 1–2 minutes. Add the Swiss chard, toss well to coat with the oil, cover, and cook until wilted, about 2 minutes. Uncover and raise the heat to high to boil away any excess liquid.

When the liquid has boiled away, add the feta cheese, cover, and cook until the cheese just begins to melt, about 30 seconds longer. If more liquid is released, carefully drain the chard in a sieve; do not drain away any of the cheese.

Transfer into a warmed serving bowl. Season to taste with salt and pepper and top with the toasted pine nuts. Serve immediately.

Serves 4

2 tablespoons pine nuts

2 tablespoons peanut or vegetable oil

2 shallots, finely chopped

2 bunches red or green Swiss chard, about 1/2 lb (250 g) each, carefully washed, stalks removed, and leaves torn into 2-inch (5-cm) pieces

1/4 cup (1 1/4 oz/37 g) crumbled feta cheese

Salt and freshly ground pepper

Stir-Fried Spinach with Garlic

This simple combination makes a great side dish for a main course of roasted vegetables or a hearty soup. A dusting of freshly grated Parmesan cheese brings all the flavors together.

1 tablespoon olive oil

2 bunches spinach, about
1/2 lb (250 g) each, carefully washed and well dried

2 cloves garlic, minced

Salt and freshly ground pepper

1 tablespoon grated Parmesan cheese

In a wok or frying pan over medium-high heat, warm the olive oil, swirling to coat the bottom and sides of the pan. When the oil is hot, add the spinach and stir and toss rapidly for about 1 minute. Cover and cook until wilted, about 2 minutes longer. Uncover and raise the heat to high to boil away any excess liquid.

Add the garlic and cook for 1 minute longer. Season to taste with salt and pepper.

Spoon into a warmed serving bowl, sprinkle with the Parmesan cheese, and toss to mix. Serve immediately.

Serves 2

Butternut Squash with Tomatoes and Leeks

This is a wonderful vegetarian main course that can be served with fried rice or crusty bread and a salad. Top with extra shredded basil just before serving, if you like.

Halve the squash and scoop out the seeds and any fibers. Peel the squash and cut into 1/4-inch (6-mm) dice.

In a wok or frying pan over medium-high heat, warm 2 tablespoons of the olive oil, swirling to coat the bottom and sides of the pan. When the oil is very hot but not quite smoking, add the squash and stir and toss every 15–20 seconds until lightly browned, 3–5 minutes. Transfer to a dish.

Add the remaining 1 tablespoon olive oil to the pan over medium-high heat, again swirling to coat the pan. When the oil is hot, add the leek and stir and toss every 15–20 seconds until softened, 2–3 minutes. Add the garlic, tomatoes, and stock and simmer for 1 minute.

Return the squash to the pan and stir and toss all the ingredients together. Cover and cook over medium-high heat until the squash is tender when pierced with a fork, 7–10 minutes. Uncover and add 1/2 teaspoon salt, 1/4 teaspoon white pepper, and the basil, stirring and tossing to combine.

Taste and adjust the seasoning. If any excess moisture remains, cook uncovered over medium-high heat until the liquid evaporates; this should take only a minute or so. Serve immediately.

Serve 4–6

1 butternut squash, about
2 lb (1 kg)

3 tablespoons olive oil

1 leek, including tender
green tops, carefully washed
(page 310) and finely chopped

1 clove garlic, minced

2 cups (12 oz/375 g) peeled,
seeded (page 313), and diced
fresh tomatoes or seeded,
well-drained, and diced
canned tomatoes

3/4 cup (6 fl oz/180 ml)
Vegetable Stock (page 300)

Salt and freshly ground white
pepper

3 tablespoons finely chopped
fresh basil

Chinese-Style Vegetables

A crisp and appealing dish of fresh green and white vegetables with the unexpected addition of pine nuts or almonds. This stir-fry is good with steamed rice mixed with finely grated lemon zest.

¹/₄ cup (2 fl oz/60 ml) cold-pressed sesame oil or safflower oil

3 celery stalks, trimmed and cut on the diagonal

¹/₂ lb (250 g) green beans, trimmed and cut on the diagonal

6 cauliflower florets, cut on the diagonal

6 broccoli florets, cut on the diagonal

1 small bok choy, leaves cut into long, thin slivers

1 cup (8 fl oz/250 ml) Vegetable Stock (page 300), heated

1 tablespoon soy sauce

¹/₂ teaspoon red pepper flakes

¹/₂ cup (3 oz/90 g) pine nuts or coarsely chopped almonds

In a large wok or frying pan over medium heat, warm the oil, swirling to coat the bottom and sides of the pan. When the oil is very hot but not quite smoking, add the celery, beans, cauliflower, broccoli, and bok choy and stir until evenly coated with the oil. Raise the heat to high and add ¹/₂ cup (4 fl oz/125 ml) of the stock, the soy sauce, and the red pepper flakes. Stir and toss until the vegetables are barely tender, 2–4 minutes. When the stock evaporates, add only enough of the remaining stock as needed to prevent sticking.

Taste and adjust the seasoning. Stir in the pine nuts or almonds and serve.

Serves 4

Fragrant Rainbow Vegetable Platter

A highly aromatic, mildly sweet-and-sour glaze coats a rainbow of vegetables in this dish. If the mushrooms are very small, leave them whole. Pair this dish with Tofu-Vegetable Fried Rice (page 271).

FOR THE SAUCE:

1 tablespoon natural rice vinegar

1 tablespoon mirin

1 teaspoon cornstarch

2 teaspoons soy sauce

1 green (spring) onion, including tender green top, minced

2 tablespoons peanut or vegetable oil

1/2 lb (250 g) fresh button mushrooms, brushed clean, stems removed, and caps halved

2 small zucchini (courgettes), cut into strips 2 inches (5 cm) long, 3/4 inch (2 cm) wide, and 1/2 inch (12 mm) thick

1 red bell pepper (capsicum), seeded, deribbed (page 308), and cut into strips 2 inches (5 cm) long and 3/4 inch (2 cm) wide

1 cup (6 oz/185 g) canned baby corn, rinsed, drained, and halved lengthwise

To make the sauce, combine the vinegar, mirin, cornstarch, soy sauce, and green onion in a small bowl and stir to dissolve the cornstarch. Set aside.

In a wok or frying pan over high heat, warm the oil, swirling to coat the bottom and sides of the pan. When the oil is very hot but not quite smoking, add the mushrooms, zucchini, and bell pepper, and stir and toss the vegetables together every 15–20 seconds until they are tender-crisp, 3–4 minutes. Add the baby corn and stir and toss for 1 minute.

Quickly stir the sauce, add to the pan, and stir and toss until the ingredients are well mixed and heated through and the sauce thickens slightly, 1 minute longer. Taste and adjust the seasoning. Serve immediately.

Serves 4

Sesame Treasure Vegetables

This is a quick and colorful vegetable dish — just what you want when a simple accompaniment is all that's needed. This dish is also good served with Steamed White Rice (page 304).

In a dry wok or frying pan over medium heat, toast the sesame seeds, stirring constantly, until lightly browned, about 1 minute. Watch carefully so they do not burn. Transfer to a dish and set aside.

Add the oil to the same pan over high heat, swirling to coat the bottom and sides of the pan. When the oil is very hot but not quite smoking, add the bell peppers and stir and toss together every 15–20 seconds until they just begin to soften, 2–3 minutes. Add the snow peas and stir and toss for 1 minute.

Stir the stir-fry sauce and add to the pan. Stir and toss until the vegetables are mixed with the other ingredients, about 1 minute. Taste and adjust the seasoning.

Drizzle with the sesame oil and the toasted sesame seeds. Serve immediately.

Serves 2 or 3

1 tablespoon sesame seeds

2 tablespoons peanut or vegetable oil

1 red bell pepper (capsicum), seeded, deribbed (page 308), and thinly sliced

1 yellow bell pepper (capsicum), seeded, deribbed (page 308), and thinly sliced

1/4 lb (125 g) snow peas (mangetouts)

All-Purpose Stir-fry Sauce (page 300)

1/2 teaspoon sesame oil

Boiled & Steamed Vegetables

Green Beans with Celery and Water Chestnuts

Fresh green beans cooked until barely tender and then tossed with crisp celery and water chestnuts is an especially refreshing combination of flavors and textures. Serve with Steamed White Rice (page 304).

½ lb (250 g) small, tender green beans, trimmed and cut in half lengthwise

4 large, tender inner celery stalks, trimmed and thinly sliced crosswise

½ cup (3 oz/90 g) thinly sliced water chestnuts

½ cup (4 fl oz/125 ml) olive oil

3 tablespoons red wine vinegar

Few drops of soy sauce

1 tablespoon heavy (double) cream

Salt and freshly ground pepper

Fill a saucepan with just enough water to cover the beans once they are added. Bring to a boil. Add the beans, cover, and cook over medium heat until barely tender, 6–7 minutes. Drain well in a colander and set aside.

Combine the beans, celery, and water chestnuts in a serving bowl.

In a small bowl, whisk together the olive oil, vinegar, soy sauce, cream, and salt and pepper to taste. Pour the dressing over the vegetables and toss well. Serve at room temperature.

Serves 4

Cucumbers and Green Peas

Cooked cucumbers are a nice addition to many dishes. Choose fresh peas with crisp, smooth, glossy, bright green pods. Frozen peas may also be used, but thaw them first, so they cook at the same rate as the cucumbers.

1 cucumber

1¹/₂ cups (12 fl oz/375 ml) Vegetable Stock (page 300)

1 cup (5 oz/155 g) English shelled peas

¹/₄ cup (2 fl oz/60 ml) heavy (double) cream

1 tablespoon unsalted butter

4 tablespoons chopped fresh flat-leaf (Italian) parsley

Salt and freshly ground pepper

Using a sharp knife or vegetable peeler, cut lengthwise strips of the peel from the cucumber to give it a striped appearance. Cut the cucumber in half lengthwise. Using a spoon, scoop out the seeds, then cut the cucumber halves crosswise into slices ³/₈ inch (1 cm) thick.

Pour the stock into a frying pan and bring to a boil. Add the cucumber slices and peas and cook, uncovered, over medium heat until nearly tender, about 4 minutes.

Remove from the heat and pour off the stock into a bowl. Set the pan with the vegetables aside. Measure out ¹/₂ cup (4 fl oz/125 ml) of the reserved stock and pour it into a small saucepan. Stir in the cream and bring to a boil over high heat. Cook, uncovered, until the sauce thickens, 3–4 minutes.

Add the butter to the pan holding the peas and cucumbers. Place over medium heat to melt the butter. Add the parsley and cook, stirring, for 1 minute. Add the sauce and simmer to allow the flavors to blend, 3–4 minutes. Season to taste with salt and pepper and serve.

Serves 4

Minted Green Peas with Hearts of Lettuce

A thoroughly satisfying vegetable dish, especially when made with fresh summer peas and tender hearts of lettuce, unadorned except for butter to enhance the fresh flavors.

Pour the stock into a frying pan and bring to a boil over medium heat.

Meanwhile, tie together the parsley sprigs, bay leaf, and mint sprig with kitchen string to make the bouquet garni. Add the bouquet garni, sugar, peas, and hearts of lettuce to the boiling stock. Simmer, uncovered, until the peas are almost tender, about 5 minutes.

Pour off all but ¹/₄ cup (2 fl oz/60 ml) of the stock and discard. Add the butter and salt and white pepper to taste to the pan. Cook, stirring, over medium heat for 2 minutes. Discard the bouquet. Cut the lettuce hearts in half.

Transfer to a bowl and sprinkle with the chopped mint.

Serves 4

1 cup (8 fl oz/250 ml) Vegetable Stock (page 300)

2 fresh flat-leaf (Italian) parsley sprigs

1 bay leaf

1 fresh mint sprig, plus 1 tablespoon finely chopped mint

¹/₂ teaspoon sugar

2 cups (10 oz/315 g) shelled English peas or thawed frozen petite peas

2 hearts of butter (Boston) lettuce

2 tablespoons unsalted butter

Salt and freshly ground white pepper

Asparagus with Vinaigrette Sauce

1 lb (500 g) asparagus

½ cup (4 fl oz/125 ml) olive oil

2 tablespoons chopped shallots

3 tablespoons red wine vinegar

1½ teaspoons Dijon mustard

Salt and freshly ground pepper

2 tablespoons chopped fresh flat-leaf (Italian) parsley

2 hard-boiled egg yolks

Cut or snap off any tough, woody ends from the asparagus and discard. Using a vegetable peeler and starting about 2 inches (5 cm) below each tip, peel off the skin of each spear.

Select a large frying pan or sauté pan large enough to hold the spears flat in a single layer and fill halfway with water. Bring to a boil, then reduce the heat so the water simmers gently with just a few bubbles breaking on the surface. Lay the asparagus spears flat in the pan (they should be covered with about 1 inch (2.5 cm) of water). Cook until tender-crisp, 4–8 minutes. Begin testing with the tip of a knife after 4 minutes; the timing will depend upon the thickness of the spears. Remove from the heat and drain well.

In a small bowl, whisk together the olive oil, shallots, vinegar, and mustard. Season to taste with salt and pepper, and add the parsley.

Arrange the spears on a warmed serving platter. Spoon the dressing over the warm asparagus. To garnish, using a wooden spoon, force the egg yolks through a fine-mesh sieve held over the asparagus.

Serves 4

Brussels Sprouts and Chestnuts

If fresh Brussels sprouts are unavailable, use frozen. Chestnuts, with their slightly sweet taste and crumbly thick texture, go well with the crisp sprouts. If fresh chestnuts are unavailable, use whole canned chestnuts.

Using a small, sharp knife, make a gash on the flat side of each chestnut (this will prevent them from bursting). Pour the stock into a saucepan and bring to a boil over high heat. Add the chestnuts, celery, and lemon zest. Reduce the heat to low, cover, and simmer until the chestnuts are tender, about 30 minutes.

Meanwhile, carefully trim the Brussels sprouts, discarding any old or wilted leaves. Place in a large frying pan in a single layer and add water to cover. Bring to a boil over high heat and add the lemon juice. Reduce the heat to medium-low and simmer, uncovered, until barely tender, 8–10 minutes. Drain well and set aside.

Drain the chestnuts well; discard the celery and lemon zest. Using a small, sharp knife, peel the chestnuts while warm, removing both the hard outer shell and the furry inner skin.

In a large frying pan over medium heat, melt the butter. Add the chestnuts, salt to taste, and the cayenne. Sauté to brown and glaze, about 5 minutes. Add the Brussels sprouts and sauté over low heat until heated through and tender, about 5 minutes. Transfer to a serving dish and serve hot.

Serves 4

12 chestnuts

3 cups (24 fl oz/750 ml) Vegetable Stock (page 300)

4 small celery stalks, without the leaves

1 strip lemon zest

2 cups (1/2 lb/250 g) small Brussels sprouts

Juice of 1/2 lemon

3 tablespoons unsalted butter

Salt

1/8 teaspoon cayenne pepper

Broccoli and Olives with Garlic and Pepper Vinaigrette

The spicy-hot vinaigrette is also good on cooked cauliflower or zucchini (courgettes). It can be made 4–6 hours in advance of combining with the broccoli. The broccoli can be cooked and chilled 2–4 hours before serving.

1 large or 2 small heads broccoli, about 1¹/₂ lb (750 g) total weight, cut into florets with stems intact and thick stems peeled

¹/₂ cup (4 fl oz/125 ml) olive oil

2 teaspoons red pepper flakes

2 tablespoons red wine vinegar

2 cloves garlic, minced

Salt and freshly ground pepper to taste

1 cup (5 oz/155 g) Gaeta or similar black olives

Bring a large pot three-fourths full of salted water to a boil. Add the broccoli and cook until tender-crisp, 3–4 minutes. Drain, being careful not to break the florets, and immediately immerse in ice water to stop the cooking and preserve the vibrant color. Drain well again and pat dry with paper towels. Cover and chill well.

In a small saucepan over medium heat, warm the olive oil until it is very hot but not smoking. Add the pepper flakes and heat until the oil is red, about 30 seconds. Remove from the heat and let cool. Strain through a fine-mesh sieve into a measuring cup. Stir in the vinegar and garlic; season with salt and ground pepper.

Just before serving, arrange the chilled broccoli on a platter. Drizzle with the vinaigrette and sprinkle with the olives. Serve immediately.

Serves 4

BOILED & STEAMED VEGETABLES

Rutabaga with Apples

Part wild cabbage, part wild turnip, with a distinctive cabbagelike flavor, rutabaga becomes a pretty yellow when cooked. Any firm, tart apple, such as Granny Smith, will work for this recipe.

Place the rutabaga slices in a large frying pan, overlapping them as little as possible. Add water just to cover and bring to a boil over high heat. Cover, reduce the heat to low, and simmer until tender, 10–15 minutes. Drain in a colander and set aside.

Place the apples in the same frying pan, overlapping them as little as possible. Add the orange juice. Cover and bring to a simmer over medium heat. Cook until soft, 5–6 minutes.

Put the apples and their cooking liquid in a food processor fitted with the metal blade. Add the rutabaga slices and process to a smooth purée. Return the purée to the frying pan and heat to serving temperature, stirring well. Add the butter and salt and white pepper to taste.

Transfer to a serving dish and garnish with any reserved cooked apple slices. Serve immediately.

Serves 4 or 5

2 rutabagas, about 1½ lb (750 g) total weight, peeled and thinly sliced

2 tart apples, peeled, cored, and thinly sliced, plus extra slices for garnish (optional)

½ cup (4 fl oz/125 ml) fresh orange juice

2 tablespoons unsalted butter

Salt and freshly ground white pepper

Turnip and Pear Purée

This is a delicious and unusual combination. The subtle flavor of the pears complements the sharp, peppery taste of the turnips. Serve in the winter alongside other hearty vegetables.

6 small, white turnips, peeled and cut crosswise into slices 1/2 inch (12 mm) thick

2 tablespoons unsalted butter

Pinch of sugar

Salt and freshly ground white pepper

2 ripe brown winter pears such as Bosc, peeled, cored, and thinly sliced lengthwise

Juice of 1/2 lemon

1 tablespoon finely grated orange zest

Place the turnip slices in a large frying pan, overlapping them as little as possible. Add water just to cover, 1 tablespoon of the butter, the sugar, and salt to taste. Bring to a boil over medium heat. Reduce the heat to low, cover, and simmer until the turnips are tender, 12–15 minutes.

Meanwhile, place the pears in a small saucepan over low heat with the lemon juice and 1/2 cup (4 fl oz/125 ml) water. Cover and simmer until soft, 5–6 minutes.

Drain the turnips and pears. Place in a food processor fitted with the metal blade and process until smooth. Transfer the purée to a saucepan and stir over high heat for a few minutes to evaporate any remaining liquid. Add the remaining 1 tablespoon butter and season to taste with salt and white pepper. Stir in the orange zest and transfer to a serving dish. Serve hot.

Serves 4

Gingered Yam and Squash Purée

This deliciously sweet dish goes well on a Thanksgiving table. Fresh ginger adds piquancy, and maple syrup adds depth to this golden orange purée. Garnish with chopped parsley, if you like.

Preheat the oven to 400°F (200°C).

Scrub the sweet potatoes to remove all dirt, then dry thoroughly with a clean kitchen towel. Rub each sweet potato with 1 teaspoon of the oil to coat evenly. Place on an ungreased baking sheet and bake for 30 minutes. Prick the skin in several places with a fork and continue to bake until tender when pierced with a knife, about 30 minutes longer. Remove from the oven and let cool.

While the sweet potatoes are baking, arrange the squash slices in a collapsible steamer basket set over 1 inch (2.5 cm) of boiling water in a saucepan with a lid. Cover and steam over medium heat until tender when pierced with a knife, 15–20 minutes. Remove from the heat and set aside.

When the sweet potatoes are cool enough to handle, cut in half, scoop out the pulp from the skins, and place in a food processor fitted with the metal blade. Add the squash, ginger, maple syrup, and butter and process to a smooth purée. Add salt and white pepper to taste.

Spoon into a serving bowl, garnish with the parsley, and serve immediately.

Serves 4–6

2 yams (orange-fleshed sweet potatoes), about 1/2 lb (250 g) each

2 teaspoons vegetable oil

1 butternut squash, about 2 lb (1 kg), peeled, seeded, and cut into slices 1 inch (2.5 cm) thick

1 1/2 teaspoons peeled and finely chopped fresh ginger

1 tablespoon maple syrup

2 tablespoons unsalted butter

Salt and freshly ground white pepper

2 tablespoons finely chopped fresh flat-leaf (Italian) parsley

New Potatoes with Lemon Butter and Fresh Herbs

For an attractive presentation, use a small, sharp knife to remove a band of skin around the middle of each potato before cooking; leave the rest of the skin intact. The green herbs add zest and color to the potatoes.

Arrange the unpeeled potatoes in a single layer in a large frying pan. Add water to cover and place over high heat. Bring to a boil, reduce the heat to low, cover, and simmer until tender but still firm, 10–12 minutes. Drain well.

In a frying pan over low heat, melt the butter with the olive oil. Add the lemon zest, chives, basil, parsley, potatoes, and salt and pepper to taste. Heat gently, stirring to coat the potatoes on all sides with the butter mixture. Add the lemon juice, stir well, and serve immediately.

Serves 4

16 small new potatoes,
1–1¹/₂ lb (500–750 g)

2 tablespoons unsalted butter

3 tablespoons olive oil

Grated zest and juice of
1 lemon

1 tablespoon chopped fresh
chives

1 tablespoon chopped fresh
basil

1 tablespoon chopped fresh
flat-leaf (Italian) parsley

Salt and freshly ground pepper

Olive Oil Mashed Potatoes

You can add herbs such as rosemary, chervil, chives, thyme, oregano, or parsley to these olive oil–enriched mashed potatoes, or mix in some grated lemon zest for a particularly lively flavor.

3 lb (1.5 kg) red potatoes, peeled and quartered

4 tablespoons (2 fl oz/60 ml) extra-virgin olive oil

2 tablespoons heavy (double) cream, warmed

¼ cup (2 oz/60 g) unsalted butter, at room temperature

2 tablespoons white wine vinegar

Salt and freshly ground pepper

Bring a saucepan three-fourths full of lightly salted water to a boil. Add the potatoes and boil until tender when pierced with a fork, about 20 minutes.

Drain the potatoes and return them to the saucepan. Place over low heat and, using a potato masher, mash the potatoes. Mix in 3 tablespoons of the olive oil, the cream, and butter. Add the vinegar and season to taste with salt and pepper.

To serve, place a mound of potatoes on each plate and use the back of a spoon to make a well in the center. Pour an equal amount of the remaining 1 tablespoon olive oil into each well. Serve immediately.

Serves 6

Chinese Cabbage with Sesame Seeds

A mild Asian vegetable with pale green leaves, Chinese or napa cabbage is more like a lettuce than a cabbage. It can be used in many different ways: shredded raw in a salad, steamed, stir-fried, or stuffed.

2 tablespoons sesame seeds

1 1/2 cups (12 fl oz/375 ml) Vegetable Stock (page 300)

4 green (spring) onions

1 small head napa cabbage, thinly sliced lengthwise and then cut in half crosswise

2 tablespoons unsalted butter

1/2 teaspoon red pepper flakes

Salt and freshly ground white pepper

In a small, dry frying pan over medium-low heat, toast the sesame seeds, stirring constantly, until lightly browned, about 1 minute. Watch carefully so that they do not burn. Transfer to a dish and set aside.

Pour the stock into a large frying pan over high heat. Bring to a boil and cook to reduce and concentrate the stock, 2–3 minutes.

Cut the green onions in half lengthwise, then cut into long, thin strips. Add to the boiling stock. Add the cabbage and reduce the heat to medium. Cook, stirring occasionally, until the cabbage is tender, about 5 minutes. The stock should be almost totally absorbed.

Add the butter and toasted sesame seeds into the cabbage and stir in the red pepper flakes. Add salt and white pepper to taste and serve.

Serves 4

Steamed Broccoli with Pine Nuts

Broccoli is available year-round, but it is at its best from autumn through spring. Look for compact, tightly furled buds, relatively slender stalks, and a deep green color.

In a dry frying pan over medium heat, toast the pine nuts, stirring constantly, until lightly browned, 1–2 minutes. Watch carefully so that they do not burn. Transfer to a dish and set aside.

Trim the ends of the broccoli stalks and cut off any coarse outer leaves. Cut off the flower heads and then divide the heads into florets with short stems; cut any large florets in half. Using a vegetable peeler, peel the thick stalks to reveal their pale green flesh. Using a sharp knife, cut the stalks on the diagonal into slices $1/3$ inch (9 mm) thick.

Arrange the broccoli in a collapsible steamer basket set over 1 inch (2.5 cm) of boiling water in a saucepan with a lid. Cover and steam until the stalks are just tender when pierced with a knife, about 5 minutes.

Transfer the broccoli to a serving dish and drizzle the melted butter over the top. Toss gently and season lightly with salt. Top with the toasted pine nuts and serve.

Serves 4

2 tablespoons pine nuts

1½ lb (750 g) broccoli

2 tablespoons unsalted butter, melted

Salt

Fresh Corn Tamales

You'll be surprised by the smooth, rich flavor of these buttery tamales from the Michoacán state in Mexico. It is essential to use only the freshest corn. Accompany with beans or a green salad.

Remove the husks in large pieces and pick the silks from the corn. Wash the husks, dry them well, and set aside.

Using a sharp knife, cut the kernels from the cobs; you should have about 5 cups (30 oz/925 g). Using a blender or a food processor, process the kernals, 1 cup (6 oz/ 185 g) at a time, at high speed, gradually adding the milk to ease the processing. The corn should have the consistency of cottage cheese. Place in a bowl, add the salt and butter, and stir to mix well.

Fill a large pan with hot water to a depth of 2-3 inches (5-7.5 cm). Line a steamer basket with the stiffest corn husks. Reserve 14-16 softer husks to use as wrappers.

On each soft husk, place a heaping spoonful of corn filling in the center. Fold the sides in loosely, overlapping them, and fold the bottom end over to rest atop the seam. The top end stays open. Layer, seam side up, in the basket. Cover with a layer of stiff husks.

Bring the water to a simmer. Cover and cook the tamales until the filling is firm (check by opening a tamale), about 1 hour. Check the water from time to time and add boiling water as needed to maintain original level. Remove from the heat and let cool for about 20 minutes so the filling will not stick to the husks.

Serve the tamales in their husks. Accompany with separate bowls of the sour cream, salsa, and cheese, if desired.

Makes 14–16 tamales; serves 4

8-10 ears of corn, husks intact

About 1/3 cup (3 fl oz/80 ml) milk

1/2 teaspoon salt

2 tablespoons unsalted butter, at room temperature

1 cup (8 fl oz/250 ml) thick sour cream

Tomato salsa (page 303) or Tomatillo Salsa (page 303)

Crumbled *queso fresco* or feta cheese, optional

Baked, Roasted & Grilled Vegetables

Baked Beets with Orange

12 small young beets with greens attached

1/2 cup (4 fl oz/125 ml) olive oil

1/4 cup (2 fl oz/60 ml) red wine vinegar

1/4 cup (2 fl oz/60 ml) fresh orange juice

3 tablespoons chopped fresh tarragon

Salt and freshly ground pepper

Preheat the oven to 350°F (180°C).

Cut off the greens from the beets, leaving about 1/2 inch (12 mm) of the stems. Discard the tough, damaged outer leaves. Thoroughly wash the beets and greens. Chop the greens coarsely.

Place the whole beets and the greens in a baking dish with a lid. Add 1/2 cup (4 fl oz/125 ml) water, cover the dish, and place in the oven. Bake until the beets are tender, about 40–50 minutes (the amount of time will depend upon the size of the beets). Remove from the oven and set aside to cool.

Trim off the stem and root ends of the beets. Peel; the skins will slip off easily. Slice the beets thinly and place on a serving plate. Using a slotted spoon, transfer the greens to the plate and arrange around the beets.

In a small bowl, stir together the olive oil, vinegar, orange juice, and 2 tablespoons of the tarragon. Season to taste with salt and pepper.

Pour the dressing evenly over the beets and greens. Garnish with the remaining 1 tablespoon tarragon and serve.

Serves 4

Baked Belgian Endive

There are many delectable ways to cook endive; it doesn't always have to go into the salad bowl. This dish makes an elegant side dish. It can also be served on its own as a light lunch with soup.

Preheat the oven to 375°F (190°C).

Trim the endive heads and remove any damaged leaves.

Pour a little of the melted butter into a baking dish. Add the endives and drizzle the remaining butter over the top. Sprinkle with the lemon juice. Pour the stock into the dish and season to taste with salt and pepper. Butter a piece of parchment paper or waxed paper and use it to cover the dish loosely, buttered side down.

Place in the oven and bake for 20 minutes. Remove the paper and baste the endives with the dish juices. Continue baking until the endives are tender and slightly golden, 20–30 minutes longer.

Dust with paprika and sprinkle with the cheeses. Continue to bake until the cheeses melt and turn golden, 5–6 minutes. Serve hot, directly from the dish.

Serves 4

4 heads Belgian endive (chicory/witloof)

3 tablespoons unsalted butter, melted

Juice of 1 lemon

1/2 cup (4 fl oz/125 ml) Vegetable Stock (page 300)

Salt and freshly ground pepper

Paprika for dusting

1/4 cup (1 oz/30 g) shredded Gruyère cheese

1/4 cup (1 oz/30 g) grated Parmesan cheese

Baked Artichokes with Mushroom Stuffing

Preheat the oven to 375°F (190°C).

Bring a large saucepan filled halfway with water to a boil. Cut off the entire stems of the artichokes so they will sit upright. Cut 1 inch (2.5 cm) off the top of each artichoke and remove the tough outer leaves. Place the artichokes upright in the saucepan and add the lemon juice. Reduce the heat to medium, cover, and simmer for 15 minutes.

Remove the artichokes and invert to drain well. When they are cool enough to handle, gently separate the leaves of each artichoke to expose the prickly choke. Using a spoon, scoop out the choke. Set the artichokes aside.

In a frying pan over medium heat, warm 2 tablespoons of the oil. Add the garlic, shallots, and mushrooms and sauté until soft, about 2 minutes. Add 2 tablespoons of the parsley, the mint, and salt and pepper to taste. Mix in the bread crumbs.

Fill each artichoke with an equal amount of the mixture. Place the artichokes upright in a baking dish and sprinkle the remaining 1 tablespoon oil around them. Pour in the warm stock. Bake until the artichokes are tender, about 30 minutes.

Remove from the oven and garnish with the remaining 1 tablespoon parsley. Serve hot or at room temperature.

Serves 4

4 artichokes

Juice of 1 lemon

3 tablespoons olive oil

2 cloves garlic, chopped

2 shallots, chopped

1/2 cup (2 oz/60 g) chopped fresh white mushrooms

3 tablespoons chopped fresh flat-leaf (Italian) parsley

1 tablespoon chopped fresh mint

Salt and freshly ground pepper

1/3 cup (1 1/2 oz/45 g) fine dried bread crumbs (page 308)

2 cups (16 fl oz/500 ml) Vegetable Stock (page 300)

Jerusalem Artichoke Gratin

A bulbous root with a sweet, slightly nutty flavor, Jerusalem artichokes, also known as sunchokes, are easier to peel when cooked. This gratinéed dish is excellent served as a main course at dinner.

1 lb (500 g) Jerusalem artichokes

3 tablespoons unsalted butter

1/2 yellow onion, chopped

1 teaspoon dried thyme

1 teaspoon dried sage

3 tablespoons all-purpose (plain) flour

2 cups (16 fl oz/500 ml) milk, warmed

Salt and freshly ground white pepper

1/4 cup (1 oz/30 g) freshly grated Parmesan cheese

Paprika for dusting

Preheat the oven to 400°F (200°C).

Fill a large saucepan with just enough water to cover the Jerusalem artichokes once they are added. Bring to a boil. Add the Jerusalem artichokes and cook, uncovered, over high heat until tender but still firm, about 15 minutes. Drain well and let cool. Peel and cut into slices 1/2 inch (12 mm) thick. Place in a bowl and set aside.

In a saucepan over medium heat, melt the butter. Add the onion, thyme, and sage and sauté for 2 minutes. Add the flour and cook, stirring, for 1 minute. Slowly add 1 cup (8 fl oz/250 ml) of the warm milk, stirring constantly. As the sauce begins to thicken, slowly stir in the remaining 1 cup (8 fl oz/250 ml) milk. Continue to stir until thickened, 1–2 minutes. Season to taste with salt and white pepper.

Mix the sauce with the Jerusalem artichokes and transfer to a 1 1/2-qt (1.5-l) baking dish. Sprinkle with the cheese and dust with paprika. Place the baking dish on a baking sheet. Bake until the sauce bubbles and the cheese is golden, 10–15 minutes.

Serve hot, directly from the baking dish.

Serves 4

Gratin of Zucchini, Eggplant, and Chickpeas

This recipe is ideal when you have a variety of vegetables on hand, as many different types can be used. Add yellow squash in place of the zucchini or a red or yellow bell pepper in place of the green one.

Pick over the chickpeas and discard any damaged peas or stones. Rinse and drain. Place in a bowl, add plenty of water to cover, and let soak for 3 hours.

Drain the chickpeas and place in a saucepan with water to cover by 2 inches (5 cm). Bring to a boil, reduce the heat to low, and simmer, uncovered, until tender, about 45–60 minutes. Drain and set aside.

Cut the eggplant and zucchini crosswise into slices 1 inch (2.5 cm) thick. Set aside. In a large frying pan over medium heat, warm the olive oil. Add the onions and bell pepper and cook, stirring occasionally, until soft, about 10 minutes. Add the eggplants and zucchini and continue to cook, stirring occasionally, until just lightly browned, about 10 minutes longer. Add the garlic and cook, stirring, for 1 minute. Raise the heat to high and add the tomatoes, stock, red pepper flakes, basil, thyme, and chickpeas. Bring to a boil over high heat. Reduce the heat to medium-low and simmer, uncovered, for 30 minutes. Season to taste with salt and pepper.

Position a rack in the upper third of the oven and preheat to 375°F (190°C). Oil a shallow 2-qt (2-l) baking dish.

Pour the vegetable mixture into the prepared dish. Sprinkle the Parmesan evenly over the top. Bake until golden and bubbling around the edges, about 20 minutes.

Let cool for 10 minutes. Spoon onto warmed plates and serve.

Serves 6

½ cup (3½ oz/105 g) dried chickpeas (garbanzo beans)

3 Asian eggplants (slender aubergines), about ¾ lb (375 g) total weight

3 zucchini (courgettes), about ¾ lb (375 g) total weight

3 tablespoons olive oil

2 small yellow onions, quartered

1 large green bell pepper (capsicum), seeded, deribbed (page 308), and cut into 1-inch (2.5-cm) squares

4 cloves garlic, finely chopped

1½ cups (9 oz/280 g) peeled, seeded (page 313), and chopped tomatoes

1 cup (8 fl oz/250 ml) Vegetable Stock (page 300)

¼ teaspoon red pepper flakes

¼ cup (¼ oz/7 g) chopped fresh basil

1 teaspoon chopped fresh thyme

Salt and freshly ground pepper

½ cup (2 oz/60 g) grated Parmesan cheese

Baked Tomatoes with Garlic, Parsley, and Bread Crumbs

For this Provençal dish, you need ripe, flavorful tomatoes. The key to success is to drain the excess water from the tomato halves so that the tops become crusty during baking and the sides do not split.

6 large, ripe but firm tomatoes

Salt and freshly ground pepper

6 tablespoons (3 fl oz/90 ml) olive oil

½ cup (2 oz/60 g) fine dried bread crumbs (page 308)

3 cloves garlic, minced

½ cup (¾ oz/20 g) chopped fresh flat-leaf (Italian) parsley

Cut the tomatoes in half crosswise. Sprinkle the cut sides with salt and drain, cut sides down, in a colander for about 10 minutes. Pat dry with paper towels.

Preheat the oven to 400°F (200°C). Select a baking dish large enough to hold all of the tomato halves in a single layer. Lightly grease the dish.

In a large sauté pan over medium-high heat, warm 2 tablespoons of the olive oil. Add half of the tomato halves, cut sides down, and fry until golden, 3–5 minutes. Transfer to the prepared dish, cut sides up. Repeat with the remaining tomato halves and 2 additional tablespoons olive oil.

Sprinkle the tomatoes with salt and pepper to taste. In a small bowl, stir together the bread crumbs, garlic, and a little of the parsley. Spread the mixture on top of the tomatoes, dividing it evenly. Drizzle evenly with the remaining 2 tablespoons oil.

Bake until puffed and juicy, 10–15 minutes. Transfer to a warmed platter and sprinkle with the remaining parsley. Serve at once.

Serves 6

Baked Tomatoes with Spinach

Stuffed ripe tomatoes are an ideal dish for summer meals. Serve with a cold soup or with a large salad, cheese, fruit, and crusty bread. As an added bonus, these tomatoes can be made ahead and served warm or cold.

Preheat the oven to 375°F (190°C).

Slice off the tops of the tomatoes and scoop out the pulp and seeds. Invert the tomatoes on a dish to drain.

In a frying pan over medium heat, melt the butter. Add the green onion and parsley and sauté for 2 minutes. Add the spinach and cook, stirring, until all the liquid has evaporated, about 2 minutes.

Slowly add the Béchamel Sauce to the pan, stirring to mix well with the spinach. Stir in $^{1}/_{2}$ cup (2 oz/60 g) of the Parmesan and season to taste with salt and pepper. Remove from the heat.

Place the tomatoes, hollow side up, in a large baking dish. Sprinkle the insides with salt and pepper. Spoon an equal amount of the spinach mixture into each tomato. Pour $^{1}/_{2}$ cup (4 fl oz/125 ml) of the stock around the tomatoes. Place in the oven and bake until the tomatoes are soft, about 40 minutes, basting with the dish juices 2 or 3 times during baking. Add the remaining $^{1}/_{2}$ cup (4 fl oz/125 ml) stock to the dish as needed for basting.

Remove from the oven and sprinkle the remaining $^{1}/_{2}$ cup (2 oz/60 g) Parmesan evenly over the tomatoes. Return to the oven until the cheese is golden, 5–6 minutes.

Serves 6

6 large ripe tomatoes

2 tablespoons unsalted butter

2 tablespoons chopped green (spring) onion, including tender green tops

2 tablespoons chopped fresh flat-leaf (Italian) parsley

2 cups (14 oz/440 g) well-drained chopped, cooked spinach (2–3 bunches)

2 cups (16 fl oz/500 ml) Béchamel Sauce (page 300)

1 cup (4 oz/120 g) grated Parmesan cheese

Salt and freshly ground pepper

1 cup (8 fl oz/250 ml) Vegetable Stock (page 300)

Baked Onions

Whole onions should be baked unpeeled; the skins help to retain the full flavor. Once slit after baking, the skins will fall away easily. Fresh basil sprigs may be substituted for the rosemary.

4 red onions

4 fresh rosemary sprigs

1/4 cup (2 fl oz/60 ml) olive oil

1 1/2 tablespoons balsamic vinegar

1 tablespoon firmly packed brown sugar

2 tablespoons red wine vinegar

3/4 cup (6 fl oz/180 ml) Vegetable Stock (page 300)

Salt and freshly ground pepper

Preheat the oven to 375°F (190°C).

Using a sharp knife, cut a thin slice off the base of each onion so they will sit upright. Cut a thin slice from the top of each onion and then cut a small slit 1/2 inch (12 mm) deep in the center. Insert a rosemary sprig into each slit. Place the onions in a small baking dish.

In a small bowl, stir together the olive oil, balsamic vinegar, brown sugar, red wine vinegar, and stock. Pour into the bottom of the dish and baste the onions. Place in the oven and bake, basting a few times with the dish juices, until the onions are soft when pierced with the tip of a sharp knife, 1–1 1/2 hours.

Before serving, split the skins with a sharp knife and remove. Season the onions to taste with salt and pepper.

Serves 4

Tomato Tart

This French-style tart could be given an Italian flair by substituting basil for the mint and mozzarella for the Gruyère. Offer it as a starter or present it as a light main course for a luncheon.

Pie Pastry (page 305)

3 large tomatoes, cut into slices 1/2 inch (12 mm) thick

Salt and freshly ground pepper

2 tablespoons Dijon mustard

3 tablespoons chopped fresh mint

1/4 (125 g) Gruyère or Emmentaler cheese, cut into 8 thin slices

2 eggs

1 cup (8 fl oz/250 ml) heavy (double) cream

On a lightly floured work surface, roll out the pastry dough into a round about 12 inches (30 cm) in diameter. Carefully transfer to a 10-inch (25-cm) tart pan with a removable bottom, or a pie pan, pressing it gently into the bottom and sides. If using a tart pan, cut off the pastry even with the rim; if using a pie pan, turn under the overhang and flute the edge decoratively. Place in the freezer for 30 minutes.

Meanwhile, using your fingers, carefully push out the seeds and watery juices from the tomato slices. Sprinkle the sliced tomatoes with salt and place in a large colander to drain for 30 minutes.

Preheat an oven to 350°F (180°C).

Remove the tomatoes from the colander and pat them dry. Using a rubber spatula, spread the mustard evenly over the bottom of the pastry shell. Sprinkle with the mint. Top evenly with the cheese, then place the tomato slices over the cheese. In a small bowl, beat together the eggs and cream until blended. Season with salt and pepper to taste. Pour over the tomatoes.

Bake until the pastry is pale gold and the custard is set, about 30 minutes. Remove from the oven, let rest for 10 minutes, then slice into thin wedges and serve.

Serves 8–10

Curried Vegetable Pizza

For this recipe, double the curry powder if you want a more fiery topping, and experiment with the combination of vegetables by using zucchini (courgettes), broccoli, cauliflower, and bell peppers (capsicums).

Make the pizza dough. In a small bowl, soak the raisins in water to cover for 30 minutes. Meanwhile, preheat the oven to 450°F (220°C). If using a baking stone or tiles, place in the oven.

In a frying pan over medium heat, warm the oil. Add the onion and fry until lightly golden, about 5 minutes. Add the eggplant, chiles, tomatoes, potato, apple, and curry powder and stir until well blended. Cover partially and cook over low heat until tender, about 30 minutes. If the mixture begins to stick to the pan bottom, add a few tablespoons water. Season to taste with salt and pepper.

Drain the raisins and add them to the frying pan along with the pine nuts. Cook, stirring occasionally, for another 2 minutes.

Shape the pizza dough and cover with the curried vegetables. Transfer the pizza to the oven and bake for 10 minutes. Reduce the oven temperature to 400°F (200°C) and bake until the crust is golden, about 10 minutes. Serve immediately.

Serves 4

Pizza Dough (page 305)

1/3 cup (2 oz/60 g) raisins

4 tablespoons (2 fl oz/60 ml) extra-virgin olive oil

1 onion, thinly sliced

1 eggplant (aubergine), about 6 oz (180 g), cut into 1/2-inch inch (12-mm) dice

2 green chile peppers such as jalapeños or poblanos, seeded and chopped (page 308)

3 fresh plum (Roma) tomatoes, peeled and chopped (page 313), or canned plum tomatoes with their liquid, chopped

1 potato, peeled and cut into 1/2-inch (12-mm) dice

1 Golden Delicious apple, peeled, cored, and diced

1 tablespoon curry powder

Salt and freshly ground pepper

6 tablespoons (2 oz/60 g) pine nuts

Baked Acorn Squash with Chutney

This treatment of acorn squash is not only delicious but makes an elegant presentation at a holiday meal. Acorn squash and pumpkin are interchangeable here, as they are in most recipes.

2 acorn squash

1 cup (8 fl oz/250 ml) Vegetable Stock (page 300)

3 tablespoons unsalted butter

3 tablespoons firmly packed brown sugar

1 teaspoon ground ginger

1/4 teaspoon ground nutmeg

Salt and freshly ground pepper

4 tablespoons (3 oz/90 g) plum or apricot chutney

Preheat the oven to 350°F (180°C).

Cut each squash in half through the stem end. Using a spoon, scrape out the seeds and any fibers and discard. Place cut sides down in a baking dish. Pour the stock into the dish. Bake for 20 minutes.

Meanwhile, in a small ovenproof bowl, combine the butter, brown sugar, ginger, and nutmeg. Place in the oven for a few minutes to melt the butter and sugar.

Remove the squash from the oven carefully. Turn skin side down in the dish and fill each hollow with 1 tablespoon of the melted butter mixture. Season to taste with salt and pepper.

Butter a piece of parchment paper or waxed paper and use it to cover the dish loosely, buttered side down. Return to the oven and bake until the squash is tender, about 30 minutes.

Place 1 tablespoon chutney in each squash half. Serve hot.

Serves 4

Gratin of Yams and Apples

In the United States, true yams can be hard to find, although the vegetable often labeled "yam," actually a type of sweet potato, is a good substitute. Both varieties have sweet, moist, dark orange flesh and reddish skin.

Preheat the oven to 350°F (180°C).

Place the yams in a large saucepan, add water to cover, and bring to a boil over high heat. Reduce the heat to medium-low and simmer, uncovered, until tender when pierced with the tip of a sharp knife, 20–30 minutes. Drain and let cool. Peel and cut crosswise into slices $1/2$ inch (12 mm) thick.

In a frying pan over medium heat, melt the butter. Add the apple slices and sauté until golden, about 3 minutes on each side. Remove from the heat.

Arrange half of the yam slices in a baking dish and season to taste with salt and pepper. In a small bowl, stir together the cream, vermouth, orange juice, and nutmeg and pour half of the mixture evenly over the yams in the dish. Cover with the apple slices and then place the remaining yam slices on top. Pour over the remaining cream mixture. Sprinkle the bread crumbs evenly over the top.

Bake until browned and bubbling, about 30 minutes. Serve hot, directly from the baking dish.

Serves 4

4 yams, 2–2½ lb (1–1.25 kg) total

2 tablespoons unsalted butter

2 green apples such as Granny Smith, cored and cut crosswise into slices ¼ inch (6 mm) thick

Salt and freshly ground pepper

1 cup (8 fl oz/250 ml) heavy (double) cream

¼ cup (2 fl oz/60 ml) sweet vermouth

¼ cup (2 fl oz/60 ml) fresh orange juice

½ teaspoon ground nutmeg

½ cup (2 oz/60 g) fine dried bread crumbs (page 308)

Baked Yams with Tomatillo Sour Cream

Spicy tomatillo cream heightens the mellow flavor of sweet potatoes. Serve as a single course for lunch or with Black Beans and Rice with Corn Salsa (page 221) for dinner.

4 uniformly sized and shaped yams (orange-fleshed sweet potatoes), 1/2–3/4 lb (250–375 g) each, unpeeled and well scrubbed

2 teaspoons vegetable oil

1/2 cup (4 fl oz/125 ml) sour cream

1–2 tablespoons Tomatillo Salsa, homemade (page 303) or purchased

1 teaspoon fresh lime juice

Salt and freshly ground pepper

1 tablespoon finely chopped fresh cilantro (fresh coriander)

Preheat the oven to 400°F (200°C).

Rub the potatoes all over with the oil and place on an ungreased baking sheet. Bake for 30 minutes. Prick the skin in a few places with a fork and continue baking until tender when pierced with the tip of a sharp knife, about 30 minutes longer.

While the potatoes are baking, in a small bowl, stir together the sour cream, salsa, lime juice, and salt and pepper to taste.

When the potatoes are done, transfer to individual plates. Using a sharp knife, split each potato open lengthwise, cutting only halfway through. Spoon a few tablespoons of the sour cream mixture into each potato, and then garnish with the cilantro. Serve immediately.

Serves 4

Baked Winter Squash

Use any flavorful, small winter squash, such as Danish, buttercup, butternut, or pumpkin for this dish. Some squashes will have more pulp than others, in which case you may need to use both shells for serving.

Preheat the oven to 375°F (190°C).

Cut the squash in half through the stem end. Place cut side down in a baking dish. Pour the stock into the dish. Bake until tender when pierced with the tip of a sharp knife, about 45 minutes.

In a frying pan over medium heat, melt 2 tablespoons of the butter. Add the onion and sauté until soft, about 2 minutes. Add 2 tablespoons of the parsley and the marjoram and sauté for 1 minute. Remove from the heat and set aside.

Using a spoon, scoop out the seeds and any fibers from the baked squash halves and discard. Scoop out the pulp, reserving one of the squash shells (see note). Place the pulp in a food processor fitted with the metal blade. Add the remaining 2 tablespoons butter and the egg yolks and process to blend. Add the cream, Parmesan, and onion mixture and again process to blend. Season to taste with salt and pepper. Spoon the squash mixture evenly into the reserved squash shell and place in a baking dish. Bake until the top is golden, 15–20 minutes.

Sprinkle the remaining 1 tablespoon parsley over the top and serve hot, spooned directly from the shell.

Serves 4

1 small winter squash, 1½–2 lb (750 g–1 kg)

1 cup (8 fl oz/250 ml) Vegetable Stock (page 300)

4 tablespoons (2 oz/60 g) unsalted butter

½ yellow onion, finely chopped

3 tablespoons chopped fresh flat-leaf (Italian) parsley

1 teaspoon dried marjoram

2 egg yolks

¼ cup (2 fl oz/60 ml) heavy (double) cream

¼ cup (1 oz/30 g) grated Parmesan cheese

Salt and freshly ground pepper

Creamy Potatoes with Rosemary

Unusual and delicious, this is a wonderful dish for guests because it can be made ahead, refrigerated, and then reheated when ready to serve. If you like, accompany it with baked leeks, mushrooms, or puréed spinach.

3 large russet potatoes, about 1³/₄ lb (875 g) total weight

2 tablespoons unsalted butter

¹/₄ cup (2 fl oz/60 ml) heavy (double) cream

2 teaspoons dried rosemary

3 egg yolks

³/₄ cup (3 oz/90 g) shredded Gruyère cheese

Salt and freshly ground white pepper

1 cup (8 fl oz/250 ml) Tomato Sauce (page 302)

Preheat the oven to 400°F (200°C). Butter a 1¹/₂-qt (1.5-l) soufflé dish and set aside.

Put the potatoes in a heavy saucepan and add water to cover. Bring to a boil over high heat. Reduce the heat to medium, cover, and boil gently until tender when pierced with the tip of a sharp knife, 25–30 minutes.

Drain the potatoes and, when cool enough to handle, peel and slice. Put through a food mill or ricer, or mash with a potato masher. Add the butter, cream, and rosemary, and mix until the potatoes are smooth. Add the egg yolks and stir to combine. Transfer to the prepared dish and fold in all but 2 tablespoons of the cheese and salt and white pepper to taste. Smooth the surface with the back of a spoon. Pour ¹/₃ cup (3 fl oz/80 ml) of the tomato sauce evenly over the top and sprinkle with the reserved 2 tablespoons cheese.

Bake until firm and golden brown, about 30 minutes.

Heat the remaining ²/₃ cup (5 fl oz/170 ml) tomato sauce and pour it into a bowl to pass at the table.

Serves 4

Potatoes Dauphinois

This rich dish originates in the Dauphiné region of southeast France. In this interpretation, eggs are omitted, but a creamier consistency is possible if crème fraîche is substituted for the half-and-half.

Preheat the oven to 350°F (180°C). Brush a 9-inch (23-cm) gratin dish with 2-inch (5-cm) sides with the melted butter.

Layer half of the potatoes in the prepared dish. Sprinkle with all of the garlic and half of the cheese. Pour ¹/₂ cup (4 fl oz/125 ml) of the half-and-half evenly over the top. Sprinkle lightly with salt to taste and a pinch of white pepper. Layer the remaining potatoes on top and then top with the remaining cheese. Again, sprinkle lightly with salt to taste and a pinch of white pepper. Pour the remaining ¹/₂ cup (4 fl oz/125 ml) half-and-half evenly over the top.

Place the dish on a baking sheet. Bake until the top is golden brown and the potatoes are tender, about 1 hour. Serve immediately.

Serves 4

1 tablespoon unsalted butter, melted

2 lb (1 kg) russet potatoes, peeled and cut into slices ¹/₄ inch (6 mm) thick

2 cloves garlic, minced

1 cup (4 oz/125 g) shredded Gruyère cheese

1 cup (8 fl oz/250 ml) half-and-half (half cream)

Salt and freshly ground white pepper

Potato-Chile Gratin

4 fresh Anaheim or poblano chile peppers

1 tablespoon vegetable oil

1 clove garlic, minced

2¹/₂ lb (1.25 kg) red potatoes, peeled and cut into slices ¹/₈ inch (3 mm) thick

1¹/₄ cups (10 fl oz/310 ml) milk

1 cup (8 fl oz/250 ml) heavy (double) cream

Salt and freshly ground pepper

1 cup (4 oz/125 g) shredded Gruyère cheese

3 tablespoons fine dried bread crumbs (page 308)

Roast and peel the chiles as you would bell peppers (page 308), then seed, derib, and cut into ¹/₄-inch (6-mm) dice. Leave the broiler on.

In a frying pan over medium heat, warm the oil. Add the diced chiles and sauté until slightly softened, 3–5 minutes. Add the garlic and sauté for 1 minute longer. Remove from the heat and set aside.

Place the potato slices in a kitchen towel and wring out all moisture. Pour the milk into a large, deep, heavy saucepan and place over medium heat. Drop in the potatoes, separating the slices as you do, and bring to a boil. Reduce the heat to low, cover, and simmer, stirring occasionally, for 10 minutes. Uncover and simmer until most of the milk has been absorbed, 3–5 minutes longer; do not scorch.

Add the cream, 1 teaspoon salt, and ¹/₈ teaspoon pepper and return to a boil. Reduce the heat to low, cover, and simmer, stirring occasionally, for 10 minutes. Uncover and simmer until nearly all the cream has been absorbed, 3–5 minutes longer; do not scorch. Taste and adjust the seasoning.

Butter a 9-inch (23-cm) flameproof baking dish with 2-inch (5-cm) sides. Transfer half of the potato mixture to the dish. Layer the chile mixture evenly on top. Cover with the remaining potatoes. Sprinkle with the cheese and then the bread crumbs. Place the dish on a baking sheet and slip under the broiler 4 inches (10 cm) from the heat source and broil (grill) until nicely browned, 8–10 minutes. Be careful, as the bread crumbs burn easily. Serve immediately.

Serves 4–6

Stuffed Potatoes
with Red Pepper Aioli

A garlicky roasted pepper mayonnaise gives a Mediterranean accent to these stuffed baked potatoes. Rubbing the potatoes with vegetable oil yields a crisp skin. For an extra-crisp skin, bake at 450°F (230°C).

2 medium-sized baking potatoes such as russet, scrubbed thoroughly to remove dirt and dried with a kitchen towel

4 teaspoons olive oil

2/3 cup (5 fl oz/160 ml) milk, warmed

3/4 cup (6 fl oz/180 ml) Red Pepper Aioli (page 303)

5 tablespoons (3 oz/90 g) freshly grated Parmesan cheese

Salt and freshly ground white pepper

2 tablespoons chopped fresh flat-leaf (Italian) parsley

Preheat the oven to 425°F (220°C).

Prick the skin in a few places with a fork. Rub each potato with 1 teaspoon of the oil to coat evenly. Place the potatoes on an ungreased baking sheet in the middle of the oven. Bake until tender when pierced with a knife or skewer, about 1 hour. The potatoes should be cooked through and slightly crisp on the outside. Remove from the oven and set aside until cool enough to handle.

Turn the oven temperature down to 400°F (200°C).

Using a sharp knife, cut out an oval of the skin on the top of each potato and remove it. Scoop out all but a thin shell of the potato pulp. Alternatively, cut each potato in half and scoop out the pulp from each half, leaving only a thin shell.

Pass the potato pulp through a potato ricer into a bowl, or place the pulp in a bowl and mash it with a potato masher. Add the milk, 1/2 cup (4 fl oz/125 ml) of the aioli, 3 tablespoons of the cheese, 1/2 teaspoon salt, and a pinch of white pepper. Stir vigorously to combine. Taste and adjust the seasoning.

Dividing the potato mixture evenly, spoon it back into the potato shells, mounding the tops attractively. Sprinkle the remaining 2 tablespoons cheese evenly over the tops of the potatoes.

Place the stuffed potatoes on an ungreased baking sheet. Bake until the potatoes are hot throughout and the cheese has melted and is bubbling, 10–15 minutes. Garnish with the remaining 1/4 cup (2 fl oz/55 ml) aioli and the parsley. Serve immediately.

Serves 4 or 8

Kohlrabi with Mustard Cream Sauce

This knobby vegetable has a taste similar to that of a turnip and can be substituted for turnips in many dishes. Because of its crisp texture, shredded kohlrabi is also ideal in a stir-fry with other vegetables.

Preheat the oven to 375°F (190°C).

Pour the stock into a saucepan and bring to a boil. Meanwhile, peel the kohlrabies and cut crosswise into slices 3/4 inch (2 cm) thick. As they are cut, place in a bowl and toss with the lemon juice, to prevent discoloration.

When the stock is boiling, add the kohlrabies. Reduce the heat, cover, and simmer until tender, about 10 minutes. Drain and set aside.

Meanwhile, make the sauce: In a saucepan over medium heat, melt the butter. Add the shallots and sauté for 1 minute. Stir in the flour and cook, stirring, until blended, 1 minute. Add the paprika. Gradually add the milk, stirring constantly with a whisk. Continue to whisk over low heat until the sauce is smooth and slightly thickened, 4–5 minutes. Mix in the mustard and vermouth, and season to taste with salt and white pepper. Remove from the heat.

Place the kohlrabies in a baking dish. Spoon the warm sauce over to cover completely. Sprinkle the bread crumbs and cheese over the top. Place in the oven and bake until the sauce bubbles and the top is golden, 15–20 minutes.

Serves 2 or 3

3 cups (24 fl oz/750 ml) Vegetable Stock (page 300)

1 lb (500 g) kohlrabies

Juice of 1 lemon

FOR THE SAUCE:

3 tablespoons unsalted butter

2 shallots, finely chopped

3 tablespoons all-purpose (plain) flour

1/2 teaspoon paprika

2 cups (16 fl oz/500 ml) milk

1 teaspoon Dijon mustard

3 tablespoons dry vermouth

Salt and freshly ground white pepper

1/4 cup (1 oz/30 g) fine dried bread crumbs (page 308)

1/2 cup (2 oz/60 g) shredded Gruyère cheese

Baked Sweet Potatoes with Crème Fraîche and Green Onions

This is a winning last-minute dish. The potatoes look pretty contrasted with the white of the crème fraîche and the green of the onions. Sour cream can be substituted for the crème fraîche.

Preheat the oven to 400°F (200°C).

Rub the sweet potatoes all over with the oil and place on an ungreased baking sheet. Bake for 30 minutes. Prick the skin in a few places with a fork, and continue baking until the potatoes are tender when pierced with the tip of a sharp knife, about 30 minutes longer.

Cut off the ends of the hot sweet potatoes and peel the potatoes if desired. Cut crosswise into slices 1 1/2 inches (4 cm) thick. Arrange a few slices, overlapping or next to one another, on each individual plate, or spoon the potatoes into a serving bowl. Garnish with the crème fraîche and green onion. Serve immediately.

Serves 4–6

2 uniformly sized and shaped sweet potatoes, 1/2–3/4 lb (250–375 g) each, unpeeled and well scrubbed

2 teaspoons vegetable oil

1/4 cup (2 fl oz/60 ml) crème fraîche (page 309)

1 tablespoon finely chopped green (spring) onion, including tender green tops

Sweet Potatoes Anna

Traditionally, French cooks prepare this dish in a specially designed round two-handled copper casserole. For this version, any heavy round pan will suffice. Make sure to use clarified butter to prevent burning.

2¹⁄₂ lb (1.25 kg) sweet potatoes, peeled and sliced ¹⁄₈ inch (3 mm) thick

1¹⁄₂ cups (³⁄₄ lb/375 g) clarified unsalted butter (page 308)

Salt and freshly ground pepper

2 tablespoons finely chopped fresh flat-leaf (Italian) parsley

Preheat the oven to 400°F (200°C). Butter a 9-inch (23-cm) straight-sided, nonstick cake pan or ovenproof frying pan.

Starting at the center of the pan and forming concentric circles, cover the bottom with a layer of sweet potatoes, overlapping the slices. Drizzle with some of the clarified butter and sprinkle with salt and pepper to taste. Continue layering in this same manner until all the potatoes have been used.

Butter one side of a piece of aluminum foil large enough to cover the pan, then cover the pan, buttered side down. Place a heavy lid (smaller than the pan) on top to weigh down the potato layers. Bake for 40 minutes. Remove the lid and foil and continue to bake until the potatoes are tender when pierced with the tip of a sharp knife and the top is golden, about 20 minutes longer; do not overcook.

Let cool for 10 minutes. Using a narrow spatula, loosen the potatoes from the pan bottom. Invert a flat round platter over the pan and, holding the platter firmly in place, invert the pan, then lift it off; excess butter will flow onto the platter as well. To remove the excess butter, tilt the platter and pour it off.

Garnish with the parsley, cut into wedges, and serve.

Serves 8

Baked Vegetables with Oregano and Dill

Easy to prepare, this Greek side dish, called *briam* in the land where it originated, can be served hot or at room temperature. Some versions call for sautéing the eggplant before combining it with other vegetables, but it is an unnecessary step.

Cut the eggplant into $1/2$-inch (12-mm) cubes. Cut the zucchini into slices $1/3$ inch (9 mm) thick. Sprinkle the eggplant and zucchini with salt and place in a colander. Let stand for 30 minutes to drain off the bitter juices and excess water. Rinse off the salt and dry well with paper towels.

Preheat the oven to 350°F (180°C). Oil a shallow 3-qt (3-l) baking dish with a lid.

In a large sauté pan over medium heat, warm the olive oil. Add the yellow onions and sauté, stirring occasionally, until tender, about 8 minutes. Add the garlic and green onions and sauté, stirring occasionally, for 3 minutes. Add the tomatoes and simmer for 2 minutes to blend the flavors. Season to taste with salt and pepper. Remove from the heat.

Place the eggplant, zucchini, potatoes, and bell peppers in a large bowl. Add the contents of the sauté pan and the oregano, dill, and parsley. Toss to mix well. Transfer to the prepared baking dish and drizzle evenly with $1/2$ cup (4 fl oz/125 ml) water. Sprinkle the bread crumbs evenly over the top.

Cover and bake for 30 minutes. Uncover and continue to bake until all the vegetables are tender when pierced with the tip of a sharp knife, about 1 hour longer. Check periodically to see if the mixture is drying out, and add water as needed.

Let cool briefly before serving, or serve at room temperature.

Serves 6

1 eggplant (aubergine), about 1 lb (500 g)

$1 1/2$ lb (750 g) zucchini (courgettes)

Salt and freshly ground pepper

$1/2$ cup (4 fl oz/125 ml) olive oil

2 large yellow onions, chopped

5 cloves garlic, minced

6 green (spring) onions, including tender green tops, chopped

3 cups (18 oz/560 g) peeled, seeded (page 313), and diced tomatoes

$1 1/2$ lb (750 g) potatoes, peeled and cut into slices $1/4$ inch (6 mm) thick

2 green bell peppers (capsicums), seeded, deribbed (page 308), and diced or sliced

1 tablespoon dried oregano

3 tablespoons chopped fresh dill

$1/4$ cup ($1/3$ oz/10 g) chopped fresh flat-leaf (Italian) parsley

$1/2$ cup (2 oz/60 g) dried bread crumbs (page 308)

Roasted Autumn Vegetables

Offer this mélange of crisp, golden brown vegetables as a side dish along-side a soup. Garnish with the sage or thyme sprigs, if using, and serve hot, warm, or at room temperature.

2 russet potatoes, about ¹/₂ lb (250 g) each

2 sweet potatoes, about ³/₄ lb (375 g) each

1 acorn squash, about 1¹/₂ lb (750 g)

2–3 tablespoons vegetable oil

Salt and freshly ground pepper

¹/₄ cup (2 oz/60 g) unsalted butter, melted

1 tablespoon chopped fresh sage or thyme or 1 teaspoon dried sage or thyme, plus sprigs for garnish (optional)

Prepare a fire for indirect-heat cooking in a covered grill (page 310). Position the grill rack 4–6 inches (10–15 cm) above the fire.

Using a vegetable peeler or a small, sharp knife, peel the russet potatoes, sweet potatoes, and acorn squash. Cut them all crosswise into slices about 1 inch (2.5 cm) thick. Scrape out the seeds and any fibers from the center of the acorn squash slices and discard. In a large bowl, toss the prepared vegetables together with the oil, 1 teaspoon salt, and ¹/₂ teaspoon pepper. Set aside.

In a small bowl, stir together the melted butter and chopped sage. Set aside. Arrange the vegetables on the center of the rack, cover the grill, and open the vents halfway. Cook for 15 minutes, then turn the slices. Cook for 15 minutes longer, then turn again and brush them with the butter mixture. Continue cooking until the vegetables are well browned and tender when pierced with the tip of a sharp knife, 10–15 minutes longer.

To serve, transfer to a platter. Garnish with the sage sprigs, if using, and serve hot, warm, or at room temperature.

Serves 4

Roasted Cajun Potatoes

Cajun spices add a lively spark to simple roasted potatoes. Serve these spiced-up favorites as a side dish for dinner. Flavorful yellow-fleshed potatoes, such as Yukon golds, are a good variety to use for this dish.

Preheat the oven to 450°F (230°C).

Peel the potatoes, then rinse under cold running water and pat dry with a clean kitchen towel. Cut each potato lengthwise into 8 wedges.

In a roasting pan, stir together the oil, shallots, garlic, 1 teaspoon salt, the paprika, cayenne, and $1/2$ teaspoon black pepper. Add the potatoes and, using a large spoon or by shaking the pan from side to side, coat them evenly with the oil mixture.

Roast the potatoes, turning them every 15 minutes, until tender and golden brown, about 45 minutes. Taste and adjust the seasoning.

Transfer to a warmed serving dish, garnish with the parsley, if desired, and serve.

Serves 4–6

2¹/₂ lb (1.25 kg) yellow, red, or white potatoes

¹/₄ cup (2 fl oz/60 ml) vegetable oil or olive oil

2 shallots, finely chopped

1 clove garlic, minced

Salt and freshly ground black pepper

¹/₂ teaspoon paprika

¹/₂ teaspoon cayenne pepper

2 tablespoons chopped fresh flat-leaf (Italian) parsley (optional)

Parmesan Roasted Potatoes

Although very little oil is used, these potatoes taste almost fried. For the best taste, be sure to buy high-quality Parmesan cheese for these crisp gems. Serve as a side dish for dinner.

3 lb (1.5 kg) russet potatoes, unpeeled and well scrubbed

3 tablespoons olive oil

Salt and freshly ground pepper

1/2 cup (2 oz/60 g) shredded Parmesan cheese

2 tablespoons finely chopped fresh flat-leaf (Italian) parsley

Preheat the oven to 450°F (230°C). Lightly grease a roasting pan.

Cut each potato into 1 1/2-inch (4-cm) cubes. Bring a large pot three-fourths full of lightly salted water to a boil. Add the potatoes and cook partially, about 5 minutes. Drain well and pat dry with a clean kitchen towel.

In a large bowl, stir together the olive oil, 1 teaspoon salt, and 1/4 teaspoon pepper. Add the potatoes and toss to coat evenly.

Spread the potatoes in the prepared pan. Roast, turning every few minutes to prevent sticking, until tender and golden brown, 20–25 minutes. Taste and adjust the seasoning with salt and pepper.

Transfer to a serving dish. Add the Parmesan and parsley and toss to coat evenly. Serve immediately.

Serves 4

Stuffed Mushrooms and Summer Squash

These stuffed vegetables can be a fine main course for a vegetarian meal, a great selection for a buffet, or a side dish. Serve with a soup such as Spring Vegetable Soup with Pesto (page 60).

12 large fresh white mushrooms, brushed clean

4 zucchini (courgettes) or yellow crookneck squash

4 tablespoons (2 fl oz/60 ml) olive oil

1 small yellow onion, chopped

1 clove garlic, minced

3/4 cup (3 oz/90 g) soda cracker crumbs or fine dried bread crumbs (page 308)

1/2 cup (2 oz/60 g) shredded Cheddar or grated Parmesan cheese

1 tablespoon chopped fresh oregano or 1 teaspoon dried oregano

Salt and freshly ground pepper

3 tablespoons heavy (double) cream

Cut or gently pull the stem from each mushroom, forming a hollow in the base of the cap to hold the stuffing; reserve the stems. Halve the squashes lengthwise and, using a teaspoon, scoop out the centers, leaving a shell about $1/3$ inch (8 mm) thick; reserve the centers. Set the prepared vegetables aside.

Prepare a fire for indirect-heat cooking in a covered grill (page 310). Oil the grill rack and position 4–6 inches (10–15 cm) above the fire.

Chop together the squash centers and mushroom stems. In a frying pan over medium-high heat, warm 2 tablespoons of the olive oil. Add the chopped squash mixture, onion, and garlic and cook, stirring occasionally, until the vegetables are tender and any liquid released during cooking has evaporated, about 7 minutes. Scrape into a large bowl and add the cracker crumbs, cheese, oregano, $1/2$ teaspoon salt, $1/4$ teaspoon pepper, and the cream. Stir and toss with a fork to combine.

Brush the outsides of the squash shells and mushroom caps with the remaining 2 tablespoons oil; sprinkle with salt. Spoon about 2 teaspoons stuffing into each mushroom cap and 2 tablespoons into each squash shell, mounding slightly.

Arrange the stuffed vegetables on the center of the rack, cover the grill, and open the vents halfway. Grill until the stuffing is browned on top and the vegetables are tender when pierced with the tip of a sharp knife, about 20 minutes.

Transfer to a platter. Serve hot or at room temperature.

Serves 3 as a main course, or 4–6 as a side dish

Stuffed Acorn Squash

Winter's acorn squashes are complemented by a savory stuffing infused with the sweetness of prunes. Serve this dish as a hearty main course or as a substantial side dish at a holiday feast.

Prepare a fire for indirect-heat cooking in a covered grill (page 310). Oil the grill rack and position 4–6 inches (10–15 cm) above the fire.

In a frying pan over medium heat, melt the butter. Add the onion and celery and cook, stirring frequently, until softened, about 5 minutes. Scrape into a large bowl and add the bread crumbs, sage, $1/2$ teaspoon salt, $1/4$ teaspoon pepper, the prunes, and the walnuts. Sprinkle 3 tablespoons water over the top. Stir and toss with a fork to combine. Set aside.

Cut out four 6-inch (15-cm) squares of aluminum foil; set aside. Using a large, sharp knife, cut each squash in half through the stem end. Using a spoon, scrape out the seeds and any fibers and discard. Season the cut sides generously with salt and pepper. Divide the bread crumb mixture evenly among the squash cavities, pressing it down lightly. To prevent the stuffing from drying out, cover each squash with a square of foil, folding it down over the sides.

Place the stuffed squashes, foil side up, on the center of the rack, cover the grill, and open the vents halfway. Cook for 45 minutes. Remove the foil and continue cooking in the covered grill until the squash is tender when pierced with the tip of a sharp knife and the stuffing is lightly browned, about 15 minutes longer.

Transfer to a warmed platter and serve at once.

Serves 4

$1/4$ cup (2 oz/60 g) unsalted butter

$1/2$ cup ($2 1/2$ oz/75 g) finely chopped yellow onion

$1/2$ cup ($2 1/2$ oz/75 g) finely chopped celery

2 cups (4 oz/125 g) fresh white bread crumbs (page 308)

1 teaspoon dried sage

Salt and freshly ground pepper

$1/2$ cup (3 oz/90 g) chopped prunes

$1/4$ cup (1 oz/30 g) chopped walnuts

2 acorn squash

Spicy Grilled Eggplant

If a charcoal grill is unavailable, bake the eggplants in the oven: Lightly grease a baking sheet and arrange the slices on it in a single layer. Bake on the top rack of a 400°F (200°C) oven, turning occasionally, until golden on both sides, 15 minutes.

Prepare a fire for direct-heat cooking in a grill (page 309). Oil the grill rack and position 4–6 inches (10–15 cm) above the fire.

Cut the eggplants crosswise into slices ¹/₄ inch (6 mm) thick. If you are using globe eggplants, place the slices in a colander and salt them liberally to draw out the moisture. Let stand for 30 minutes. Rinse with water and pat dry with paper towels. If you are using slender eggplants, there is no need to salt them.

Brush the eggplant slices with 4 tablespoons (2 fl oz/60 ml) of the olive oil. Season to taste with salt and pepper.

Arrange the eggplant slices on the rack and grill, turning occasionally, until they are tender and golden, 10–12 minutes.

Meanwhile, in a small bowl, stir together the garlic, the remaining 2 tablespoons olive oil, and the vinegar.

Place the eggplant on a serving platter and drizzle the garlic-oil mixture over the top. Sprinkle with the red pepper flakes and parsley and serve.

Serves 6

9 Asian eggplants (slender aubergines) or 2 small globe eggplants (aubergines), about 2 lb (1 kg) total weight

Salt and freshly ground pepper

6 tablespoons (3 fl oz/90 ml) olive oil

3 cloves garlic, minced

1 tablespoon red wine vinegar

¹/₄ teaspoon red pepper flakes

2 tablespoons chopped fresh flat-leaf (Italian) parsley

Corn in the Husk

You're in for a treat if you haven't grilled corn before. Do not worry if the husks burn and char; the kernels underneath stay moist. Serve with salt, pepper, and plenty of softened butter.

8 ears of corn, in the husk

1/4 cup (2 oz/60 g) unsalted butter, at room temperature

Salt and freshly ground pepper

Prepare a fire for direct-heat cooking in a grill (page 309). Position the grill rack 4–6 inches (10–15 cm) above the fire.

Carefully peel back the husks on each ear of corn, but do not detach. Remove and discard the silks. Rub each ear of corn with $^{1}/_{2}$ tablespoon butter and sprinkle to taste with salt and pepper. Pull the husks back up around the corn and tie them snugly at the top with kitchen string. Arrange the corn on the rack. Grill, turning frequently, until the husks are blackened in spots, about 12 minutes.

Cut off the string, remove the husks, and serve immediately.

Serves 4

Slow-Cooked Onions with Tarragon-Mustard Sauce

Roasting vegetables over coals heightens their natural flavors. Whole onions become especially sweet when prepared on a grill. Try serving these alongside pasta or Risotto with Saffron (page 255).

Prepare a fire for indirect-heat cooking in a covered grill (page 310). Oil the grill rack and position 4–6 inches (10–15 cm) above the fire.

To make the sauce, in a small bowl, whisk together the vinegar and mustard. Slowly add the olive oil, whisking constantly to form a smooth, creamy sauce. Whisk in the tarragon, $1/4$ teaspoon salt, and a pinch of pepper. Cover and set aside.

Peel the onions gently; take care to keep their layers intact at the root ends, which will help hold them together during cooking. Using a sharp knife and starting at the stem end, slice an **X** in each onion to within about 1 inch (2.5 cm) of the root end. In a large bowl, toss the onions with the 3 tablespoons olive oil, $1/2$ teaspoon salt, and $1/4$ teaspoon pepper.

Place the onions on the center of the rack, cover the grill, and open the vents halfway. Cook, turning the onions every 15–20 minutes, until they are tender when pierced with the tip of a sharp knife, 45–50 minutes total.

To serve, transfer the onions to a platter and drizzle some of the sauce over them. Serve hot, warm, or at room temperature. Pass the remaining sauce at the table.

Serves 4

FOR THE SAUCE:

2 tablespoons white wine vinegar or tarragon vinegar

2 tablespoons Dijon mustard

$1/3$ cup (3 fl oz/80 ml) olive oil

2 tablespoons chopped fresh tarragon or 1 teaspoon dried tarragon

Salt and freshly ground pepper

4 yellow onions

3 tablespoons olive oil

Salt and freshly ground pepper

Grilled Tomatoes and Green Onions

Firm tomatoes, even those that are slightly green, should be used for this recipe.
They are less juicy and hold their shape better when grilled than fully ripe ones.
The basil in the basting sauce can be replaced with chopped tarragon.

1/3 cup (3 fl oz/80 ml) olive oil

1 tablespoon fresh lemon juice or wine vinegar

2 tablespoons chopped fresh basil

1 tablespoon chopped shallots

Salt and freshly ground pepper

3 large tomatoes, cut into slices 1/2–3/4 inch (12 mm–2 cm) thick

10–12 green (spring) onions, trimmed, including 4 inches (10 cm) of green tops

Sprigs of fresh basil or flat-leaf (Italian) parsley for garnish

Prepare a fire for direct-heat cooking in a grill (page 309). Position the grill rack 4–6 inches (10–15 cm) above the fire.

In a small bowl, stir together the olive oil, lemon juice, chopped basil, shallots, 1/2 teaspoon salt, and 1/4 teaspoon pepper.

Arrange the tomatoes and green onions on the rack. Grill, turning them two or three times and brushing with the olive oil mixture, about 5 minutes. If the onions are large, they might take 1 or 2 minutes longer.

Transfer the tomatoes and onions to a platter and garnish with basil or parsley sprigs.

Serves 4–6

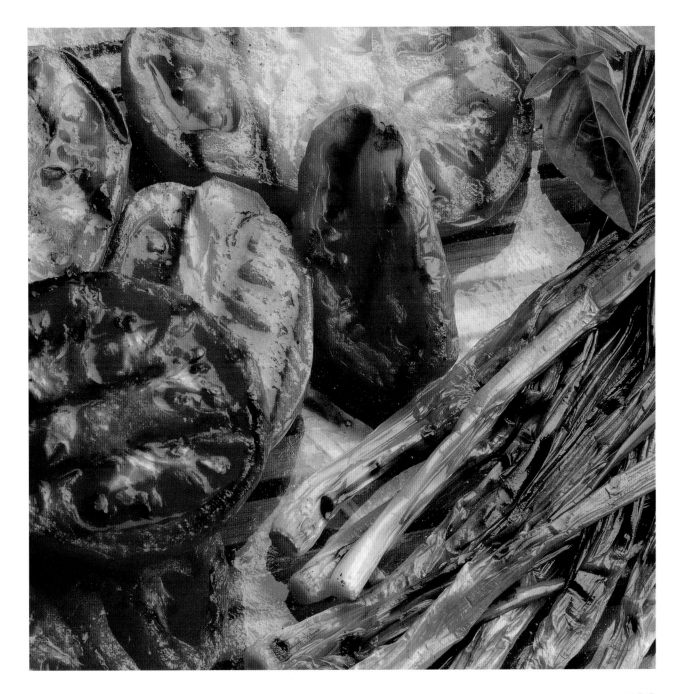

Grilled Summer Vegetables

How wonderful it is to find summer's harvest in the markets and bring it home to prepare on your outdoor grill. Increase the vegetables as needed to serve more guests, or add others to the variety suggested here.

Cut the zucchini, crookneck squash, and eggplants lengthwise into 3 slices. Cut the pattypan squash and tomatoes in half crosswise. If using green onions, trim to equal lengths, including the tender green tops. If using red onions, cut in half crosswise. Place all the vegetables in a large glass or ceramic dish and sprinkle the basil over them.

To make the marinade, stir together the olive oil, vinegar, lemon juice, garlic, sage, chives, and salt and pepper to taste. Pour the marinade evenly over the vegetables and let stand at room temperature for 1 hour, turning the vegetables once.

Prepare a fire for direct-heat cooking (page 309) in a grill. Oil the grill rack and position 4–6 inches (10–15 cm) above the fire. Arrange the vegetables on the rack and grill until tender, 3–6 minutes on each side, depending upon the vegetable.

Alternatively, preheat a broiler (grill). Arrange the vegetables in a shallow flame-proof pan and place under the broiler 3–4 inches (7.5–10 cm) from the heat source. Broil (grill) 3–5 minutes on each side, depending upon the vegetable.

Serves 4

2 zucchini (courgettes), trimmed but unpeeled

2 yellow crookneck squash, trimmed but unpeeled

2 Asian eggplants (slender aubergines), trimmed but unpeeled

2–4 pattypan squash

2 large ripe tomatoes

4 green (spring) onions or 2 red onions

1/2 cup (1 oz/30 g) chopped fresh basil

FOR THE MARINADE:

1/2 cup (4 fl oz/125 ml) olive oil

3 tablespoons red wine vinegar

2 tablespoons fresh lemon juice

2 cloves garlic, cut in half

1 tablespoon chopped fresh sage or 1 teaspoon dried sage

3 tablespoons chopped fresh chives or mint

Salt and freshly ground pepper

Grilled Vegetable Skewers
with Romesco Sauce

In Spain, the zesty almond-pepper sauce known as romesco is a classic accompaniment to grilled fish. It is equally delicious spooned over vegetables. Garnish with fresh flat-leaf (Italian) parsley, if you wish.

Romesco Sauce (page 301)

24 fresh whole mushrooms, 1 lb (500 g) total weight, brushed clean

6 Asian eggplants (slender aubergines), 1 lb (500 g) total weight, cut crosswise into slices ³/4 inch (2 cm) thick

6 long, thin zucchini (courgettes), 1¹/4 lb (625 g) total weight, cut crosswise into slices 1 inch (2.5 cm) thick

12 cherry tomatoes

Prepare the Romesco Sauce. Set aside.

Place 12 bamboo skewers in water to cover for 30 minutes. Prepare a fire for direct-heat cooking in a grill (page 309). Position the rack 4–6 inches (10–15 cm) above the fire. Drain the skewers. Thread the eggplant slices, mushrooms, zucchini slices, and tomatoes onto the skewers, alternating the vegetables and distributing them evenly and piercing the eggplant and zucchini slices through the skin sides (see photo). Brush the vegetables with olive oil. Place the skewers on the grill rack and grill, turning occasionally, until tender when pierced with the tip of a sharp knife, 10–15 minutes.

Place 2 skewers on each serving plate and garnish with parsley sprigs and serve. Pass the sauce at the table.

Serves 6

Mixed Vegetable Grill

Here is a suggested medley of vegetables, but improvise and use whatever is in season. Very firm vegetables will grill more quickly and evenly if you first cook them in boiling water until just tender.

In a small bowl, whisk together the olive oil, lemon juice, cilantro, 1 teaspoon salt, and 1/4 teaspoon pepper; set aside.

Bring a large pot three-fourths full of lightly salted water to a rapid boil. Add the fennel and cook until just tender when pierced with the tip of a sharp knife, 7–10 minutes. Using a slotted spoon, transfer to a colander to drain thoroughly. Drop the artichokes into the boiling water and cook until just tender when pierced, 5–10 minutes. Spoon them out, drain well, and cut in half lengthwise; set aside. Add the garlic heads to the boiling water and blanch for about 5 minutes; spoon them out, drain well, and set aside. Then blanch the Belgian endives for about 1 minute; drain well, and cut in half lengthwise. Set aside.

Cut or snap off any tough, woody ends from the asparagus spears and discard. Using a vegetable peeler and starting about 2 inches (5 cm) below the tip, peel off the skin from each spear.

Prepare a fire for direct-heat cooking in a grill (page 309). Oil the grill rack and position 4–6 inches (10–15 cm) above the fire. Arrange the vegetables on the rack. Grill the fennel halves, artichoke halves, whole garlic heads, and onion slices for about 12 minutes, the pepper halves and mushrooms for about 10 minutes, the endive halves for about 8 minutes, and the asparagus for 4–8 minutes, depending upon size. As the vegetables cook, turn them two or three times and brush with the olive oil mixture. Serve warm or at room temperature.

Serves 6

3/4 cup (6 fl oz/180 ml) olive oil

3 tablespoons fresh lemon juice

3 tablespoons chopped fresh cilantro (fresh coriander)

Salt and freshly ground pepper

2 fennel bulbs, stalks and any bruised outer leaves removed, cut in half lengthwise

4 baby artichokes, trimmed (page 308)

2 whole heads garlic, unpeeled

2 Belgian endives (chicory/witloof), trimmed

12–16 thin asparagus spears, about 12 oz (375 g)

1 large red onion, cut crosswise into slices 1/2 inch (12 mm) thick

2 Anaheim chile peppers, cut in half lengthwise, seeded, and deribbed (page 308)

8 oz (250 g) fresh shiitake mushrooms, brushed clean and stemmed

Beans & Legumes

Three-Bean Vegetarian Chili

This chili is versatile: Try serving it warm as an appetizer dip with tortilla chips or as a filling for burritos. Virtually any dried beans can be substituted for the beans given here. Seeding the fresh chile peppers reduces the spiciness.

3/4 cup (5 oz/155 g) dried pinto beans

3/4 cup (5 oz/155 g) dried red kidney beans

3/4 cup (5 oz/155 g) dried black beans

1/3 cup (3 oz/80 ml) olive oil

3 yellow onions, chopped

2 or 3 fresh serrano or jalapeño chiles, seeded (if desired) and minced

6 large cloves of garlic, minced

6 tablespoons (1 oz/30 g) chili powder

2 1/2 tablespoons ground cumin

1/4 teaspoon cayenne pepper

3/4 teaspoon dried oregano

2 cans (28 oz/875 g each) crushed plum (Roma) tomatoes

Salt and freshly ground black pepper

1/2 cup (2 oz/60 g) finely shredded Colby or Monterey jack cheese (optional)

Fresh cilantro (fresh coriander) leaves for garnish (optional)

Pick over the beans and discard any damaged beans or stones. Rinse the beans. Place in a bowl, add plenty of water to cover, and soak for about 3 hours. Drain the beans and set aside.

In a large, heavy saucepan over low heat, warm the olive oil. Add the onions and chiles and sauté, stirring, until the onions are soft, about 10 minutes. Add the garlic, chili powder, cumin, cayenne, and oregano and sauté, stirring, for 2 minutes. Add the beans, tomatoes, and water to cover by 3 inches (7.5 cm). Bring to a boil, reduce the heat to low, and simmer, uncovered, until the beans are very tender and begin to fall apart, 2 1/2–3 hours; add more water as needed if the beans begin to dry out but are not yet cooked.

Season to taste with salt and black pepper. Ladle into individual bowls, garnish with the cheese and cilantro, and serve.

Serves 6

Chili with Cornmeal Dumplings

This chili is a substantial meal. You can garnish this hearty one-dish vegetarian meal with sour cream or plain low-fat yogurt in place of the cheese. Sprinkle cilantro on top, if you like.

In a heavy-bottomed soup pot over medium-high heat, warm the olive oil. Add the bell peppers and onion and sauté, stirring, until the onion is translucent, about 5 minutes. Add the kidney beans and their liquid, tomatoes and their juices, chili powder, and hot-pepper sauce. Mix until well blended and bring to a simmer. Reduce the heat to medium-low, cover, and simmer gently for 20 minutes. Season to taste with salt and pepper.

Add the cornmeal dumplings to the top of the stew, cover, and cook as directed.

To serve, spoon the stew and dumplings into warmed bowls and sprinkle with the cheese, if using, and cilantro.

Serves 6

2 teaspoons olive oil

2 green bell peppers (capsicums), seeded, deribbed (page 308), and cut lengthwise into 1/2-inch (12-mm) strips

1 large sweet onion, cut in half and then into slices 1/2 inch (12 mm) thick

2 cans (19 oz/590 g each) red kidney beans, with liquid

2 cups (12 oz/375 g) canned tomato chunks in purée, with juices

1 tablespoon chili powder

3–5 dashes hot-pepper sauce such as Tabasco

Salt and freshly ground pepper

Cornmeal Dumplings (page 304)

1 cup (4 oz/125 g) shredded Colby or Monterey jack cheese (optional)

2 tablespoons chopped fresh cilantro (fresh coriander)

Refried Pinto Beans

Refried beans are usually made with a good amount of fat. This version reduces the fat, but is still full of flavor. Garnish with sour cream, sliced avocado, and Tomato Salsa (page 303). Seed the chiles for a milder dish.

1½ cups (10½ oz/330 g) dried pinto or red kidney beans

¼ cup (2 oz/60 g) vegetable oil

1 yellow onion, minced

2 serrano or jalapeño chiles, seeded (if desired) and minced

4 cloves garlic, minced

1 teaspoon dried oregano

½ teaspoon ground cumin

1 tomato, diced

Salt and freshly ground pepper

Pick over the beans and discard any damaged beans or stones. Rinse the beans. Place in a bowl, add plenty of water to cover, and soak for about 3 hours.

Drain the beans and place in a saucepan with water to cover by 2 inches (5 cm). Bring to a boil, reduce the heat to low, and simmer, uncovered, until the skins begin to crack and the beans are tender, 50–60 minutes. Drain, reserving the liquid.

In a large nonstick frying pan over low heat, warm the vegetable oil. Add the onion, chiles, garlic, oregano, and cumin and sauté, stirring, until the onion is very soft, about 15 minutes.

Add the tomato, beans, and salt and pepper to taste. With the pan still on the heat, mash with a potato masher or wooden spoon until creamy, adding some of the reserved bean cooking liquid if necessary to achieve the proper consistency.

Transfer to a warmed serving dish and serve.

Serves 6

Vegetarian Burritos

The term burrito pays tribute to little burros — pack animals capable of carrying abundant cargo. By all means, vary the vegetable mixture depending upon what is in season at your market.

In a large frying pan over medium heat, warm the oil. Add the onion, carrots, garlic, chile, oregano, and cumin and sauté until tender, about 10 minutes. Add the zucchini, bell pepper, corn, and kidney beans and cook until the zucchini is tender-crisp, 6–8 minutes longer.

Warm a nonstick frying pan over medium heat and heat the tortillas, turning once. Alternatively, enclose the tortillas in plastic wrap and place in a microwave oven for about 30 seconds. Place an equal amount of the vegetables in the center of each tortilla. Fold in the sides, overlapping them, then fold over the ends to rest atop the seam.

Serve the burritos immediately. Accompany with the cheese, shredded lettuce, and salsa in separate bowls on the side for spooning over the top.

Makes 12 burritos; serves 6

2 tablespoons vegetable oil

1 large onion, finely chopped

2 large carrots, peeled and thinly sliced

1 clove garlic, minced

1 fresh jalapeño or serrano chile pepper, seeded, deribbed and finely chopped

1 teaspoon dried oregano, crumbled

$1/2$ teaspoon ground cumin

2 cups (10 oz/315 g) diced zucchini (courgette)

1 green or red bell pepper (capsicum), seeded, deribbed (page 308), and chopped

1 cup (6 oz/185 g) fresh or frozen corn kernals

1 can (1 lb/500 g) kidney beans, drained

12 flour tortillas, each 8 inches (20 cm) in diameter

1 cup (4 oz/125 g) shredded Cheddar cheese

Shredded lettuce

Tomato Salsa (page 303) or Tomatillo Salsa (page 303)

Baked Adzuki Beans with Eggplant and Tomatoes

Traditionally made to use up leftovers, this versatile dish is called a *tian* in Provence. Any dried beans can be substituted. To julienne fresh herb leaves, stack in a pile, roll tightly, and slice thinly crosswise.

1 cup (7 oz/220 g) dried adzuki beans

6 fresh parsley stems

Pinch of fresh thyme leaves

1 bay leaf

2 small eggplants (aubergines), 1½ lb (750 g) total weight, trimmed but unpeeled, cut into 1-inch (2.5-cm) cubes

Salt and freshly ground pepper

6 tablespoons (3 fl oz/90 ml) olive oil

1 yellow onion, finely chopped

2½ cups (15 oz/470 g) peeled, seeded (page 313), and chopped tomatoes

1 cup (8 fl oz/250 ml) Vegetable Stock (page 300)

½ teaspoon ground allspice

¼ teaspoon red pepper flakes

4 tablespoons fresh basil leaves, cut into julienne (see note)

½ cup (2 oz/60 g) grated Parmesan cheese

Pick over the beans and discard any damaged beans or stones. Rinse the beans to remove any dirt or grit. Place in a bowl, add water to cover and soak for about 3 hours. Drain the beans and place in a saucepan with water to cover by 2 inches (5 cm). Combine the parsley stems, thyme, and bay leaf in a small piece of cheesecloth (muslin), bring the corners together, and tie with kitchen string to form a bouquet garni. Add to the saucepan. Bring to a boil, reduce the heat to low, and simmer, uncovered, until the beans are tender, about 20 minutes. Drain and set aside.

Meanwhile, place the eggplant cubes in a colander and sprinkle with salt. Let drain for 30 minutes. Rinse and pat dry with paper towels.

Preheat the oven to 375°F (190°C). Oil a large baking dish. In a large frying pan over medium-high heat, warm 4 tablespoons (2 fl oz/60 ml) of the olive oil. Add the eggplant and sauté until lightly browned on all sides, 10–15 minutes. Transfer to a bowl.

Add the remaining 2 tablespoons olive oil to the pan over medium heat. Add the onion and sauté, stirring, until soft, about 10 minutes. Add the tomatoes and stock and simmer slowly for 5 minutes. Add the eggplant, allspice, red pepper flakes, basil, and beans. Season to taste with salt and pepper.

Transfer the mixture to the prepared baking dish. Sprinkle with the Parmesan. Bake until golden brown, about 20 minutes. Serve hot, directly from the dish.

Serves 6

Spiced Black-eyed Peas with Yogurt and Ginger

Serve these East Indian–inspired black-eyed peas as a vegetarian main course with steamed basmati rice. Garnish with ¼ cup (⅓ oz/10 g) chopped fresh cilantro (fresh coriander) if you like.

Pick over the peas and discard any damaged peas or stones. Rinse the peas. Place in a bowl, add plenty of water to cover, and soak for about 3 hours.

Drain the peas and place in a saucepan with water to cover by 2 inches (5 cm). Bring to a boil, reduce the heat to low, and simmer, uncovered, until almost tender, about 35 minutes. Drain the peas, reserving the liquid. Set aside.

In a large frying pan over low heat, warm the olive oil. Add the onions and sauté, stirring, until soft, about 10 minutes. Add the ginger, garlic, coriander, cumin, and cardamom and sauté, stirring, for 2 minutes. Add the tomatoes, cover, and cook for 2 minutes longer. Uncover and raise the heat to medium. Add 1 tablespoon of the yogurt and stir until it is fully incorporated into the sauce. Continue in the same manner with the remaining yogurt, adding 1 tablespoon at a time.

Add the peas, ½ cup (4 fl oz/125 ml) of the reserved cooking liquid, salt to taste, and the cayenne. Cover and simmer over medium heat for 15 minutes. Uncover and continue to cook, stirring occasionally, until the liquid is very thick, 3–5 minutes.

Transfer to a platter, garnish with the cilantro, and serve.

Serves 6

1½ cups (10½ oz/330 g) dried black-eyed peas

¼ cup (2 fl oz/60 ml) olive oil

2 yellow onions, minced

4 tablespoons peeled and minced fresh ginger

6 cloves garlic, minced

1 teaspoon ground coriander

¾ teaspoon ground cumin

¼ teaspoon ground cardamom

2 tomatoes, chopped

½ cup (4 oz/125 g) plain yogurt

Salt

¼ teaspoon cayenne pepper

¼ cup (⅓ oz/10 g) chopped fresh cilantro (fresh coriander)

Mexican Layered Tortillas and Pinto Beans

Many thanks go to Nancy Gokey, a well-seasoned New England cook, for providing the recipe for this tasty dish. Garnish with a dollop of guacamole (page 14) or sour cream mixed with chopped green (spring) onions, or both, if you like.

Pick over the beans and discard any damaged beans or stones. Rinse the beans. Place in a bowl, add plenty of water to cover, and soak for about 3 hours.

Drain the beans and place in a saucepan with water to cover by 2 inches (5 cm). Bring to a boil, reduce the heat to low, and simmer, uncovered, until the skins begin to crack and the beans are tender, 45–60 minutes. Drain.

In a frying pan, combine the beans, onions, garlic, bell peppers, canned tomatoes and their juices, cayenne pepper (if using), chili powder, cumin, and salt and black pepper to taste. Bring to a simmer and cook, stirring occasionally, for 20 minutes.

Meanwhile, preheat the oven to 350°F (180°C)

Spread one-third of the bean mixture in a 9-by-13-inch (23-by-33-cm) baking dish. Top with 4 of the tortillas, overlapping evenly, and 1 cup (4 oz/125 g) of the cheese. Repeat the layers, using half of the remaining bean mixture and all of the tortillas and cheese. Top with the remaining bean mixture. Cover with aluminum foil and bake until the edges are bubbling, about 35 minutes.

Scatter the lettuce and fresh tomatoes evenly over the top and serve immediately.

Serves 6

3/4 cup (5 oz/155 g) dried pinto or red kidney beans

2 yellow onions, chopped

3 cloves garlic, minced

2 small green bell peppers (capsicums), seeded, deribbed (page 308), and chopped

1 can (28 oz/875 g) plum (Roma) tomatoes, drained, with juices reserved, and chopped

1/4–1/2 teaspoon cayenne pepper (optional)

6 tablespoons (1 oz/30 g) chili powder

1 tablespoon ground cumin

Salt and freshly ground black pepper

8 corn tortillas, each 6 inches (15 cm) in diameter

2 cups (8 oz/250 g) shredded Cheddar or Monterey jack cheese

2 cups (4 oz/125 g) coarsely chopped lettuce

2 tomatoes, coarsely chopped

Open-Faced Bean-and-Cheese Sandwiches

Excellent as a luncheon or brunch dish, this popular Mexico City creation goes well with scrambled eggs or a simple green salad. Lengths of French bread may be substituted for the individual rolls.

6 French rolls, split horizontally

Unsalted butter

1 cup (8 fl oz/250 ml) Refried Pinto Beans (page 210)

2 lb (1 kg) Cheddar cheese, thinly sliced

1 cup (8 fl oz/250 ml) Tomato Salsa (page 303)

Preheat a broiler (grill).

If you like, spread the cut sides of the rolls with butter or margarine. Then spread each with about 1 rounded tablespoon of the refried beans. Top with the cheese slices. Arrange on a broiler tray and slip under the broiler. Broil (grill) until the cheese melts. Serve immediately with the salsa.

Make 12 sandwiches; serves 6

Black Beans and Rice with Corn Salsa

Pick over the beans and discard any misshapen beans or stones. Rinse the beans and drain. Place in a bowl, add plenty of water to cover, and let soak for 3 hours. Seed and derib the bell pepper, and cut into ¹/₂-inch (12-mm) dice.

Drain the beans and place in a saucepan with the yellow onion, bell pepper, and water to cover by 2 inches (5 cm). Bring to a boil over high heat. Reduce the heat to medium-low and simmer, uncovered, until the beans are tender, about 1 hour. Remove from the heat and reserve the beans in their cooking liquid.

While the beans are cooking, make the salsa: Bring a saucepan three-fourths full of water to a boil. Add the corn kernels and boil for 30 seconds. Drain, place in a bowl, and let cool. Add the chiles, lime juice, red onion, cilantro, and salt and pepper to taste. Mix well and set aside.

In a large frying pan over medium-low heat, warm the olive oil. Add the garlic, parsley, cilantro, brown sugar, cumin, oregano, 1¹/₂ teaspoons salt, and pepper to taste. Sauté, stirring occasionally, until the garlic is golden, about 10 minutes.

Rinse and drain the rice. In a heavy saucepan, combine 2 cups (16 fl oz/500 ml) water and ¹/₂ teaspoon salt and bring to a boil. Add the rice, stir once, then cover, reduce the heat to low, and cook for 20 minutes. Uncover and check to see if the rice is tender and the water is absorbed. If not, re-cover and cook for a few minutes longer.

Meanwhile, add the wine to the garlic mixture and simmer over high heat until the wine is reduced by one-fourth, about 5 minutes. Reduce the heat to medium, add the beans and their cooking liquid, and simmer, uncovered, until the liquid has evaporated, about 15 minutes.

Spoon the rice into individual bowls. Top with the beans and the salsa and serve.

Serves 6

2 cups (14 oz/440 g) dried black beans

1 large green bell pepper (capsicum)

1 large yellow onion, chopped

FOR THE CORN SALSA:

Kernels from 3 ears of fresh corn (about 2 cups/12 oz/375 g)

2 fresh jalapeño chiles, seeded and minced

2 tablespoons fresh lime juice

¹/₂ cup (2¹/₂ oz/75 g) finely chopped red onion

¹/₃ cup (¹/₂ oz/15 g) chopped fresh cilantro (fresh coriander)

Salt and freshly ground pepper

¹/₄ cup (2 fl oz/60 ml) olive oil

6 cloves garlic, finely chopped

¹/₃ cup (¹/₂ oz/15 g) chopped fresh flat–leaf (Italian) parsley

³/₄ cup (1 oz/30 g) chopped fresh cilantro (fresh coriander)

1 tablespoon brown sugar

1 tablespoon ground cumin

1¹/₂ teaspoons dried oregano

Salt and freshly ground pepper

1 cup (7 oz/220 g) basmati rice

³/₄ cup (6 fl oz/180 ml) dry white wine

Chickpeas with Zucchini and Tomatoes

You can use 1 cup (7 oz/220 g) dried chickpeas in place of the canned. Soak the dried chickpeas for 3 hours in water, then drain and proceed as directed, increasing the cooking time to 1 hour to cook the chickpeas until tender.

2 tablespoons olive oil

2 cloves garlic, minced

1 large sweet onion, cut into wedges 1/2 inch (12 mm) thick

2 zucchini (courgettes), cut crosswise into slices 1/2 inch (12 mm) thick

1 red bell pepper (capsicum), seeded, deribbed (page 308), and cut lengthwise into 1/2-inch (12-mm) strips

1 lb (500 g) cherry tomatoes

1/2 cup (4 fl oz/125 ml) dry red wine

1 1/2 cups (12 oz/375 g) canned tomato chunks in purée, with juices

1 can (20 oz/625 g) chickpeas (garbanzo beans), drained

1/2 teaspoon dried oregano

1/2 teaspoon dried basil

Salt and freshly ground pepper

In a large heavy-bottomed soup pot over medium heat, warm the olive oil. Add the garlic, onion, and zucchini and sauté, stirring, until the onion is translucent, about 10 minutes. Add the bell pepper, cherry tomatoes, wine, canned tomatoes and juices, chickpeas, oregano, and basil. Stir well and bring to a simmer. Reduce the heat to medium-low, cover, and simmer gently until the stew is slightly thickened and the vegetables are tender, 25 minutes. Season to taste with salt and pepper.

Spoon into warmed shallow bowls or plates and serve.

Serves 4

Lima Beans with Vegetables

Bulgur or kasha is a wonderful accompaniment to this savory vegetable dish.
If you like, garnish it with garlic-flavored croutons or toasted sesame seeds.
A bouquet garni is a combination of herbs and spices that will enhance the flavor.

Pick over the beans and discard any damaged beans or stones. Rinse the beans. Place in a bowl, add plenty of water to cover, and let stand for at least 4 hours or overnight. Drain the lima beans, rinse, and set aside.

In a large, heavy-bottomed soup pot over medium heat, warm the olive oil. Add the onion, carrots, and celery and sauté, stirring, until the vegetables just start to turn golden, about 10 minutes. Add the stock and, using a large spoon, deglaze the pot over medium-high heat by stirring to dislodge any browned bits from the bottom of the pot. Meanwhile, tie together the parsley sprigs, bay leaf, and mint sprig with kitchen string to make the bouquet garni. Add the bouquet garni, lima beans, and tomatoes. Stir well and bring to a simmer. Reduce the heat to medium-low, cover, and simmer gently until the carrots are tender and the liquid has thickened slightly, about 20 minutes. Remove the bouquet garni and discard. Season to taste with salt and pepper.

Spoon into warmed shallow bowls or plates and serve.

Serves 4

6 peppercorns

1 bay leaf

1 clove garlic, sliced

3 fresh flat-leaf (Italian) parsley sprigs

1 cup (7 oz/220 g) dried lima beans

2 tablespoons olive oil

1 large sweet onion, cut into 1-inch (2.5-cm) pieces

3 carrots, peeled and cut into 1-inch (2.5-cm) pieces

2 celery stalks, coarsely chopped

1 cup (8 fl oz/250 ml) Vegetable Stock (page 300)

2 tomatoes, cut into 3/4-inch (2-cm) wedges

Salt and freshly ground pepper

Spiced Lentils

For the best texture, make this dish no more than several hours in advance. If you make it ahead, fold in half of the mint, then add the rest just before serving.

2 cups (14 oz/440 g) green or brown lentils

1 bay leaf

1 teaspoon salt

1/2 cup (4 fl oz/125 ml) plus 3 tablespoons olive oil

1/4 cup (2 fl oz/60 ml) lemon juice

2 cups (8 oz/250 g) chopped yellow onions

1 teaspoon minced garlic

2 tablespoons ground cumin

1 teaspoon ground coriander

Grated zest of 1 lemon

1/2 cup (3/4 oz/20 g) chopped fresh mint

Salt and freshly ground pepper

In a deep saucepan, combine the lentils and bay leaf. Add water to cover by 3 inches (7.5 cm) and bring to a boil over high heat. Add the salt, reduce the heat to low, cover, and simmer until the lentils are tender but still firm. Green lentils can take as long as 45 minutes, while brown lentils can take as little as 15 minutes, so keep testing. When the lentils are done, drain well and place in a bowl. Add the 1/2 cup (4 fl oz/125 ml) olive oil and the lemon juice, toss well, and set aside.

In a large frying pan over medium heat, warm the 3 tablespoons oil. Add the onions and sauté until tender and translucent, about 10 minutes. Add the garlic, cumin, coriander, and lemon zest and continue to sauté until the garlic is soft and the flavors are blended, 2–3 minutes longer.

Add the cooked onion mixture to the lentils and mix well. Fold in the mint and season with salt and pepper. Serve at room temperature.

Serves 6

Falafel Burgers
with Tahini Mayonnaise

In Syria, Lebanon, Israel, and Egypt, this is street food, but arguably some of the most nutritious and flavorful of its kind in the world. Falafel mix is available at well-stocked supermarkets and natural-food stores.

In a bowl, stir together the falafel mix and the cold water. Let stand until the mixture thickens, about 30 minutes.

In a deep saucepan, pour in canola oil to a depth of 1 inch (2.5 cm). Heat to 375°F (190°C) on a deep-frying thermometer, or until a small drop of the falafel mixture sizzles immediately upon contact with the oil. While the oil is heating, using your hands, form the falafel mixture into 6 patties, each $2^{1}/_{2}$ inches (6 cm) in diameter and $^{1}/_{2}$ inch (12 mm) thick.

Slip the patties into the hot oil a few at a time and fry, turning once, until golden on both sides, about 6 minutes total. Using tongs or a slotted spoon, transfer the patties to paper towels and keep them warm while you fry the remaining patties.

Place a falafel burger on the roll with a spoonful of the tahini mayonnaise, some lettuce leaf strips, a tomato slice, and a slice of red onion. Cap with the top of the roll and serve immediately.

Serves 6

2 cups (10 oz/315 g) dry falafel mix

$1^{1}/_{3}$ cups (11 fl oz/330 ml) cold water

Canola oil for deep-frying

6 crusty round rolls, each $2^{1}/_{2}$ inches (6 cm) in diameter, halved

6 large romaine (cos) lettuce leaves, carefully washed, well dried, and cut crosswise into strips 1 inch (2.5 cm) wide

1 large tomato, cut into 6 thin slices

1 large red onion, cut into 6 thin slices (optional)

$^{1}/_{2}$ cup (4 fl oz/125 ml) Tahini Mayonnaise (page 303)

Pasta, Polenta & Rice

Fettuccine with Roasted Garlic and Chile

For this recipe, the garlic sauce can be replaced with an onion sauce: Roast 3 small brown-skinned onions, using the same method as for the garlic heads, peel them and puree with the oil in a food processor.

6 whole heads garlic

1¼ lb (600 g) fettuccine

6 tablespoons (3 fl oz/90 ml) extra-virgin olive oil

Salt

Pinch of ground dried chile flakes

Toasted Bread Crumbs (page 303) for garnish (optional)

Preheat an oven to 350°F (180°C). Wrap each head of garlic separately in aluminum foil. Place the garlic on a rack in the center of the oven and bake for 45 minutes. Remove the garlic heads from the oven and set aside to cool slightly so that they can be handled.

In a large pot bring 6 qt (6l) salted water to a boil. Add the fettuccine to the boiling water and cook until al dente, 9–12 minutes or according to the package directions.

Meanwhile, unwrap the garlic heads, separate the cloves and squeeze the garlic cloves from their papery sheaths into a hot serving bowl. Add the olive oil and season to taste with salt. Sprinkle with the chile flakes and blend together well with a fork. Set aside.

Drain the pasta and transfer it to the serving bowl. Toss the pasta with the sauce and sprinkle on the bread crumbs if using. Serve immediately.

Serves 6

Spaghetti with Marinara Sauce

This basic Italian-style tomato sauce complements a wide variety of pastas. The recipe yields about 4 cups (32 fl oz/1 l) sauce, enough for 1 pound (500 g) of pasta. It will keep several days in the refrigerator or several months in the freezer.

To make the sauce, in a saucepan over medium-low heat, warm the olive oil. Add the onion, garlic, and mushrooms and cook, stirring often until the vegetables are soft, about 7 minutes.

Add the tomatoes, wine, tomato paste, and thyme and stir to combine. Bring to a boil over medium-high heat, then return the heat to medium-low and simmer, uncovered, stirring occasionally, until the sauce thickens slightly, 10–15 minutes. Season to taste with salt and pepper.

Meanwhile, bring a large pot three-fourths full of lightly salted water to a boil. Add the spaghetti to the boiling water, stir well, and cook until al dente, about 10 minutes or according to the package directions.

Drain the spaghetti and place in a warmed shallow serving bowl. Pour the sauce over and toss briefly to combine. Serve at once. Pass the Parmesan at the table.

Serves 6

FOR THE SAUCE:

2 tablespoons olive oil

1 yellow onion, chopped

2 cloves garlic, minced

1/4 lb (125 g) fresh white mushrooms, brushed clean and sliced

1 can (28 oz/875 g) crushed tomatoes in purée

1/3 cup (3 fl oz/80 ml) dry red or white wine or water

1/4 cup (2 oz/60 g) tomato paste

1/2 teaspoon dried thyme, or oregano, or mixed Italian herbs

Salt and freshly ground pepper

1 lb (500 g) dried spaghetti

1 cup (4 oz/125 g) grated Parmesan cheese

Spaghetti with Summer Garden Purée

Sun-ripened tomatoes join with celery, zucchini, parsley, and olive oil to produce a creamy, garden-fresh sauce that is equally good warm or at room temperature.

10 oz (300 g) ripe tomatoes, peeled (page 313) and halved

1 zucchini (courgette)

1 lb (500 g) dried spaghetti

$1/2$ stalk white or green celery, trimmed and cut crosswise into slices $3/4$ inch (2 cm) thick

Handful of fresh flat-leaf (Italian) parsley leaves

$1/2$ cup (4 fl oz/120 ml) extra-virgin olive oil

Freshly ground pepper

Sprinkle the tomato halves with a little salt. Place them cut side down in a colander for about 1 hour, to drain off excess juice.

Using a vegetable peeler, remove the green skin from the zucchini and set it aside. The zucchini itself can be saved and used in a soup.

In a large pot bring 6 qt (6l) salted water to a boil. Add the spaghetti and boil until al dente, about 10 minutes or according to the package directions.

Meanwhile, in a blender or food processor, combine the tomatoes, celery, zucchini skins, parsley, olive oil, and salt and pepper to taste. Process until smooth and creamy.

Drain the pasta and arrange it on a platter. Pour the sauce over the top and toss well. This dish may be served immediately or at room temperature

Serves 6

Radiatori with Avocado

Although this is a warm dish, it is also excellent served cold. To do so, toss the pasta with oil after draining, and then let cool. Just before serving, toss the pasta with the avocado, tomato, and parsley.

In a large pot bring 6 qt (6l) salted water to boil. Add the radiatori and cook until al dente, about 10 minutes or according to the package directions.

Meanwhile, cut the avocado in half. Remove the pit, then peel the halves and cut them lengthwise into thin slices. Place the slices in a bowl and sprinkle them with lemon juice, chile, and salt to taste. Add the olive oil and stir gently.

Drain the pasta and transfer it to a platter. Pour the avocado mixture over the pasta, then toss together gently. Transfer to a serving bowl and serve immediately.

Serves 6

1¼ lb (600 g) dried radiatori

1 avocado

Juice of 1 lemon

Pinch of ground dried chile

Salt

6 tablespoons (3 fl oz/90ml) extra-virgin olive oil

2 ripe tomatoes, peeled (page 313) and diced

1 tablespoon finely chopped fresh flat-leaf (Italian) parsley

Fettuccine with Cranberry Beans and Pesto

Feel free to substitute other beans in this recipe: red or white kidney beans, cannellini beans, chickpeas (garbanzo beans), small white (navy) beans, or black-eyed peas. Different pasta types may be substituted as well.

1 cup (7 oz/220 g) dried cranberry (borlotti) beans

1½ cups (1½ oz/45 g) firmly packed fresh basil leaves, plus whole leaves for garnish

1 cup (4 oz/125 g) grated romano, pecorino, or Parmesan cheese

10 tablespoons (6 fl oz/180 ml) extra-virgin olive oil

1 large yellow onion, chopped

4 cloves garlic, minced

2 cups (16 fl oz/500 ml) Vegetable Stock (page 300) or water

1 lb (500 g) dried fettucine

½ cup (2½ oz/75 g) pine nuts, toasted (page 311)

Salt and freshly ground pepper

Pick over the beans and discard any damaged beans or stones. Rinse the beans. Place in a bowl, add plenty of water to cover, and soak for about 3 hours.

Drain the beans and place in a saucepan with water to cover by 2 inches (5 cm). Bring to a boil, reduce the heat to low, and simmer, uncovered, until tender, 40–50 minutes. Drain and set aside.

In a blender or in a food processor fitted with the metal blade, combine the 1½ cups (1½ oz/45 g) basil, the cheese, and 6 tablespoons (3 fl oz/90 ml) of the olive oil. Process until smooth. Set aside.

In a large frying pan over medium heat, warm the remaining 4 tablespoons (2 fl oz/60 ml) olive oil. Add the onion and garlic and sauté, stirring, until soft, about 10 minutes. Add the stock and the beans. Bring to a boil, reduce the heat to low, and simmer, uncovered, until the stock is reduced by one-fourth, 5–10 minutes.

Meanwhile, bring a large pot three-fourths full of water to a boil. Add salt to taste and the fettuccine and cook until al dente, 9–12 minutes or according to the package directions. Drain and place in a warmed serving bowl.

Add the bean mixture, basil mixture, pine nuts, and salt and pepper to taste to the bowl with the pasta and toss well. Garnish with basil leaves and serve.

Serves 6

Curry-Flavored Fettuccine

Adding flavoring—vegetables, herbs, spices—to regular fresh pasta dough has long been popular in Italy. Here, curry powder adds an exotic touch and a warm golden tint to the cream sauce.

2 cups (10 oz/300 g) shelled peas

1/2 cup (4 fl oz/120 ml) heavy (double) cream

1/4 cup (2 oz/60 g) unsalted butter

2 tablespoons curry powder

1 lb (500 g) dried fettuccine

Salt and freshly ground pepper

In a large pot bring 5 qt (5l) salted water to a boil. Add the peas and boil for 5 minutes.

Meanwhile, in a saucepan combine the cream, butter, and curry powder. Bring slowly to a boil over low heat and boil, stirring, for 2 minutes.

Bring a large pot three-fourths full of water to a boil. Add salt to taste and the fettuccine. Cook until al dente, 9–12 minutes or according to the package directions. Drain and place in a warmed serving bowl. Pour the cream-butter mixture over the top and season to taste with salt and pepper. Toss gently and serve immediately.

Serves 6

Penne with Carrots and Chevre

The sweet flavor of carrots brings out a corresponding sweetness in fresh, creamy goat cheese. While regular pasta may be used, green spinach pasta makes a beautiful backdrop to the other ingredients.

In a large pot bring 5 qt (5l) salted water to a boil.

While the water is heating, in a large frying pan heat the olive oil over medium heat. Add the carrots and sauté, stirring occasionally, until tender when pierced with a fork, about 10 minutes. Season to taste with salt.

Add the penne to the boiling water and cook until barely al dente, 10–12 minutes or according to the package directions. Meanwhile, crumble the chevre onto a plate and set aside.

Drain the pasta and transfer it to the frying pan containing the carrots. Cook over medium heat, stirring frequently, for about 2 minutes.

Arrange the pasta on a warm platter. Sprinkle the crumbled cheese and parsley over the top and serve at once.

Serves 6

6 tablespoons (3 fl oz/90 ml) extra-virgin olive oil

10 oz (300 g) carrots, peeled and cut crosswise into slices about 1/16 inch (2 mm) thick

Salt

1 lb (480 g) dried penne

6 oz (180 g) chevre

1 tablespoon chopped fresh flat-leaf (Italian) parsley

Baked Penne with Three Cheeses

Other short dried pastas — fusilli, farfalle, elbow macaroni — can be used in place of the penne. This recipe can also be made in individual 5-inch (13-cm) round gratin dishes, in which case the baking time should be reduced by 5–10 minutes.

In a large saucepan over medium heat, melt the butter. Whisk in the flour and cook, stirring constantly, for 2 minutes; do not brown. Gradually whisk in the milk and cook, stirring constantly, until the sauce is smooth and thickened, about 5 minutes. Add the fontina, Gorgonzola, and Parmesan and stir until the cheeses melt. Season to taste with salt and pepper. Remove from the heat; set aside.

Preheat the oven to 375°F (190°C). Lightly grease a shallow 2 1/2-qt (2.5-l) baking dish or six, 5-inch (13-cm) gratin dishes.

Meanwhile, bring a large pot three-fourths full of lightly salted water to a boil. Add the pasta and cook until al dente, 10–12 minutes or according to package directions. Drain and add to the sauce. Toss gently to mix.

Transfer the pasta and sauce to the prepared dish. Sprinkle the top evenly with the bread crumbs. Bake until the top is golden brown and the sauce is bubbling, 25–30 minutes.

Let cool for 5 minutes, then spoon into warmed bowls if necessary and serve.

Serves 6

6 tablespoons (3 oz/90 g) unsalted butter

6 tablespoons (2 oz/60 g) all-purpose (plain) flour

4 cups (32 fl oz/1 l) milk

1 1/2 cups (6 oz/185 g) shredded fontina cheese

1/2 lb (250 g) Gorgonzola cheese, cut into small pieces

1 cup (4 oz/125 g) grated Parmesan cheese

Salt and freshly ground pepper

3/4 lb (375 g) dried penne

1/2 cup (1 oz/30 g) fresh bread crumbs (page 308)

Pasta Primavera

In Italian, primavera means "spring," so be sure to use the first tiny vegetables of the season. After draining the pasta, add it to the sauce; the hot pasta will continue to absorb moisture, enabling it to become evenly coated with sauce.

3 tablespoons unsalted butter

½ cup (2½ oz/75 g) asparagus tips, cut on the diagonal

½ cup (2½ oz/75 g) small, tender green beans, trimmed

½ cup (2½ oz/75 g) small shelled English peas

½ cup (2½ oz/75 g) sliced yellow crookneck squash

¾ cup (6 fl oz/180 ml) heavy (double) cream

Salt and freshly ground pepper

1 teaspoon olive oil

1 lb (500 g) dried fettuccine or spaghetti

Freshly grated Parmesan cheese for garnish

In a large sauté pan over medium heat, melt the butter. Add the asparagus, green beans, peas, and squash and sauté, stirring, until tender-crisp, about 5 minutes. Add the cream and season to taste with salt and pepper. Boil briskly, stirring for 1–2 minutes to reduce slightly. Remove from the heat and cover to keep warm.

Meanwhile, bring a large pot three-fourths full of lightly salted water to a boil. Add 1 teaspoon salt and the olive oil. Add the pasta and stir gently. Boil, stirring occasionally, until al dente, 6–10 minutes or according to package directions.

Drain the pasta in a colander and, acting quickly, immediately add it to the cooked sauce. Toss well and promptly divide among warmed plates. Garnish with Parmesan cheese. Serve immediately.

Serves 4

Green and White Lasagne

½ lb (250 g) dried lasagne
noodles

2 cups (16 oz/500 g) ricotta
cheese

⅓ cup (1½ oz/45 g) freshly
grated Parmesan cheese

Salt and freshly ground pepper

¼ cup (2 fl oz/60 ml) extra-
virgin olive oil

2 yellow onions, thinly sliced

4 zucchini (courgettes), 1 lb
(500 g) total weight, trimmed
and thinly sliced crosswise

1 lb (500 g) fresh mushrooms,
brushed clean and thinly
sliced

3 cloves garlic, minced

¼ cup (2 oz/60 g) unsalted
butter

¼ cup (1½ oz/45 g)
all-purpose (plain) flour

3 cups (24 fl oz/750 ml) milk

Freshly grated nutmeg

40 fresh basil leaves

½ lb (250 g) whole-milk
mozzarella, shredded

Bring a large pot three-fourths full of lightly salted water to a boil. Add the lasagne noodles and cook until al dente, 10–12 minutes or according to the package directions. Meanwhile, fill a bowl with cold water. When the pasta is done, drain and place in the bowl of water to cool. After 5 minutes, drain the pasta again and lay the pieces in a single layer on a baking sheet. Cover with plastic wrap and set aside.

In a small bowl, stir together the ricotta, Parmesan, and salt and pepper to taste until mixed. Set aside. In a frying pan over medium heat, warm the olive oil. Add the onions and cook, stirring occasionally, until soft, about 10 minutes. Add the zucchini, mushrooms, and garlic and continue to cook, stirring occasionally until the vegetables are tender and any moisture has evaporated, 10–12 minutes. Season with salt and pepper. Set aside.

In a saucepan over low heat, melt the butter. Whisk in the flour and cook, stirring, for 2 minutes. Gradually whisk in the milk and cook, stirring, until the sauce is smooth and thickened, 3–4 minutes. Season with salt, pepper, and nutmeg. Position a rack in the upper third of the oven and preheat to 375°F (190°C). Oil a 9-by-13-inch (23-by-33-cm) baking dish. Cover the bottom of the baking dish with a layer of lasagne noodles. Spoon one-third of the ricotta mixture over the noodles. Sprinkle one-third of the reserved vegetables over the ricotta layer and then top with one-third of the white sauce. Distribute one-third of the basil leaves evenly over the sauce. Repeat the layers twice more, ending with the basil. Sprinkle the cheese evenly over the top. Bake until golden and bubbling around the edges, 30–40 minutes. Let cool briefly, then cut into squares to serve.

Serves 8–10

Ricotta and Spinach Dumplings with Pesto

Place the freshly washed spinach with just the water clinging to it in a large frying pan over high heat. Cook, using tongs to gently toss the spinach, until it wilts, about 2 minutes. Transfer to a colander and press out the excess water with the back of a large spoon. Wrap the spinach in a clean kitchen towel or paper towels and wring out any excess moisture. Transfer to a cutting board and chop finely.

In a bowl, combine the chopped spinach, $^1/_2$ cup (2 oz/60 g) of the Parmesan, $^1/_2$ cup (2$^1/_2$ oz/75 g) of the flour, the ricotta, and the eggs. Season with the nutmeg and salt and pepper to taste and stir well. Spread another $^1/_2$ cup (2$^1/_2$ oz/75 g) of the flour on a plate. Using a spoon, shape the dough into walnut-sized oval dumplings and, working with 2 or 3 dumplings at a time, dredge them in the flour. If the dough is too wet and will not form a ball, add more flour, 1 tablespoon at a time, until it holds a nice shape.

Preheat the oven to 350°F (180°C). Bring a large pot three-fourths full of lightly salted water to a boil. Add the dumplings, a few at a time, and boil until they rise to the surface, 5–7 minutes. Using a slotted spoon, transfer the dumplings to a lightly greased 2-qt (2-l) baking dish. Drizzle with the olive oil and toss gently to coat. Bake until the dumplings are heated throughout, 10–15 minutes.

To serve, spoon the pesto onto a warmed platter or individual plates and arrange the dumplings on top. Sprinkle with the remaining $^1/_2$ cup (2 oz/60 g) Parmesan. Serve at once.

Makes about 36 dumplings; serves 6

3 lb (1.5 kg) spinach, stemmed, carefully washed

1 cup (4 oz/120 g) grated or shredded Parmesan cheese

1 cup (5 oz/150 g) all-purpose (plain) flour, plus more as needed

1$^1/_2$ cups (12 oz/375 g) ricotta cheese

3 eggs, lightly beaten

Large pinch of freshly grated nutmeg

Salt and freshly ground pepper

3 tablespoons extra-virgin olive oil

1$^1/_4$ cups (10 fl oz/310 ml) Pesto Sauce (page 301)

Noodles with Spicy Peanut Sauce

You will need a regular hand blender or a small food processor to mix the peanut sauce. Use Chinese mein noodles made without eggs for this classic dish; look for them in Asian markets and well-stocked food stores.

Bring a large pot three-fourths full of water to a boil. Add the noodles and boil for 2 minutes. Drain well and set aside.

In a wok or frying pan over high heat, warm 2 tablespoons of the oil, swirling to coat the bottom and sides of the pan. When the oil is very hot but not quite smoking, add the carrots and stir and toss every 15–20 seconds until just tender, 3–4 minutes. Add the green onions and stir and toss for 1 minute.

Push the carrot-onion mixture to the side of the pan and add the remaining 1 tablespoon oil over medium-high heat, again swirling to coat the pan. When the oil is hot, add the drained noodles and, using 2 tongs or 2 large forks, stir and toss every 15–20 seconds for 2 minutes, being careful to keep the noodles from sticking together and heating them evenly until very hot. Remove from the heat and immediately add the peanut sauce. Toss until the noodles and vegetables are evenly coated with the sauce.

Taste and adjust the seasoning. Serve immediately.

Serves 4–6

1 lb (500 g) fresh Chinese mein noodles

3 tablespoons peanut or vegetable oil

2 carrots, peeled and cut into thin strips 2 inches (5 cm) long and 1/4 inch (6 mm) wide

4 green (spring) onions, including tender green tops, cut into 2-inch (5-cm) lengths and then halved lengthwise

Spicy Peanut Sauce (page 302)

Polenta Triangles with Saffron Tomato Sauce

FOR THE POLENTA:

6 cups (48 fl oz/1.5 l) water

Salt and freshly ground pepper

1¼ cups (7½ oz/235 g) polenta or coarse-grind cornmeal

⅓ cup (1½ oz/45 g) freshly grated Parmesan cheese, plus extra for serving

2 teaspoons chopped fresh rosemary, plus 6 sprigs for garnish (optional)

2 tablespoons olive oil

1 large yellow onion, chopped

¼ cup (2 fl oz/60 ml) red wine

1 tablespoon balsamic vinegar

⅛ teaspoon red pepper flakes

1 tablespoon tomato paste

¼ teaspoon dried oregano

4 cups (28 oz/875 g) peeled, seeded (page 313), and finely chopped plum (Roma) tomatoes

Salt and freshly ground pepper

1 teaspoon saffron threads

2 cups (10 oz/315 g) all-purpose (plain) flour

Canola oil for deep-frying

To make the polenta, butter a 9-inch (23-cm) square pan and set aside. In a large saucepan, bring the water to a boil. Add 1 teaspoon salt and slowly stir in the polenta. Cook over medium heat, stirring, until the polenta pulls away from the sides of the pan, 20–30 minutes. Stir in the Parmesan, rosemary, and salt and pepper to taste. Pour the polenta into the prepared pan and smooth the top. Cover and refrigerate to cool completely.

While the polenta is cooling, but before frying the triangles, in a large frying pan over medium heat, warm the olive oil. Add the onion and sauté, stirring, for 10 minutes. Stir in the wine, vinegar, red pepper flakes, tomato paste, oregano, tomatoes, and salt and pepper to taste. Reduce the heat to low and simmer, uncovered, until the sauce begins to thicken, about 20 minutes. Add the saffron and simmer for 5 minutes longer.

Remove the sauce from the heat and let cool slightly. Using a blender or a food processor fitted with the metal blade, purée the sauce until smooth. Transfer to a saucepan and keep warm while you fry the polenta.

Pour canola oil to a depth of ½-inch (12 mm) in a large, deep frying pan and heat until it registers 400°F (200°C) on a deep-fat frying thermometer.

Cut the polenta into nine 3-inch (7.5-cm) squares. Cut each square into 2 triangles; remove from the pan. Place the flour in a shallow bowl and, working with a few triangles as a time, toss in the flour to dust lightly. Slip the triangles into the hot oil a few at a time and fry, turning once, until golden brown, about 4–6 minutes. Using a slotted spoon, transfer to paper towels to drain briefly.

To serve, arrange the triangles on a platter or individual plates. Spoon the tomato sauce over the polenta and sprinkle with the cheese. Garnish with rosemary sprigs, if desired, and serve.

Serves 6

Polenta with Pesto

Lightly grease a 9-inch (23-cm) round pie pan.

To make the polenta, in a saucepan, combine 1 1/2 cups (12 fl oz/375 ml) water, the milk, butter, 1 teaspoon salt, and the red pepper flakes and bring to a boil over high heat. Slowly pour in the polenta, whisking constantly so that it does not lump. Reduce the heat to low and cook, stirring frequently, until quite thick, 10–15 minutes; it should have the consistency of cooked oatmeal. Spread evenly in the prepared pie pan, then cover with plastic wrap and chill until firm, about 1 1/2 hours.

Meanwhile, make the pesto: In a food processor fitted with the metal blade, place the basil, parsley, and garlic. Process until puréed. With the motor running, pour the olive oil through the food tube of the processor in a thin, steady stream. Add 1/2 teaspoon salt and the Parmesan and process until smooth. If the pesto seems too thick, add 1–2 tablespoons water. You should have at least 3/4 cup (6 fl oz/180 ml).

Cut the polenta into 8 wedges and carefully remove from the pie pan with a spatula. Lightly grease a large, nonstick frying pan and place over medium-high heat. Add the polenta wedges and cook, turning once, until lightly browned, about 3 minutes on each side.

To serve, transfer the wedges to a warmed platter or individual plates. Spoon half of the pesto over the wedges. Pass the remaining pesto at the table.

Serves 4

FOR THE POLENTA:

1 1/2 cups (12 fl oz/375 ml) water

1 1/2 cups (12 fl oz/375 ml) nonfat milk

1 tablespoon unsalted butter

Salt

Pinch of red pepper flakes

3/4 cup (4 oz/125 g) polenta or yellow cornmeal

FOR THE PESTO:

3 cups (3 oz/90 g) loosely packed fresh basil leaves

1/2 cup (1/2 oz/15 g) fresh flat-leaf (Italian) parsley

2 large cloves garlic

1/4 cup (2 fl oz/60 ml) olive oil

Salt

1/4 cup (1 oz/30 g) grated Parmesan cheese

Polenta with Vegetable Ragout

Polenta pairs well with vegetables. This hearty ragout makes for a substantial main course. Let the finished dish cool for 10 minutes before serving, otherwise it will be too hot.

Salt and freshly ground pepper

1³/4 cups (10¹/2 oz/330 g) polenta

2 tablespoons olive oil

1 small yellow onion, chopped

1 celery stalk, chopped

1 small carrot, peeled and chopped

1 clove garlic, minced

2 teaspoons chopped sage

¹/2 teaspoon chopped thyme

1 teaspoon chopped rosemary

4 cups (28 oz/875 g) peeled, seeded (page 313) and finely chopped tomatoes

5 tablespoons (2¹/2 oz/75 g) unsalted butter

¹/4 cup (1¹/2 oz/45 g) all-purpose (plain) flour

3 cups (24 fl oz/750 ml) milk

Large pinch of grated nutmeg

1 cup (4 oz/125 g) grated Parmesan cheese

In a large, heavy saucepan over high heat, bring 7 cups (56 fl oz/1.75 l) water to a boil. Add 1 teaspoon salt and then slowly pour in the polenta, stirring constantly. Reduce the heat to medium and cook, stirring, until the polenta pulls away from the sides of the pan, 20–30 minutes. Season to taste with salt and pepper. Turn out onto a smooth work surface and, using a rubber spatula, spread it evenly to form a sheet ¹/2 inch (12 mm) thick. Let cool completely.

In a sauté pan over medium-low heat, warm the olive oil. Add the onion, celery, carrot, garlic, sage, thyme, and rosemary. Cook, stirring, until the onion is soft, 15 minutes. Add the tomatoes and any juices and simmer, stirring until thick, 20-25 minutes. Remove from the heat. Using a round cutter 2¹/2 inches (6 cm) in diameter, cut out as many rounds as possible from the polenta sheet. Arrange half of the rounds in a single layer on the bottom of a 9-by-13-inch (23-by-33-cm) baking dish.

Preheat the oven to 350°F (180°C). In a saucepan over low heat, melt the butter. Whisk in the flour and cook, whisking constantly, for 2 minutes; do not brown. Add the milk, whisking constantly. Continue to whisk until smooth and thickened, 3–4 minutes. Season with salt and pepper and the nutmeg. Remove from the heat.

Spoon half of the white sauce evenly over the polenta rounds. Spread with half of the tomato sauce. Repeat layering with the remaining polenta, white sauce, and tomato sauce. Sprinkle with the Parmesan. Bake until golden on top and bubbling around the edges, about 20 minutes. Let cool for 10 minutes, then serve.

Serves 6

Beet and Goat Cheese Risotto

Just two beets, shredded raw and added toward the end of cooking, give this risotto a dazzlingly vivid red color. The goat cheese makes this dish equally suitable as a side dish or as a main course.

In a saucepan over medium-high heat, bring the stock to a simmer. Adjust the heat to keep the liquid hot.

In a large, heavy saucepan over medium heat, warm the olive oil. Add the shallots and sauté until translucent, about 2 minutes. Add the rice and stir until white spots appear in the center of the grains, about 1 minute. Add a ladleful of the hot stock, reduce the heat to maintain a simmer, and cook, stirring constantly, until the liquid is absorbed, about 2 minutes. Continue adding the liquid, a ladleful at a time and stirring constantly, until the rice is just tender but slightly firm in the center and the mixture is creamy, 20–25 minutes longer.

Stir in the shredded beets and the orange juice. Continue cooking and stirring until the beets are heated through, about 2 minutes. Season to taste with salt and pepper.

To serve, spoon onto warmed individual plates and crumble the goat cheese evenly on top. Garnish with the chives, parsley, and lemon zest.

Serves 6

8 cups (64 fl oz/2 l) Vegetable Stock (page 300) or broth

3 tablespoons extra-virgin olive oil

2 shallots, finely chopped

2¹⁄₂ cups (17¹⁄₂ oz/545 g) Arborio rice

2 beets, trimmed, peeled, and coarsely shredded

1 cup (8 fl oz/250 ml) fresh orange juice

Salt and freshly ground pepper

6 oz (185 g) fresh goat cheese

2 tablespoons snipped fresh chives

2 tablespoons coarsely chopped fresh flat-leaf (Italian) parsley

2 tablespoons grated orange zest

Risotto with Saffron

Always use a starchy rice such as Arborio or Carnaroli when making risotto; the round grains cook to a creamy yet firm consistency. The stock must be added a little at a time so that the grains swell slowly and evenly.

In a saucepan over medium heat, combine the stock and 2 cups (16 fl oz/500 ml) water to make a light stock and bring to a simmer.

In a large, heavy saucepan over medium heat, melt 4 tablespoons (2 oz/60 g) of the butter with the olive oil. Add the onion and sauté, stirring, until soft, about 5 minutes. Add the rice and stir until slightly translucent, 1–2 minutes.

Start adding the hot stock to the pan, ¹/₂ cup (4 fl oz/125 ml) at a time, stirring constantly. Continue to cook over medium-low heat, stirring frequently and gradually adding more stock.

After 20 minutes, dissolve the saffron in the remaining simmering stock and continue adding the stock to the rice until it is creamy and the grains are tender to the bite, 5–10 minutes longer; if needed, add an additional ¹/₂ cup (4 fl oz/ 125 ml) water, first brought to a simmer. Stir in the cheese and the remaining 2 tablespoons butter. Season to taste with salt and pepper. Serve at once.

Serves 4 as a first course, 2–3 as a main course

2 cups (16 fl oz/500 ml) Vegetable Stock (page 300)

6 tablespoons (3 oz/90 g) unsalted butter

2 tablespoons olive oil

1 yellow onion, finely chopped

1 cup (7 oz/220 g) Arborio rice

Large pinch of saffron threads

³/₄ cup (3 oz/90 g) grated Parmesan cheese

Salt and freshly ground pepper

Risotto with Mozzarella and Sun-Dried Tomatoes

Use fresh mozzarella cheese packed in water. The results are impressive: the cheese melts into threads, giving the risotto an intriguing texture and full flavor. Garnish with fresh basil leaves.

5½ cups (44 fl oz/1.35 l) Vegetable Stock (page 300)

⅓ cup (3 oz/90 g) oil-packed sun-dried tomatoes

1 yellow onion, chopped

2 cups (14 oz/440 g) Arborio rice

1 cup (4 oz/125 g) shredded fresh mozzarella cheese

1 cup (4 oz/125 g) grated Parmesan cheese

¼ cup (⅓ oz/10 g) finely chopped fresh basil, plus whole leaves for garnish

Salt and freshly ground pepper

In a saucepan over medium-high heat, bring the stock to a simmer. Adjust the heat to keep the liquid hot.

Drain the sun-dried tomatoes and reserve the oil. Add olive oil if needed to the oil from the jar to equal 4 tablespoons (2 fl oz/60 ml). Chop the sun-dried tomatoes and set aside.

In a large, heavy saucepan over medium-low heat, warm 2 tablespoons of the reserved oil. Add the onion and sauté until translucent, about 8 minutes. Add the rice and stir until white spots appear in the center of the grains, about 1 minute. Add a ladleful of the hot stock, adjust the heat to maintain a simmer, and cook, stirring constantly, until the liquid is absorbed, about 2 minutes. Continue adding the liquid, a ladleful at a time and stirring constantly, until the rice is just tender but slightly firm in the center and mixture is creamy, 20–25 minutes longer.

Add the mozzarella, Parmesan, sun-dried tomatoes, chopped basil, and the remaining 2 tablespoons oil and season with salt and pepper. Stir to mix well.

To serve, spoon onto warmed individual plates and garnish with the basil leaves.

Serves 6

Risotto Pancakes

Place the risotto in a bowl and gently mix in the egg.

In a large, nonstick frying pan over medium heat, melt 1 tablespoon of the butter. Working in batches and adding more butter as needed to prevent sticking, drop the risotto mixture into the pan to make 6 pancakes. Using a spatula, gently press down on the risotto mixture to make round pancakes and fry until light brown on the bottom, about 3 minutes.

Flip the pancakes and sprinkle each one with 1 tablespoon of the Parmesan cheese. Cover and cook until the cheese melts, about 1 minute. Uncover and continue frying until light brown on the bottom, about 2 minutes longer.

To serve, transfer to a warmed platter or individual plates. Pass the additional cheese at the table.

Serves 6

Classic Risotto (page 304)

1 egg, lightly beaten

2 tablespoons unsalted butter

6 tablespoons (1 1/2 oz/45 g) grated Parmesan cheese, plus extra for serving

Grape Leaves Stuffed with Rice

These popular rice-stuffed grape leaves, known as dolmas, can be served hot or at room temperature. Accompany with sliced cucumbers tossed with plain yogurt, mint, and freshly ground pepper.

1 jar (8 oz/250 g) grape leaves, drained

FOR THE FILLING:

1 tablespoon olive oil

1 cup (5 oz/155 g) yellow onion, finely chopped

2 cloves garlic, finely chopped

1/2 cup (2 1/2 oz/75 g) pine nuts

1/2 cup (2 1/2 oz/75 g) finely chopped pitted green olives

2 cups (10 oz/315 g) Steamed White Rice (page 304), cooled

Salt and freshly ground pepper

FOR THE SAUCE:

2 tablespoons unsalted butter

2 tablespoons all-purpose (plain) flour

1 1/2 cups (12 fl oz/375 ml) Vegetable Stock (page 300)

1 tablespoon fresh lemon juice

1 cup (8 oz/250 g) plain yogurt

Salt and freshly ground pepper

2 tablespoons finely chopped fresh mint

Rinse the grape leaves in cool water and pat dry with paper towels. Set aside.

To make the filling, in a saucepan over medium heat, warm the olive oil. Add the onion and garlic and sauté, stirring, until the onion is translucent, about 5 minutes. Remove from the heat and add the pine nuts, olives, rice, and salt and pepper to taste. Mix well.

Place each grape leaf, shiny side down, on a work surface and place 1 rounded tablespoonful of the filling in the bottom center. Fold the sides of each leaf inward over the filling and then roll up tightly. Set aside, seam side down.

To make the sauce, in a large, heavy-bottomed soup pot over medium heat, melt the butter. Whisk in the flour and cook, whisking constantly, for 2–3 minutes. Whisk in the stock and lemon juice.

Carefully place the stuffed grape leaves, seam sides down, in the pot, layering them if necessary. Cover and cook over medium-low heat until the sauce has thickened and the flavors have blended, about 45 minutes; do not allow to boil.

Using a slotted spoon, transfer the stuffed leaves to a serving platter or individual plates. Reduce the heat to very low and whisk the yogurt into the sauce. Do not allow the sauce to boil or it may separate. Season to taste with salt and pepper. Spoon the sauce over the stuffed grape leaves, garnish with the mint, and serve.

Makes about 25 stuffed grape leaves; serves 4–6 as a main course

Peppers Stuffed with Rice, Tomatoes, and Corn

Peppers stuffed with rice, tomatoes, and corn make a colorful and attractive presentation. Serve hot or at room temperature. You can choose a mixture or the same color of peppers, if you like.

In a frying pan over medium heat, add the tomato sauce, rice, 1 1/2 cups (12 fl oz/ 375 ml) water, and 1/2 teaspoon salt. Bring to a boil, reduce the heat to low, cover, and cook, without stirring, until the rice is almost tender, 15–20 minutes. Remove from the heat and let cool. Mix in the corn, basil, and salt and pepper to taste.

Preheat the oven to 375°F (190°C).

Cut off the tops from the peppers and remove and discard the seeds and ribs. In a saucepan large enough to hold the bell peppers, bring the stock to a boil. Place the peppers in the stock and simmer for 3 minutes. Drain, reserving the stock.

Fill the peppers with the cooled rice mixture. Stand them in a baking dish in which they fit closely together. Pour the reserved stock into the dish and cover with aluminum foil. Bake for 15 minutes. Remove the foil and continue to bake until the rice is tender, about 15 minutes longer.

Transfer to a platter; serve hot or at room temperature.

Serves 6

1/2 cup (4 fl oz/125 ml) Tomato Sauce (page 302)

1 cup (7 oz/220 g) short-grain white rice

Salt and freshly ground pepper

Kernels from 1 ear of corn, boiled for 1 minute and drained

3 tablespoons chopped fresh basil

6 small red bell peppers (capsicums)

1 cup (8 fl oz/250 ml) Vegetable Stock (page 300) or water

Brown Rice Vegetable Loaf with Yogurt Sauce

This recipe is also quite good made with a combination of short-grain white rice and wild rice. A few mint leaves make a nice garnish and will add color to the plate. Spoon the yogurt sauce onto the vegetable loaf or pass it at the table.

Rinse the rice well and drain. Place in a heavy saucepan with 2 cups (16 fl oz/500 ml) water and $1/2$ teaspoon salt. Bring to a boil, reduce the heat to low, cover, and cook, without stirring, for 45 minutes; do not remove the cover. Uncover and check to see if the rice is tender and the water is absorbed. If not, recover and cook for a few minutes longer until the rice is done. Remove from the heat, fluff the grains with a fork, and let cool.

Meanwhile, preheat the oven to 375°F (190°C). While the oven is heating and the rice is cooling, coarsely grate the zucchini, drain in a colander for about 20 minutes, and squeeze dry with a clean kitchen towel.

In a frying pan over medium heat, warm the olive oil. Add the green onions and sauté, stirring, until soft, about 7 minutes. Add the mushrooms and sauté until their released liquid evaporates, 3–5 minutes. Transfer the onions and mushrooms to a large bowl; let cool. Add the cooked rice, zucchini, carrots, pine nuts, parsley, cheese, eggs, and salt and pepper to taste. Mix well.

Lightly grease a 5-by-9-by-3-inch (13-by-23-by-7.5 cm) loaf pan and line the bottom and sides with parchment paper. Transfer the rice mixture to the prepared pan and cover with aluminum foil. Place the loaf pan in a baking pan; pour hot water into the baking pan to reach halfway up the sides of the loaf pan. Bake until set, 50–60 minutes. Let cool for 20 minutes, then unmold onto a platter.

In a small bowl, whisk together the yogurt, mint, garlic, and salt and pepper to taste. Using a serrated knife, cut the loaf into slices $3/4$ inch (2 cm) thick. Serve hot, topped with the yogurt sauce.

Serves 6

3/4 cup (5 oz/155 g) brown rice

Salt and freshly ground pepper

2 zucchini (courgettes)

3 tablespoons olive oil

1 bunch green (spring) onions, including tender green tops, thinly sliced

1 cup (3 oz/90 g) finely chopped fresh white mushrooms

2 carrots, peeled and coarsely grated

$1/2$ cup ($2 1/2$ oz/75 g) pine nuts, toasted (page 311)

4 tablespoons chopped fresh flat-leaf (Italian) parsley

$1/2$ cup ($2 1/2$ oz/75 g) crumbled feta cheese

2 eggs, lightly beaten

1 cup (8 oz/250 g) plain yogurt

$1 1/2$ tablespoons chopped fresh mint

1 clove garlic, minced

Warm Green Beans and Brown Rice
with Sesame Dressing

½ cup (3½ oz/105 g) brown rice

1 cup (8 fl oz/250 ml) Vegetable Stock (page 300) or water

Salt and freshly ground pepper

1 teaspoon Dijon mustard

1 clove garlic, minced

1½ tablespoons rice vinegar or fresh lemon juice

2 tablespoons soy sauce

2 teaspoons Asian sesame oil

2 tablespoons corn oil

1¼ lb (625 g) green beans, trimmed and cut on the diagonal into 1½-inch (4-cm) lengths

1 tablespoon sesame seeds

½ cup (3 oz/90 g) raw peanuts, toasted (page 311)

Rinse the rice well and drain. Place in a heavy saucepan with the stock and ¼ teaspoon salt. Bring to a boil, reduce heat to low, cover, and cook, without stirring, for 45 minutes; do not remove the cover. Uncover and check to see if the rice is tender and the water is absorbed. If not, re-cover and cook for a few minutes longer until the rice is done. Uncover and fluff the grains with a fork.

Meanwhile, in a small bowl, whisk together the mustard, garlic, vinegar, soy sauce, sesame oil, corn oil, and salt and pepper to taste. Set aside.

When the rice is almost ready, bring a saucepan three-fourths full of lightly salted water to a boil. Add the green beans and cook until just tender, 5–7 minutes.

While the green beans are cooking, place the sesame seeds in a small, dry frying pan over medium heat and toast, stirring constantly, until golden, 2–3 minutes. Watch carefully so that they do not burn. Transfer to a dish and set aside.

Drain the beans and place in a deep bowl. Immediately add the hot rice, the peanuts, and the dressing and toss to mix well. Place on a platter, garnish with the toasted sesame seeds, and serve at once.

Serves 6

Vegetable Curry with Brown Rice

Rinse the rice well and drain. In a heavy saucepan over high heat, combine 3 cups (24 fl oz/750 ml) water and $1/2$ teaspoon salt and bring to a boil. Add the rice, stir once or twice, and reduce the heat to low. Cover and cook, without stirring, for 45 minutes; do not remove the cover.

Meanwhile, in a large soup pot over medium-high heat, melt the butter. Add the onions, celery, and carrots and cook, stirring occasionally, until the onions are soft, about 10 minutes. Reduce the heat to medium, add the jalapeño and garlic, and cook, stirring, for 2 minutes to blend the flavors. Sprinkle the flour over the vegetables and continue to cook, stirring, for 2 minutes longer.

Cut the potatoes in half. Add them to the vegetables along with the stock, curry powder, ginger, and coconut milk.

Cover and simmer gently, stirring occasionally, for 15 minutes. Add the cauliflower and broccoli and continue to simmer, stirring occasionally, until the vegetables are tender when pierced with the tip of a sharp knife, about 20 minutes longer.

After the rice has cooked for 45 minutes, uncover and check if it is tender and the water is absorbed. If not, re-cover and cook for a few minutes longer.

Spoon the rice onto a large platter or individual plates. Make a well in the center and spoon the curry into the well. Serve immediately.

Serves 6

1 cup (7 oz/220 g) short- or long-grain brown rice

Salt

3 tablespoons unsalted butter

2 yellow onions, quartered

2 celery stalks, finely diced

2 carrots, peeled and cut into slices $1/2$ inch (12 mm) thick

1 fresh jalapeño or serrano chile, seeded and minced

4 cloves garlic, minced

2 tablespoons all-purpose (plain) flour

6 small red potatoes, $3/4$ lb (375 g) total weight

3 cups (24 fl oz/750 ml) Vegetable Stock (page 300)

3 tablespoons curry powder

2 tablespoons peeled and minced or grated fresh ginger

$1/4$ cup (2 fl oz/60 ml) canned coconut milk

3 cups *each* (12 oz/375 g) broccoli and cauliflower florets

Cabbage Stuffed with Brown Rice in Tomato Sauce

This version of traditional baked stuffed cabbage is made easier by eliminating the blanching of the cabbage leaves. Instead, the leaves are frozen and then defrosted, which wilts them so they can be rolled easily.

1 head green cabbage, placed in the freezer overnight, then thawed at room temperature

FOR THE FILLING:

2 cups (10 oz/315 g) cooled, cooked brown rice

1 egg, beaten

1 cup (6 oz/185 g) golden raisins (sultanas)

1/2 cup (2 oz/60 g) chopped walnuts

1/2 cup (2 1/2 oz/75 g) finely chopped yellow onion

Salt and freshly ground pepper

FOR THE SAUCE:

2 tablespoons olive oil

2 sweet onions

2 cloves garlic, finely chopped

1 can (28 oz/875 g) whole tomatoes in purée, with juices

1 cup (8 fl oz/250 ml) Vegetable Stock (page 300)

2 tablespoons brown sugar

1 tablespoon fresh lemon juice

Salt and freshly ground pepper

Using a small, sharp knife, cut out the core from the base of the cabbage. Separate the leaves from the cabbage head and set aside.

To make the filling, in a bowl, combine the rice, egg, raisins, walnuts, onion 1/2 teaspoon salt, and 1/4 teaspoon pepper. Mix until well blended. Place about 1/4 cup (1 1/2 oz/45 g) of the filling in the bottom center of each cabbage leaf, fold in the sides of each leaf, and then roll up each leaf tightly. Set the stuffed leaves, seam sides down, aside.

Coarsely chop the onions. Set aside.

To make the sauce, in a large heavy-bottomed soup pot over medium heat, warm the olive oil. Add the onions and garlic and sauté, stirring, until the onions are soft, about 10 minutes. Add the tomatoes with their juices, the stock, brown sugar, and lemon juice and stir well.

Carefully add the stuffed cabbage leaves to the sauce, seam sides down. Reduce the heat to low, cover, and simmer very gently until the cabbage is cooked and the flavors are blended, about 40 minutes. Do not allow the sauce to boil, or the cabbage rolls may break apart. Season to taste with salt and pepper.

To serve, using a large serving spoon, carefully transfer the cabbage rolls to warmed shallow bowls and spoon the sauce over the top.

Makes about 12 cabbage rolls; serves 6

Tofu-Vegetable Fried Rice

This delicious version of fried rice leaves out the usual chicken and replaces it with tofu, also known as bean curd. Tofu is available in soft and firm forms; select the latter for this recipe.

Place the rice in a bowl. Wet your fingers and rub the rice between them until the grains are separated. Set aside.

In a wok or frying pan over medium heat, warm 1 tablespoon of the oil, swirling to coat the bottom and sides of the pan. When the oil is hot, add the eggs and stir constantly until soft curds form, about 1 minute. Transfer to a bowl and set aside.

Add another 1 tablespoon oil to the pan over medium-high heat, again swirling to coat the pan. When the oil is hot but not quite smoking, add the tofu and stir and toss every 20–30 seconds until it begins to brown, 4–5 minutes. Add the vinegar; cook, stirring once, for 30 seconds. Add to the bowl holding the eggs.

Add another 1 tablespoon oil to the pan over medium-high heat, again swirling to coat the pan. When hot, add the leek and stir and toss until slightly softened, 2–3 minutes. Add another 1 tablespoon oil to the pan over medium-high heat, again swirling to coat. When the oil is hot but not quite smoking, add the broccoli, carrot, zucchini, and cabbage to the leek and stir and toss the vegetables together every 15–20 seconds until they just begin to soften, 2–3 minutes. Add the sherry and stir and toss for 1 minute longer. Add to the bowl with the eggs and tofu.

Add the remaining 2 tablespoons oil to the pan over medium-high heat, again swirling to coat the pan. When hot, add the rice and stir and toss every 20–30 seconds until lightly browned, about 5 minutes. Add the stock, soy sauce, water chestnuts, and green onions and stir to combine. Add the tofu, vegetables, and eggs and stir and toss until the egg is in small pieces and the mixture is heated through, about 1 minute longer. Taste and adjust the seasonings. Serve immediately.

Serves 6–8

---

4 cups (1¼ lb/625 g) Steamed White Rice (page 304), cooled

6 tablespoons (3 fl oz/90 ml) peanut or vegetable oil

2 eggs, lightly beaten

½ lb (250 g) tofu, cut into ½-inch (12-mm) cubes

1 tablespoon balsamic vinegar

1 leek, including tender green tops, carefully washed (page 310) and finely chopped

1 cup (2 oz/60 g) broccoli florets

1 carrot, peeled and cut into 1-inch (2.5-cm) pieces

1 zucchini (courgette), trimmed and finely chopped

2 cups (6 oz/185 g) finely chopped napa cabbage

1 teaspoon dry sherry

¼ cup (2 fl oz/60 ml) Vegetable Stock (page 300)

2 tablespoons soy sauce

½ cup (2 oz/60 g) canned water chestnuts, rinsed, well drained, and sliced

2 tablespoons thinly sliced green (spring) onions, including tender green tops

Basmati Rice with Dried Fruits and Nuts

Sweet additions of dried fruits, spices, and nuts bring this dish to life. Dried apples, cherries, and golden raisins can be used in place of the fruits listed, and almonds, pine nuts, walnuts, cashews, or pistachios can replace the pecans.

¹/₄ cup (2 oz/60 g) unsalted butter

1 small yellow onion, minced

1¹/₂ cups (10¹/₂ oz/330 g) basmati rice

Salt and freshly ground pepper

¹/₄ teaspoon ground cinnamon

¹/₄ teaspoon ground allspice

¹/₄ cup (1¹/₂ oz/45 g) raisins

¹/₄ cup (1 oz/30 g) dried cranberries

¹/₂ cup (2 oz/60 g) dried apricot halves, coarsely chopped

¹/₂ cup (2 oz/60 g) pecans, toasted (page 311) and coarsely chopped

In a saucepan over medium heat, melt the butter. Add the onion and sauté, stirring, until soft, about 10 minutes.

Meanwhile, rinse the rice well and drain. When the onion is ready, add the rice, 3¹/₄ cups (26 fl oz/810 ml) water, ³/₄ teaspoon salt, pepper to taste, cinnamon, allspice, raisins, cranberries, and apricots to the saucepan. Bring to a boil, reduce the heat to low, cover, and cook, without stirring, for 20 minutes; do not remove the cover. After 20 minutes, uncover and check to see if the rice is tender and the water is absorbed. If not, re-cover and cook for a few minutes longer until the rice is done.

Add the pecans and toss gently to combine. Transfer to a warmed dish and serve.

Serves 6

Vegetable Fried Rice

Dried mushrooms can be used in place of fresh: Soak 6 dried shiitake mushrooms in boiling water to cover for 20 minutes; drain, remove the stems, and cut the caps into slices ½ inch (12 mm) thick.

3 cups (15 oz/470 g) Steamed White Rice (page 304), cooled

2 eggs

4 tablespoons (2 fl oz/60 ml) peanut or vegetable oil

1 cup (2 oz/60 g) small broccoli florets

1 carrot, peeled and cut into 1-inch (2.5-cm) pieces

6 fresh mushrooms, brushed clean and cut into slices ½ inch (12 mm) thick

1 teaspoon dry sherry

Kernels from 2 ears of fresh corn (about 1 cup/6 oz/185 g)

¼ cup (2 fl oz/60 ml) Vegetable Stock (page 300)

2 tablespoons soy sauce

2 tablespoons thinly sliced green (spring) onion, including tender green tops

½ cup (3 oz/90 g) unsalted roasted peanuts (optional)

Place the rice in a bowl. Wet your fingers and rub the rice between them until the grains are separated. Set aside.

In a small bowl, beat the eggs lightly. In a wok or frying pan over medium heat, warm 1 tablespoon of the oil, swirling to coat the bottom and sides of the pan. When the oil is hot, add the eggs and stir constantly until soft curds form, about 1 minute. Transfer to a bowl and set aside.

Add another 1 tablespoon oil to the pan over medium-high heat, swirling to coat the pan. When the oil is very hot but not quite smoking, add the broccoli, carrot, and mushrooms and stir and toss the vegetables together about every 15–20 seconds until they just begin to soften, 2–3 minutes. Add the sherry and stir and toss for another minute. Add the corn and stir and toss for 1 minute longer. Add to the bowl holding the eggs.

Add the remaining 2 tablespoons oil to the pan over medium-high heat, again swirling to coat the pan. When the oil is hot, add the rice and stir and toss every 20–30 seconds until it is lightly browned, about 5 minutes. Add the stock, soy sauce, and green onion and stir to combine. Add the reserved vegetables and eggs and the peanuts, if using, and stir and toss until the egg is in small pieces and the mixture is heated through, about 1 minute longer.

Taste and adjust the seasoning. Serve immediately.

Serves 4–6

Wild and White Rice Pilaf with Leeks and Walnuts

This dish is hearty enough to be a main course. Garnish this dish with fried leeks, which also add more crunch to the rice. Chopped chives can also be sprinkled on top.

Cut 2 of the leeks into ¹/₂-inch (12-mm) dice. In a saucepan over medium heat, melt the butter. Add the leeks and sauté, stirring, until soft, about 10 minutes.

Meanwhile, rinse the wild rice well and drain. Add to the leeks and stir for 1 minute. Add the stock and ³/₄ teaspoon salt and bring to a boil. Reduce the heat to low, cover, and cook for 25 minutes. Uncover, add the white rice, and stir once. Re-cover and continue to cook, without stirring, for 20 minutes; do not remove the cover. Uncover and check to see if the rice is tender and the water is absorbed. If not, re-cover and cook for a few minutes longer until the rice is done. Add the walnuts and pepper to taste to the rice and toss to mix well. Set aside.

To make the fried leeks, slice the 2 remaining leeks into very thin strips about 2 inches (5 cm) long. In a deep frying pan, pour in peanut or corn oil to a depth of 1 inch (2.5 cm) and heat to 375°F (190°C). Deep-fry the leeks until golden. Using a slotted spoon, transfer to paper towels to drain.

Transfer to a platter and garnish with the chives and fried leeks. Serve immediately.

Serves 6

4 leeks including tender green tops, carefully washed (page 310)

3 tablespoons unsalted butter

¹/₂ cup (3 oz/90 g) wild rice

3 cups (24 fl oz/750 ml) Vegetable Stock (page 300)

Salt and freshly ground pepper

³/₄ cup (5 oz/155 g) long-grain white rice

¹/₂ cup (2 oz/60 g) walnut pieces, toasted (page 311) and chopped

2 tablespoon chopped fresh chives

Peanut or corn oil for deep-frying

Eggs & Cheese

Scrambled Egg Enchiladas

Here is a tasty alternative to enchiladas filled with meat or cheese. Accompany with black beans and guacamole (page 14) at brunch or lunchtime. Garnish with red onions thinly sliced into rings, if you like.

2½ lb (1.25 kg) large ripe tomatoes

1 or 2 fresh jalapeño or serrano chile peppers, seeded if desired

¼ white onion, cut up, plus 1 tablespoon minced onion

1 clove garlic

1 tablespoon salt

7 tablespoons (3½ fl oz/ 105 ml) corn oil or other vegetable oil

12 corn tortillas

6 eggs, lightly beaten

½ cup (4 fl oz/125 ml) thick sour cream

⅔ cup (3½ oz/100 g) crumbled queso fresco or feta cheese

4 lettuce leaves, shredded

Red onions for garnish (optional)

Place the tomatoes in a saucepan over high heat and add water to cover. Bring to a boil and remove from the heat. Drain well. Peel the tomatoes (page 313), coarsely chop and place in a blender or in a food processor fitted with the metal blade. Add the chiles, cut-up onion, garlic, and salt and process to form a smooth purée.

In a saucepan over medium heat, warm 1 tablespoon of the oil. Add the purée and cook, uncovered, until thickened, about 10 minutes. Cover and keep hot.

Heat the remaining 6 tablespoons (3 fl oz/90 ml) oil in a frying pan over high heat. Add the tortillas, one at a time, and fry to soften, a few seconds on each side. Using tongs, transfer to paper towels to drain, then stack and cover to keep warm.

Reduce the heat to medium and add the 1 tablespoon minced onion to the oil remaining in the pan. Sauté until slightly translucent, about 30 seconds. Add the beaten eggs and cook, stirring frequently, until done but not too dry.

Place an equal amount of the egg mixture on each tortilla, roll up into a cylinder and place on a platter. Cover with the warm tomato sauce. Dollop with the sour cream, then sprinkle with the cheese and lettuce. Garnish with the red onion rings, if desired, and serve immediately.

Serves 6

Poached Eggs in Swiss Chard Nests

A little vinegar added to the poaching water helps to coagulate egg whites. You can cook the eggs for this dish in advance and store them in a bowl of water; reheat in a pan of simmering water before serving.

Cut the center stems from the chard leaves. Keeping the stems separate from the leaves, rinse well and drain. Cut the stems crosswise into thin slices; chop the leaves coarsely.

In a large frying pan over medium-low heat, melt 2 tablespoons of the butter with the olive oil. Add the stems and sauté, stirring, for 5 minutes. Add the leaves and continue to sauté, stirring often, until wilted, about 2 minutes longer. Add $1/2$ cup (4 fl oz/125 ml) water and a pinch of salt, cover, reduce the heat to low, and simmer until tender, 10–15 minutes. Drain the chard and return it to the pan. Season to taste with salt and pepper. Cover to keep warm.

Meanwhile, fill a nonstick 12-inch (30-cm) sauté pan halfway with water. Add the vinegar and $1/2$ teaspoon salt and bring the water to a simmer over high heat. Reduce the heat to low to maintain a gentle simmer. Using a saucer, slip 1 egg at a time into the water. When the whites have firmed up slightly, spoon the barely simmering water over the eggs and continue to cook until the whites are set, milky looking, and opaque and the yolks are just glazed but still soft, 2–3 minutes.

Meanwhile, cut the remaining 2 tablespoons butter into small pieces and stir into the chard, tossing to coat evenly. Divide the chard among 4 warmed plates and make a nest in the center of each mound.

Remove the eggs from the water and trim any untidy edges. Place an egg in each chard nest and serve at once.

Serves 4

2 lb (1 kg) Swiss chard

4 tablespoons (2 oz/60 g) unsalted butter

2 tablespoons olive oil

Salt and freshly ground pepper

1 teaspoon white wine vinegar

4 eggs, at room temperature

Wild Rice–Mushroom Custards

For these delicious custards, select fresh wild mushrooms such as chanterelles, morels, porcini (cèpes), or shiitakes. Garnish each custard with fresh chopped parsley.

1/2 oz (15 g) dried wild mushrooms

2 cups (16 fl oz/500 ml) boiling water, plus more as needed

1/2 cup (3 oz/90 g) wild rice, well rinsed and drained

Salt and freshly ground pepper

2 tablespoons unsalted butter

1 lb (500 g) fresh wild mushrooms, brushed clean and halved

1/4 teaspoon chopped thyme

3 egg yolks, plus 2 whole eggs, lightly beaten

1 cup (8 fl oz/250 ml) half-and-half (half cream)

1/4 cup (1 oz/30 g) pecan halves, chopped

1 cup (8 fl oz/250 ml) heavy (double) cream

1/4 cup (1 oz/30 g) grated Parmesan cheese

1 tablespoon chopped fresh flat-leaf (Italian) parsley

In a bowl, combine the dried mushrooms and 1/2 cup (4 fl oz/125 ml) of the boiling water; let stand for 30 minutes. Drain, reserving the liquid. Squeeze out any excess liquid, then chop finely. Strain the liquid through a sieve lined with cheesecloth (muslin). Reserve the liquid and mushrooms separately. Add the rice, the remaining 1 1/2 cups (12 fl oz/375 ml) boiling water, and 1/2 teaspoon salt in a saucepan over medium-low heat. Cover and cook, without stirring, until the rice is tender and no water remains, 40 minutes. Remove from the heat and let cool. In a frying pan over medium-high heat, melt the butter. Add all of the mushrooms and cook, stirring, until soft and the moisture has evaporated, 10 minutes. Finely chop half of the mushrooms and place in a bowl. Reserve the unchopped mushrooms in the pan.

Add the thyme, eggs, half-and-half, cooked wild rice, pecans, and salt and pepper to the bowl; mix well. Preheat the oven to 350°F (180°C). Butter six 1/2-cup (4–fl oz/125-ml) ramekins. Place them in a baking dish and pour boiling water into the dish to reach halfway up the sides. Divide the rice mixture evenly in the ramekins. Bake until a knife inserted into the center comes out clean, 30–35 minutes. Remove the dish from the oven, then lift out the ramekins. About 10 minutes before the custards are ready, in a saucepan, combine the cream, the reserved soaking liquid, and the Parmesan. Place over medium heat and simmer until reduced by one-third, 10 minutes. Season with salt. Keep warm. Place the pan holding the reserved unchopped mushrooms over medium heat and reheat, stirring, for 2 minutes.

To serve, spoon the warm sauce onto individual plates. Invert 1 custard onto the center of each plate. Distribute the unchopped mushrooms around each custard.

Serves 6

Farmers' Market Corn Custard

Make this delicious side dish when young corn has been freshly picked and is still very sweet; as ears of corn age, the natural sugar in the kernels turns to starch.

Preheat an oven to 375°F (190°C). Grease a shallow 1-qt (1-l) baking dish with the butter. Pull the green husks off the corn, remove the silk filaments and then wipe the ears clean with a paper towel.

Working with 1 ear of corn at a time, place stem-end down in a shallow bowl. Using a sharp, heavy knife, make a lengthwise cut down the center of each row of kernels. Then, holding the ear at a 30-degree angle and using the dull side of the knife blade at a 90-degree angle to the ear, carefully scrape all of the pulp out of the kernels. Repeat with the remaining ears of corn. There should be about 2 cups (12 oz/375 g) of kernels, pulp, and juice.

Using a fork, stir the cream into the corn and season to taste with salt, pepper, and nutmeg, mixing well. Transfer the mixture to the prepared baking dish. Bake until the custard has thickened and puffed up slightly and the surface is lightly browned, 30–35 minutes. Serve immediately.

Serves 4

1 tablespoon unsalted butter, at room temperature

4 or 5 ears very fresh corn

1/3 cup (3 fl oz/80 ml) heavy (double) cream

Salt and freshly ground pepper

Pinch of ground nutmeg

Savory Rice Custard with Roasted Garlic

Preheat the oven to 350°F (180°C). Remove the papery sheaths from the garlic heads and place the garlic in a small baking dish. Drizzle with 1 tablespoon of the olive oil and ¼ cup (2 fl oz/60 ml) water. Cover and bake until soft, about 45 minutes. Pass the heads through a food mill or potato ricer to extract the pulp; discard the skins and set the pulp aside. Alternatively, separate into cloves and squeeze the pulp form the skins by hand.

Meanwhile, in a saucepan, bring 1⅓ cups (11 fl oz/330 ml) water and ½ teaspoon salt to a boil. Slowly add the rice, reduce the heat to low, cover, and cook, without stirring, for 20 minutes; do not remove the cover. Uncover and check to see if the rice is tender and the water is absorbed. If not, re-cover and cook for a few minutes longer until the rice is done. Remove from the heat, fluff the grains with a fork, and place in a bowl to cool.

In a frying pan over medium heat, warm the remaining ½ tablespoon olive oil. Add the onion and sauté, stirring, until soft, about 10 minutes. Transfer to a bowl and add the garlic pulp, cooled rice, egg yolks, whole eggs, cream, thyme, Parmesan, and salt and pepper to taste; mix well.

Lightly grease six ½-cup (4–fl oz/125-ml) ramekins. Place them in a baking dish and pour boiling water into the baking dish to reach halfway up the sides of the ramekins. Divide the rice mixture evenly among the ramekins.

Bake until the custards are firm and a knife inserted in the center comes out clean, 30–35 minutes.

Remove the ramekins from the baking dish. Serve hot or warm.

Serves 6

2 heads garlic

1½ tablespoons olive oil

Salt and freshly ground pepper

⅔ cup (5 oz/155 g) short-grain white rice

¼ cup (1½ oz/45 g) minced yellow onion

2 egg yolks, lightly beaten

2 whole eggs, lightly beaten

1 cup (8 fl oz/250 ml) heavy (double) cream

½ teaspoon chopped fresh thyme

½ cup (2 oz/60 g) grated Parmesan cheese

Boiling water, as needed

Sweet Potato Pudding

Serve this spice-laced pudding with soup and a green salad for a winter meal. Because it can be prepared in advance and has an appealing golden crust, this dish is ideal for a dinner party.

3 sweet potatoes, about 1¹/₂ lb (750 g) total weight

¹/₃ cup (3 fl oz/80 ml) heavy (double) cream

4 eggs

3 tablespoons unsalted butter, melted

2 tablespoons bourbon

1¹/₂ teaspoons fresh lemon juice

1 tablespoon grated lemon zest

¹/₂ teaspoon freshly grated nutmeg

¹/₂ teaspoon ground cinnamon

1 teaspoon ground ginger

Salt

Pecan halves for garnish (optional)

Preheat the oven to 375°F (190°C). Butter a 1–1¹/₂-qt (1–1.5-l) soufflé dish.

Place the unpeeled sweet potatoes in a large saucepan, add cold water to cover, and bring to a boil over high heat. Reduce the heat to medium-low, cover, and simmer until the potatoes are tender when pierced with the tip of a sharp knife, 30–40 minutes. Drain and let cool.

Peel the sweet potatoes. Transfer to a food processor fitted with the metal blade and purée until smooth. Add the cream, eggs, and melted butter and process to blend. Add the bourbon, lemon juice and zest, nutmeg, cinnamon, and ginger and process again to mix. Season to taste with salt and process for a few seconds to blend the ingredients.

Spoon into the prepared dish. Place in a large baking pan and pour in hot water to reach halfway up the sides of the dish. Place in the oven and bake until puffed and golden brown on top, about 40 minutes.

Garnish the top with the pecan halves, if desired. Serve hot, directly from the soufflé dish.

Serves 4 or 5

Corn Pudding

This is a delightful summer recipe that pairs perfectly with outdoor grilled foods, so use fresh corn when it's in season. You can make the pudding year-round, as it's also delicious with canned corn.

3 eggs

2 cups (12 oz/375 g) fresh corn kernels (from 3–4 ears) or drained canned corn kernels

2 tablespoons chopped green (spring) onion, including tender green tops

1/2 cup (2½ oz/75 g) chopped red bell pepper (capsicum)

5 tablespoons all-purpose (plain) flour

Salt

1/2 teaspoon paprika

1/4 teaspoon cayenne pepper

1/4 cup (2 oz/60 g) unsalted butter, melted

1 cup (8 fl oz/250 ml) half-and-half (half cream)

Preheat the oven to 350°F (180°C). Butter a 1½-qt (1.5-l) soufflé dish and set aside.

In a large bowl, beat the eggs until light and frothy. Stir in the corn, green onion, and bell pepper.

In a small bowl, stir together the flour, salt to taste, the paprika, and the cayenne. Add to the corn mixture, stirring to blend. Stir in the melted butter and the half-and-half and mix well. Pour into the prepared dish and place the dish in a baking pan. Pour hot water into the pan to reach about one-fourth of the way up the sides of the dish.

Place in the oven and bake until the top is golden and a knife inserted in the center comes out clean, about 40 minutes. Let rest for 5 minutes before serving.

Serves 4

Spinach Ring

This recipe can be assembled in advance and refrigerated before baking. If using a ring mold, try filling the center or surrounding edges with New Potatoes with Lemon Butter and Fresh Herbs (page 141).

Preheat the oven to 375°F (190°C). Butter a 1¹/₂-qt (1.5-l) ring mold or soufflé dish.

Place the spinach in a food processor fitted with the metal blade and purée until smooth. Melt 1 tablespoon of the butter in a sauté pan over medium heat. Add the spinach, raise the heat to high, and cook, stirring, until all moisture has cooked away, 1–2 minutes.

Reduce the heat to medium and stir in the flour and salt and pepper to taste. Slowly pour in the warm milk, stirring constantly until smooth and thickened. Cook over low heat, stirring constantly, for 2 minutes. Add the paprika and cook for about 4 minutes longer.

Remove from the heat and add ¹/₂ cup (2 oz/60 g) of the Parmesan and the remaining 1 tablespoon butter. Stir in the eggs and pour into the prepared mold or dish. (If using a soufflé dish, mound the surface into a dome.) Sprinkle the top with the remaining ¹/₄ cup (1 oz/30 g) cheese. Place in a baking pan and pour hot water into the pan to reach halfway up the sides of the mold or dish. Bake until firm and lightly browned, 30–40 minutes.

Remove from the oven and let sit for a few minutes. Run a knife around the edges, then invert onto a serving plate. Serve hot.

Serves 4

2 cups (14 oz/440 g) well-drained cooked spinach (2–3 bunches)

2 tablespoons unsalted butter

1¹/₂ tablespoons all-purpose (plain) flour

Salt and freshly ground pepper

¹/₂ cup (4 fl oz/125 ml) milk, warmed

¹/₂ teaspoon paprika

³/₄ cup (3 oz/90 g) grated Parmesan cheese

3 eggs, well beaten

Leek and Goat Cheese Tart

To make the pastry, in a bowl, mix together the flour and salt. Add the butter and, using an electric mixer fitted with the paddle attachment on low speed or your fingers, beat or rub in the butter until it resembles coarse meal. Sprinkle in the water, a little at a time, and beat just until the mixture holds together.

Gather the dough into a ball and flatten into a 6-inch (15-cm) round. Wrap in plastic wrap; chill in the refrigerator for 1 hour.

Meanwhile, to begin making the filling, in a large frying pan over medium-low heat, melt the butter. Add the leeks and cook, stirring occasionally, until soft and no moisture remains in the pan, about 30 minutes. Season to taste with salt and pepper. Transfer to a bowl and let cool.

On a well-floured work surface, roll out the pastry into a round 10 inches (25 cm) in diameter. Drape the pastry over the rolling pin and carefully transfer it to a 9-inch (23-cm) tart pan with a removable bottom. Press the pastry firmly but gently into the pan. Trim the edges even with the rim. Freeze the pastry shell until firm, about 20 minutes.

Meanwhile, preheat the oven to 325°F (165°C).

Line the pastry shell with aluminum foil and fill with dried beans or pie weights. Bake until the pastry turns golden on the edges, about 15 minutes. Remove the beans and foil and continue to bake until lightly golden, 3–5 minutes longer.

Meanwhile, finish making the filling: Crumble the goat cheese into a bowl. Add the Parmesan, half-and-half, eggs, and salt and pepper to taste and whisk until blended. Stir in the leeks. Pour the filling into the warm prebaked tart shell. Bake until set and a thin skewer inserted into the center comes out clean, 20–30 minutes.

Let cool for 5 minutes, then cut into wedges and serve.

Serves 6–8

FOR THE PASTRY:

1 cup (5 oz/155 g) all-purpose (plain) flour

1/4 teaspoon salt

1/2 cup (4 oz/125 g) unsalted butter, cut into 1-inch (2.5-cm) pieces

2–4 tablespoons water

FOR THE FILLING:

2 tablespoons unsalted butter

3 leeks, white parts and 2 inches (5 cm) of the green, carefully washed (page 310), well dried, and cut into 3/4-inch (2-cm) dice

Salt and freshly ground pepper

1/4 lb (125 g) fresh goat cheese

1/4 cup (1 oz/30 g) grated Parmesan cheese

3/4 cup (6 fl oz/180 ml) half-and-half (half cream)

3 eggs

Grilled Cheese Tortilla "Sandwiches"

In this dish, two tortillas are perfectly aligned to form a sandwichlike stack of melted Cheddar, mushrooms, and roasted peppers. Serve with Refried Pinto Beans (page 210).

2 teaspoons unsalted butter

1 cup (3 oz/90 g) sliced fresh mushrooms

12 flour tortillas

1 lb (480 g) Cheddar cheese, shredded

3 fresh poblano chile peppers, about 7 oz (220 g) total weight, roasted, peeled and cut into long, thin strips (page 308)

Guacamole (page 14)

Tomato Salsa (page 303)

In a frying pan over medium heat, melt the butter. Add the mushrooms and sauté until tender, 3–5 minutes. Remove from the heat.

In a nonstick frying pan over medium heat, place a tortilla and top with one-sixth each of the cheese, sautéed mushrooms, and chiles. Top with a second tortilla and press down slightly. Cook until the cheese melts and the bottom is lightly browned, about 2 minutes. Turn the "sandwich" over and cook on the second side until golden brown, about 1 minute.

Remove from the pan and repeat with the remaining ingredients. Cut each sandwich in half or quarters. Serve immediately with guacamole and salsa in separate bowls on the side.

Serves 6

Zucchini Frittata

Frittata is the term for a type of rustic Italian flat omelet. Slice the zucchini thinly for the best texture. Salting the slices helps to draw out excess moisture before they are combined with the eggs.

Evenly spread one-third of the zucchini slices in a colander set over a bowl. Sprinkle with salt. Spread half of the remaining slices over the first layer of zucchini, salt them, then spread and salt the remainder. Set aside to drain for 30 minutes. Then, pick up the zucchini in small handfuls and squeeze out the juices. Set aside.

Preheat the oven to 350°F (180°C).

In a bowl, using a fork, beat the eggs until lightly frothy. Add the zucchini and half of the Parmesan and stir gently to combine; season to taste with pepper.

In a 10-inch (25-cm) ovenproof, nonstick frying pan over medium heat, melt the butter with the olive oil. Add the egg mixture, spreading it evenly. Sprinkle with the remaining Parmesan. Place in the oven and bake until set but still slightly moist, about 20 minutes.

Serve the frittata directly from the pan, or loosen the edges with a knife tip and slide it out or invert onto a warmed platter. Cut into wedges and top with the tomato sauce. Serve at once.

Serves 4–6

1½ lb (750 g) small zucchini (courgettes), trimmed and cut crosswise into very thin slices

Salt

10 eggs

¼ cup (1 oz/30 g) grated Parmesan cheese

Freshly ground pepper

2 tablespoons unsalted butter

2 tablespoons olive oil

Tomato Sauce (page 302)

Wild Rice and Blue Cheese Skillet Soufflé

This easy-to-make soufflé differs from a traditional soufflé in that the eggs are not separated and it is baked in a frying pan rather than a straight-sided soufflé dish. Serve it for breakfast, lunch, or a light dinner main course.

¹/₄ cup (1¹/₂ oz/45 g) wild rice

1 cup (8 fl oz/250 ml) boiling water

Salt and freshly ground pepper

2 tablespoons milk or cream

3 oz (90 g) blue cheese such as Maytag, Roquefort, or Gorgonzola, crumbled

6 eggs, lightly beaten

3 tablespoons olive oil

1 yellow onion, chopped

2 cloves garlic, minced

³/₄ lb (375 g) spinach, carefully washed, well dried, and coarsely chopped

6 tablespoons (1¹/₂ oz/45 g) grated Parmesan cheese

Rinse the rice well and drain. Place in a saucepan and add the boiling water and ¹/₂ teaspoon salt. Bring to a boil, reduce the heat to medium-low, cover, and cook, without stirring, until the rice is tender, about 40 minutes. Check the pan from time to time and add a little water if the pan is dry but the rice is not yet ready. Remove from the heat, fluff the grains with a fork, and let cool completely.

In a bowl, using a fork, mash together the milk and blue cheese. Add the eggs and rice; mix well. Set aside.

Preheat the broiler (grill).

In a 9-inch (23-cm) nonstick flameproof frying pan over medium heat, warm the olive oil. Add the onion and garlic and sautè until soft, about 10 minutes. Add the spinach and salt and pepper to taste and stir until the spinach begins to wilt, about 2 minutes.

Add the egg mixture to the pan holding the spinach and stir together. Cook over medium heat, without stirring, until the eggs are set at the bottom, 2–3 minutes.

Sprinkle the surface with the Parmesan. Slip under the broiler and broil (grill) until puffed and golden, 2–3 minutes. Serve immediately, directly from the pan.

Serves 4–6

Classic Cheese Soufflé

The name soufflé comes from the french word *souffler*, which means "to puff up." For the maximum volume, the egg whites must be beaten to soft (not stiff) peaks and then evenly folded into the soufflé base.

3 tablespoons unsalted butter

4 tablespoons (1 oz/30 g) grated Parmesan cheese

2 tablespoons all-purpose (plain) flour

1 cup (8 fl oz/250 ml) milk, warmed

1 cup (4 oz/125 g) shredded Gruyère cheese

4 large eggs, at room temperature, separated

Salt and freshly ground white pepper

Pinch of ground nutmeg

Preheat the oven to 375°F (190°C). Lightly grease a 1-qt (1-l) soufflé dish with 1 tablespoon of the butter and dust with 2 tablespoons of the Parmesan. Set aside.

In a saucepan over low heat, melt the remaining 2 tablespoons butter. Using a wooden spoon, stir in the flour; continue to stir until golden. Whisk in the warm milk, then stir over medium heat until the mixture is thick and smooth. Reduce the heat to low and simmer, stirring constantly, until very thick, 3–4 minutes. Remove from the heat. Stir in the Gruyère cheese and the remaining 2 tablespoons Parmesan until melted.

In a small bowl, lightly beat the egg yolks. Beat 3 tablespoons of the hot cheese mixture into the yolks, then gradually beat the yolk mixture into the cheese mixture. Season lightly with salt and white pepper and the nutmeg. Set aside.

In a large bowl, using a balloon whisk or an electric mixer, beat the egg whites to soft peaks. Stir one-fourth of the whites into the cheese sauce to lighten it, then, working in 2 or 3 more batches, add the remaining whites and quickly fold them in. Spoon into the prepared dish.

Bake until well risen, golden brown, and a skewer inserted into the center comes out moist, about 25 minutes. Serve at once.

Serves 4

Yam Soufflé with Pecan Topping

To make this rich soufflé, choose the reddish yam-type sweet potato for its creamy flesh. If you like, use 1½ teaspoons pumpkin pie spice in place of the cinnamon, ginger, allspice, and nutmeg.

Preheat the oven to 350°F (180°C). Place the pecans on a baking sheet and toast in the oven until lightly browned, 5–7 minutes. Transfer to a bowl, add the ginger-snaps and the ¼ cup (2 oz/60 g) dark brown sugar, and stir to mix. Set aside.

Raise the oven temperature to 400°F (200°C). Butter a deep-sided 2-qt (2-l) baking dish or soufflé dish. Scrub the outsides of the unpeeled yams well. Wrap each yam in aluminum foil and place on a baking sheet in the middle of the oven. Bake until very soft when pierced with the tip of a sharp knife, 45–60 minutes. Remove from the oven and let cool. Reduce the oven temperature to 350° F (180°C).

Scoop the pulp from the potatoes and measure out 4 cups (2 lb/1 kg). Place in a bowl and add the half-and-half, melted butter, orange juice, the 3 tablespoons dark brown sugar, the marmalade, and the cinnamon, ginger, and allspice. Using an electric mixer on low speed, beat until combined. Taste and adjust the spices. Add the egg yolks, one at a time, beating well after each addition. Set aside.

In a large bowl, using an electric mixer with clean beaters, beat the egg whites until foamy. Add the salt and cream of tartar and continue beating until stiff peaks form. Gently fold the egg whites into the potato mixture until no white streaks remain. Spoon into the prepared dish. Sprinkle evenly with the pecan mixture. Dot with the butter pieces. Bake until puffed and browned, 1–1¼ hours. If the topping begins to brown too much, cover loosely with aluminum foil. Serve immediately.

Serves 8–10

½ cup (2 oz/60 g) coarsely chopped pecans

10 gingersnap cookies, coarsely chopped

¼ cup (2 oz/60 g) plus 3 tablespoons firmly packed dark brown sugar

4 yams (orange-fleshed sweet potatoes), about ½ lb (250 g) each

½ cup (4 fl oz/125 ml) half-and-half (half cream)

2 tablespoons unsalted butter, melted, plus 2 tablespoons, cut into small pieces

½ cup (4 fl oz/125 ml) freshly squeezed orange juice

3 tablespoons orange marmalade

½ teaspoon *each* ground cinnamon, ground ginger, and ground allspice

¼ teaspoon ground nutmeg

4 egg yolks

5 egg whites

¼ teaspoon salt

¼ teaspoon cream of tartar

Caramelized Onion and Cheddar Soufflé

This savory soufflé is delicious and can be served as a main course. Make sure your guests are seated and waiting for the soufflé when it is removed from the oven, as it must be served immediately because it will sink quickly.

In a frying pan over medium-low heat, warm the oil. Add the onions and thyme, cover, and cook, stirring occasionally, until very soft, about 20 minutes. Uncover and continue to cook, stirring occasionally, until lightly golden, about 30 minutes longer. Season to taste with salt and pepper. Transfer the onions to a sieve set over a bowl; set aside to drain.

Position a rack in the lower third of the oven and preheat to 350°F (180°C). Butter a 2-qt (2-l) soufflé dish.

In a saucepan over medium-high heat, combine the milk and half-and-half and bring to a boil. Meanwhile, in another saucepan over low heat, melt the butter. Whisk the flour into the butter. Cook, whisking constantly, for 2 minutes. Slowly pour the hot milk mixture into the butter mixture, whisking vigorously. Cook, stirring, until thick and smooth, 2–3 minutes. Transfer to a bowl and let cool for 10 minutes.

Add the drained onions to the pan with the sauce and mix well. Stir in the egg yolks, one at a time. Add the cheese and mix well. Season with salt and pepper.

In a clean bowl, beat the egg whites until stiff peaks form. Fold half of the egg whites into the cheese base. Then fold in the remaining egg whites just until combined; do not overmix. Pour the mixture into the prepared soufflé dish and sprinkle with the Parmesan. Bake until well browned and firmly set when gently shaken, 40–50 minutes. Serve immediately.

Serves 6–8

3 tablespoons vegetable oil

3 yellow onions, 1¼ lb (625 g) total weight, thinly sliced

½ teaspoon chopped fresh thyme

Salt and freshly ground pepper

1 cup (8 fl oz/250 ml) milk

1 cup (8 fl oz/250 ml) half-and-half (half cream)

5 tablespoons (2½ oz/75 g) unsalted butter

5 tablespoons (1½ oz/45 g) all-purpose (plain) flour

6 eggs, separated

1¼ cups (5 oz/155 g) coarsely shredded Cheddar cheese

¼ cup (1 oz/30 g) freshly grated Parmesan cheese

Basic Recipes & Techniques

These basic recipes and techniques are used throughout *Vegetarian*. Once you have mastered them, you'll turn to them again and again to create delicious meals.

Vegetable Stock

This stock should be simmered for only 1–1 1/2 hours to ensure a sweet, fresh flavor. Any number of vegetables can be used for a wide range of results: leeks, celery, tomatoes, potatoes, mushrooms, green beans, squash, garlic, fennel, eggplant (aubergine), cabbage, and greens such as spinach, Swiss chard, or lettuce. Avoid cauliflower, Brussels sprouts, artichokes, and beets or beet greens because of their strong flavors.

10 cups (3 lb/1.5 kg) cut-up assorted fresh vegetables *(see above)*

1 yellow onion, coarsely chopped

1 carrot, peeled and coarsely chopped

12 fresh parsley sprigs

Pinch of fresh thyme leaves

1 bay leaf

Place the assorted vegetables, onion, and carrot in a large stockpot. On the center of a small square of cheesecloth (muslin), place the parsley stems, thyme, and bay leaf. Bring the corners together and tie securely with kitchen string to form a bundle. Add to the pot along with cold water to cover the vegetables by 3 inches (7.5 cm).

Bring to a boil over high heat, then immediately reduce the heat to low and simmer gently, uncovered, until the stock is aromatic and has a good flavor, 1–1 1/2 hours. Add water as needed to maintain the original level.

Remove from the heat and pour the stock through a fine-mesh sieve into a clean container. Use immediately, or cover and refrigerate for up to 1 week or freeze for up to 2 months.

Makes 2–3 qt (2–3 l)

All-Purpose Stir-fry Sauce

This sauce can be stored in a tightly covered container for up to 1 week in the refrigerator. If you do make it in advance, add the green onion just before using.

3 tablespoons soy sauce

1 teaspoon peeled and finely chopped fresh ginger

1 small clove garlic, minced

1 green (spring) onion, including tender green tops, finely chopped

1/2 teaspoon Chile Oil (page 302)

In a small bowl, combine the soy sauce, ginger, garlic, green onion, and chile oil and stir well.

Makes about 1/4 cup (2 fl oz/60 ml)

Béchamel Sauce

This classic sauce, sometimes simply called white sauce, adds a rich and creamy quality to many dishes. It can be spooned over hot cooked vegetables just before serving, or mixed with them to make an easy yet elegant creamed vegetable course.

3 tablespoons unsalted butter

3 tablespoons all-purpose (plain) flour

1 teaspoon paprika

1 bay leaf

2 cups (16 fl oz/500 ml) milk, warmed

Salt and freshly ground white pepper

Melt the butter in a saucepan over medium heat. Stir in the flour and cook, stirring, until blended, 1 minute. Add the paprika and bay leaf.

Gradually add the milk, whisking constantly. Continue to whisk over low heat until the sauce is smooth and slightly thickened, 4–5 minutes. Season to taste with salt and white pepper.

Raise the heat to medium and simmer to allow the flavors to blend, 2–3 minutes. Discard the bay leaf before using.

Makes about 2 cups (16 fl oz/500 ml)

Caper Sauce

2 tablespoons well-drained capers, chopped

2 tablespoons chopped fresh parsley

2 tablespoons chopped green (spring) onions, including tender green tops

1/3 cup (3 fl oz/80 ml) dry white wine

Juice of 1/2 lemon

1 cup (8 fl oz/250 ml) mayonnaise

Salt and freshly ground pepper

Place the capers, parsley, green onions, wine, and lemon juice in a small saucepan. Cook over high heat, stirring, until the wine is reduced by one-fourth, just a few minutes. Place the mayonnaise in a bowl and stir in the caper mixture. Season to taste with salt and pepper.

Makes about 1 cup (8 fl oz/250 ml)

Harissa Sauce

Harissa is a spicy red pepper condiment from North Africa. It is usually sold in specialty-food stores or ethnic markets.

1 cup (8 fl oz/250 ml) broth from stew or Vegetable Stock (page 300)

2 teaspoons harissa

1 tablespoon fresh lemon juice

1 tablespoon chopped fresh cilantro (fresh coriander)

Salt and freshly ground pepper

In a bowl, stir together the broth, harissa, lemon juice, cilantro, and salt and pepper to taste. Mix until well blended.

Makes about 1 cup (8 fl oz/250 ml)

Pesto Sauce

Pesto—a pungent sauce of basil and olive oil—is a versatile condiment that is delicious on baked, steamed, or mashed potatoes and pasta.

2 cloves garlic

2 cups (2 oz/60 g) firmly packed fresh basil leaves (about 2 bunches)

1/2 cup (1/2 oz/15 g) firmly packed fresh flat-leaf (Italian) parsley leaves

2 tablespoons pine nuts

1/2 cup (4 fl oz/125 ml) olive oil

1/4 teaspoon freshly ground pepper

3/4 cup (3 oz/90 g) grated Parmesan cheese

In a food processor fitted with the metal blade or a blender, process the garlic to a smooth purée.

Add the basil and parsley and process to chop finely. Add the pine nuts and process to chop finely. With the motor running, slowly pour in the olive oil through the food tube in a fine, steady stream. Add the pepper and cheese and process until well blended, stopping the motor as needed to scrape down the sides. Taste and adjust the seasoning.

Store refrigerated in a tightly covered container for up to 5 days.

Makes about 1 1/4 cups (10 fl oz/310 ml)

Romesco Sauce

This zesty almond-pepper sauce is delicious spooned over vegetables.

4 tablespoons (2 fl oz/60 ml) extra-virgin olive oil

2 slices coarse-textured white bread

1/4 cup 1 1/2 oz/45 g) blanched almonds

1 cup (6 oz/185 g) peeled, seeded, and chopped tomatoes (fresh or canned)

1 clove garlic, minced

2 teaspoons sweet paprika

1/4 teaspoon red pepper flakes

3 tablespoons red wine vinegar

Salt and freshly ground pepper

In a frying pan over medium heat, warm 2 tablespoons of the olive oil. Add the bread and fry, turning once or twice with tongs, until golden on both sides, about 2 minutes. Transfer the bread to a food processor fitted with the metal blade.

Add the almonds to the oil remaining in the frying pan and sauté, stirring, until golden, about 2 minutes. Transfer the almonds to the processor, along with the tomatoes, garlic, paprika, and red pepper flakes. In a small cup, combine the red wine vinegar and the remaining 2 tablespoons olive oil. With the processor motor running, pour in the olive oil mixture in a slow, steady stream. Season to taste with salt and pepper. Pour the sauce into a serving bowl and let stand for 2 hours before serving.

Makes 1 cup (8 fl oz/250 ml)

Spicy Peanut Sauce

2/3 cup (6 oz/185 g) smooth peanut butter

1/4 cup (2 fl oz/60 ml) water

1/2 cup (4 fl oz/125 ml) soy sauce

2 tablespoons Asian sesame oil

2 tablespoons dry sherry

4 teaspoons rice vinegar

1/4 cup (3 oz/90 g) honey

4 cloves garlic, minced

2 teaspoons peeled and minced fresh ginger

1 tablespoon Chile Oil (page 302), or to taste

Combine all of the ingredients in a blender or in a small food processor fitted with the metal blade. Blend or process until well mixed and smooth.

Makes about 1 cup (8 fl oz/250 ml)

Tomato Sauce

You will want to have some of this easy-to-make sauce on hand at all times. It will keep, covered, in the refrigerator for 4 or 5 days. Serve the sauce hot or at room temperature.

2 tablespoons olive oil

1 clove garlic, cut in half

6 plum (Roma) tomatoes, halved lengthwise

1 teaspoon dried oregano

1/2 teaspoon dried mint

Warm the oil in a small sauté pan over medium heat. Add the garlic, tomatoes, oregano, and mint. Cover and cook for 5 minutes.

Uncover and break up the tomatoes with a wooden spoon. Stir to mix well. Re-cover and simmer over low heat for 10 minutes.

Using a wooden spoon, force the tomato mixture through a sieve set over a small bowl. If serving hot, reheat gently.

Makes about 1 cup (8 fl oz/250 ml)

Balsamic and Red Wine Vinegar Dressing

This versatile dressing is delicious with any salad of mixed greens, beans, or legumes. To vary the flavor, use all red wine vinegar or all balsamic vinegar, as you wish. Then taste and adjust with more oil or vinegar, if needed. Be sure to whisk the dressing well just before using.

5 tablespoons (3 fl oz/80 ml) extra-virgin olive oil

1 tablespoon red wine vinegar

1 tablespoon balsamic vinegar

Salt and freshly ground pepper

In a bowl, whisk together the olive oil, red wine vinegar, and balsamic vinegar. Season to taste with salt and pepper.

Makes about 1/2 cup (4 fl oz/125 ml)

Chile Oil

While preparing this oil, do not lean directly over the pan as the oil heats, because the pepper flakes release very pungent fumes that may irritate your eyes. If you like, leave the pepper flakes in the oil; they will make it hotter the longer it stands. The oil keeps indefinitely in a small glass jar with a tight-fitting lid in the refrigerator.

4 tablespoons red pepper flakes

1 cup (8 fl oz/250 ml) peanut, canola, or safflower oil

In a small saucepan over medium heat, combine the pepper flakes and oil. Bring almost to a boil, then turn off the heat and let cool. Strain into a glass container with a lid.

Makes 1 cup (8 fl oz/250 ml)

Garlic Mayonnaise

Just a few tips will make preparing this mayonnaise easier. First, make sure all the ingredients are at room temperature and check that your eggs are fresh and haven't passed their expiration date. Begin by making an emulsion with the egg yolk, mustard, and just 1 tablespoon of the oil, then add the remaining oil very slowly.

1 egg yolk

1 teaspoon Dijon mustard

1/3 cup (3 fl oz/80 ml) olive oil

1/3 cup (3 fl oz/80 ml) safflower oil or peanut oil

Salt and freshly ground pepper

Juice of 1/2 lemon

3 cloves garlic, minced

In a bowl, whisk together the egg yolk, mustard, and about 1 tablespoon of the olive oil until a smooth emulsion forms. Combine the remaining olive oil and the safflower oil in a cup with a spout. Drop by drop, begin adding the oil mixture to the emulsion while whisking constantly. Continue to add the oil in this manner, whisking constantly and increasing the flow into a thin, steady stream as it is incorporated, until the mixture has the consistency of mayonnaise. Season to taste with salt and pepper and the lemon juice. Add the garlic and stir until well mixed.

Makes about 1 cup (8 fl oz/250 ml)

Tahini Mayonnaise

Tahini is a smooth, rich paste ground from sesame seeds and used in Middle Eastern cooking to enrich the flavor and texture of both savory and sweet dishes. It is usually sold in jars or cans in ethnic markets and can also be found in well-stocked food stores.

½ cup Garlic Mayonnaise (page 302)

1 tablespoon tahini

1 teaspoon ground cumin

2 teaspoons warm water

Salt and freshly ground pepper

Place the garlic mayonnaise in a bowl. Adding a little at a time, whisk in the tahini. When all of the tahini has been added, whisk in the cumin, warm water, and salt and pepper to taste.

Makes about 1 cup (8 fl oz/250 ml)

Red Pepper Aioli

1 red bell pepper (capsicum)

4 cloves garlic

1 cup (8 fl oz/250 ml) mayonnaise

Salt and freshly ground white pepper

Pinch of cayenne pepper

Roast and peel the bell pepper (page 308). Remove the seeds and ribs and chop the pepper.

In a blender or food processor fitted with the metal blade, add the garlic and process until puréed. Add the roasted pepper and process until well blended. Add the mayonnaise and process just until mixed. Add salt and white pepper to taste and the cayenne pepper.

Store refrigerated in a tightly covered container for up to 1 week.

Makes about 1¼ cups (10 fl oz/310 ml)

Tomato Salsa

2 tomatoes, peeled, seeded (page 313), and chopped

¼ cup (1½ oz/45 g) minced red onion

½ fresh jalapeño pepper, seeded and minced

1–2 tablespoons fresh lime juice

2 tablespoons chopped fresh cilantro (fresh coriander), plus more if needed

Salt and freshly ground pepper

Stir together the tomatoes, red onion, jalapeño, lime juice, cilantro, and salt and pepper to taste in a bowl.

Makes about 1 cup (8 fl oz/250 ml)

Tomatillo Salsa

2 cans (12 oz/375 g each) tomatillos, drained and chopped

⅓ cup (½ oz/15 g), chopped fresh cilantro (fresh coriander)

¼ cup (1½ oz/45 g) minced red onion

2 tablespoons fresh lime juice

½ fresh jalapeño or serrano chile, seeded and minced

Salt and freshly ground pepper

In a bowl, stir together the tomatillos, cilantro, onion, lime juice, jalapeño, and salt and pepper to taste.

Serves 6

Toasted Bread Crumbs

1 loaf coarse country bread, 1½ lb (750 g), crusts removed

1 teaspoon *each* salt and pepper

½ cup (4 oz/125 g) unsalted butter, melted, or ½ cup (4 oz/125 g) olive oil

Preheat the oven to 350°F (180°C). Break up the bread into chunks and place in a food processor. Using on-off pulses, process until the bread is broken up into coarse crumbs. Spread the crumbs onto a baking sheet. In a small bowl, stir the salt and pepper into the butter or oil. Drizzle over the bread.

Bake, stirring occasionally for even browning, until golden, about 20 minutes. Remove from the oven, let cool, and transfer to a container with a tight-fitting lid. Store at room temperature for up to 2 days.

Makes 1½ cups (6 oz/185 g)

Classic Risotto

If the rice is still firm after all of the liquid has been used up, add hot water and cook until creamy.

6 cups (48 fl oz/1.4 l) Vegetable Stock (page 300)

2 tablespoons unsalted butter

1 yellow onion, chopped

2½ cups (17½ oz/545 g) Arborio rice

⅔ cup (5 fl oz/160 ml) dry white wine

1¾ cups (7 oz/220 g) grated Parmesan cheese

Salt and freshly ground pepper

Pour the stock into a saucepan and bring to a simmer. Adjust the heat to keep the liquid hot.

In a large, heavy saucepan over low heat, melt the butter. Add the onion and sauté until translucent, about 8 minutes. Add the rice and stir until white spots appear in the center of the grains, about 1 minute. Add the wine and stir until absorbed, about 2 minutes.

Add one ladleful of the hot stock, adjust the heat to maintain a gentle simmer, and cook, stirring constantly, until the liquid is absorbed, about 2 minutes.

Continue adding the stock, one ladleful at a time and stirring constantly, until the rice is just tender but slightly firm in the center and the mixture is creamy, 20–25 minutes longer.

Add the cheese and season with salt and pepper. Stir to mix well.

Spoon into warmed shallow bowls or onto plates, or arrange on a warmed platter, and serve at once.

Makes 6 cups (30 oz/940 g)

Cornmeal Dumplings

1 cup (5 oz/155 g) fine-grind cornmeal

2 teaspoons baking powder

¼ teaspoon baking soda (bicarbonate of soda)

½ teaspoon salt

1 egg, beaten

¾ cup (6 fl oz/180 ml) milk

In a bowl, sift together the cornmeal, baking powder, baking soda, and salt. Add the egg and milk and mix with a fork until the cornmeal is absorbed.

Bring the stew to a gentle boil.

To cook the dumplings on top of the stew, dip a large metal spoon into cold water, then scoop out a spoonful of the moist dumpling dough and drop it on top of the stew. Repeat with the remaining dough. Try to have the dumplings rest on something solid in the stew; do not allow them to float in the liquid. If there is too much liquid for the dumplings to rest on solid ingredients, remove as much of the liquid as necessary and return it to the stew before serving. Cover and cook the dumplings over medium heat until a toothpick inserted into the center of a dumpling comes out clean, about 12 minutes.

Makes about 16 dumplings; serves 4

Steamed White Rice

This simply cooked rice is the traditional accompaniment for stir-fries. Its mild taste and whiteness contrast well with the more definite flavors and brighter colors of most stir-fry dishes. Left to cool, the steamed rice can also be used for making fried rice.

1 cup (7 oz/220 g) long-grain white rice

1½ cups (12 fl oz/375 ml) water

Place the rice in a colander and rinse with cold water to remove excess starch. Drain well.

Combine the rice and the water in a saucepan over medium-high heat. Bring to a boil and boil, uncovered, until most of the water evaporates and there are crater-like holes in the surface of the rice, about 10 minutes.

Reduce the heat to low, cover tightly, and simmer until the rice is tender, 10–15 minutes longer. Remove from the heat and let stand, covered, for about 10 minutes before serving.

Just before serving, fluff the rice with a fork, then serve immediately.

Makes about 3 cups (15 oz/470 g); serves 4–6

Pie Pastry

1/2 cup (4 oz/125 g) chilled
unsalted butter or vegetable
shortening (vegetable lard), or
half of each

1 1/2 cups (7 1/2 oz/235 g)
all-purpose (plain) flour

1 tablespoon sugar

1/2 teaspoon salt

3–4 tablespoons cold water

To make the dough by hand, cut the butter and/or shortening into small bits. Combine the flour, sugar, and salt in a bowl. Add the butter and/or shortening. With your fingertips, 2 knives, or a pastry blender, quickly blend the ingredients together until the mixture resembles coarse crumbs. Sprinkle on the water 1 tablespoon at a time, stirring and tossing with a fork after each addition. Add just enough water for the dough to come together in a rough mass.

To make the dough in a food processor, cut the butter and/or shortening into large pieces. Place the flour, sugar, salt, and butter and/or shortening in the work bowl. Process with rapid on-off pulses until the mixture resembles cornmeal; do not overprocess or the pastry will be tough. Add the water, a little at a time, and process until blended; do not let the mixture form a ball. Stop and feel the dough (take care not to touch the blade); it should be just damp enough to mass together. If necessary, add more water by tea-spoonfuls, processing for just an instant after each addition.

To roll out the dough, turn it out onto a lightly floured board. Using floured hands, pat the dough into a smooth cake. Roll out the dough and transfer it to the pan as directed in the recipe. Put the pie shell in the freezer and let it rest for at least 30 minutes before baking.

Makes 12 oz (375 g)

Pizza Dough

Here is an all-purpose pizza dough that complements both traditional and modern pizzas.

1 tablespoon active dry yeast

3/4 cup plus 2 tablespoons
(7 fl oz/210 ml) lukewarm water
(105°F/40°C)

2 3/4 cups (11 oz/360 g)
all-purpose (plain) flour, plus
1/2 cup (2 oz/60 g) for working

1 teaspoon salt

1 tablespoon extra-virgin olive oil

In a small bowl dissolve the yeast in the water and let stand until slightly foamy on top, about 10 minutes.

In a large bowl stir together the 2 3/4 cups (11 oz/360 g) flour and the salt and form into a mound. Make a well in the center and add the yeast mixture to the well. Using a fork and stirring in a circular motion, gradually pull the flour into the yeast mixture. Continue stirring until a dough forms.

Lightly flour a work surface with some of the 1/2 cup (2 oz/60 g) flour and transfer the dough to it. Using the heel of your hand, knead the dough until it is smooth and elastic, about 10 minutes. Form the dough into a ball.

Brush a large bowl with the oil and place the dough in it. Cover with plastic wrap and let rise at room temperature until doubled, 1–2 hours.

Turn the dough out onto a surface dusted with the remaining flour. Punch the dough down and, using your hand, begin to press it out gently into the desired shape. Then, place one hand in the center of the dough and, with the other hand, pull, lift and stretch the dough, gradually working your way all around the edge, until it is the desired thickness, about 1/4 inch (6 mm) thick for a crusty pizza base and 1/2 inch (12 mm) thick for a softer one. Flip the dough over from time to time as you work with it. (Or roll out the dough with a rolling pin.) The dough should be slightly thinner in the middle than at the edge. Lift the edge of the pizza to form a slight rim.

Transfer the dough to a baker's peel or baking sheet, cover with a cotton towel and let rise again until almost doubled, about 20 minutes. Top and bake as directed in the individual recipes

Makes 1 1/4 lb (600 g) dough, enough for a 12-inch (30-cm) thin-crust pizza or a 9-inch (24-cm) thick-crust pizza

CHOOSING & STORING VEGETABLES

Below are simple guidelines for selecting the best-quality ingredients and maintaining them in optimum condition.

Artichokes, leaf vegetables, peas, and beans Refrigerate in open plastic bags for up to 3 days.

Cabbage family Refrigerate cabbages, Brussels sprouts, kohlrabi, cauliflower, bok choy, and broccoli in open paper bags for up to 3 days.

Corn Refrigerate unhusked in open plastic bags for up to 2 days.

Mushrooms Refrigerate in open paper bags for up to 3 days.

Onions Keep dry-skinned onions loose in a cool, dark, dry place for up to several weeks. Refrigerate green (spring) onions and leeks for up to 1 week.

Peas and Beans Refrigerate fresh peas and beans in an open plastic bag for up to 3 days.

Root vegetables Store all kinds of mature potatoes, as well as rutabagas, for up to several weeks in open paper bags in a cool, dark, dry, airy place. Refrigerate new potatoes and Jerusalem artichokes in open plastic bags for up to 3 days; beets, celery root (celeriac), and parsnips for up to 1 week; and carrots and turnips for up to 2 weeks.

Stalks Refrigerate asparagus in an open plastic bag for up to 2 days, and celery and fennel bulbs in an open plastic bag for up to 5 days.

Fruit vegetables and squashes Eat fresh, ripe tomatoes immediately; store underripe tomatoes at a cool room temperature. Refrigerate cucumbers, zucchini (courgettes), bell peppers (capsicums), and eggplants (aubergines) unwrapped for up to several days, and okra in an open plastic bag for the same amount of time. Store hard-shelled squashes at room temperature for up to several weeks.

PREPARING VEGETABLES

1. Chopping an onion
To chop an onion, first trim off its stem and root ends, then cut in half vertically. Peel off the skin. From the stem end, cut thick parallel slices toward but not all the way through the root end. Cut crosswise to chop the onion coarsely.

2. Chopping finely
For a finer chop, gather a pile of coarsely chopped vegetables. Using a chef's knife, steady the knife tip with one hand while rocking the blade and moving it back and forth through the pile.

3. Cutting uniform dice
To dice, first cut into uniform strips; here, a bell pepper (capsicum) has been halved, stemmed, seeded, deribbed, and cut lengthwise into strips ¹/₂ inch (12 mm) wide. Hold the strips together and cut crosswise at the same width.

4. Baking
For baked recipes requiring basting, select a baking dish large enough to allow the juices to collect and be spooned up for drizzling over the vegetables.

5. Boiling vegetable pieces
Bring a saucepan of water to a boil and then add the vegetables—here, carrots. Continue boiling until the vegetables reach the desired degree of doneness.

6. Boiling whole vegetables
Select a pan that will hold the vegetables comfortably. Fill with enough water to cover, then bring to a boil before the vegetables are added.

7. Sautéing in a frying pan
For rapid sautéing, select a wide frying pan with sloping sides that allow moisture to escape rapidly. Heat oil in the pan over medium heat, add the cut-up vegetables, and stir vigorously.

8. Steaming
To assemble a steamer, place a steaming rack inside a saucepan into which it fits snugly. Add water to just below the bottom of the rack, then lay the vegetables on the rack. Cover and bring to a boil until the vegetables are ready. Or use a 2 piece steaming pot made for this purpose.

9. Stir-frying in a wok
A wok has a spherical shape that allows vegetables, to be tossed rapidly for quick cooking. Heat oil in the wok over medium-high heat, add vegetables and use a large spatula or spoon to keep the vegetables in constant motion.

Glossary

Artichoke Also known as globe artichoke. The large flower bud of a type of thistle, grown primarily in the Mediterranean and in California. The tightly packed cluster of tough, pointed, prickly leaves conceals tender, gray-green flesh at the vegetable's center—the heart.

TRIMMING ARTICHOKES

While trimming, dip artichokes repeatedly in a mixture of water and lemon juice to prevent discoloring. First, cut or snap off the artichoke's stem at the base. Cut off the stem and trim off the thorny leaf tops with a serrated knife. Starting at the base, break off the toughest outer leaves, snapping them downward.

For an artichoke heart, continue snapping off leaves until only a cone of them remains. Cut these off to reveal the prickly choke; scrape it out. Pare off the remaining tough green outer skin.

Asparagus At their best in April and May, these bright green, purplish green, or sometimes pale ivory-green spears should be trimmed before cooking. Look for firm, brightly colored spears with tightly furled tips.

Bell Pepper Sweet-fleshed, bell-shaped members of the pepper family, also known as capsicums. Most commonly sold in the unripe green form, although ripened red, yellow, orange, brown, and purple varieties are also available.

To prepare a raw bell pepper, cut it in half lengthwise with a sharp knife. Pull out the stem section from each half, along with the cluster of seeds attached to it. Remove any remaining seeds, along with any thin white membranes, or ribs, to which they are attached. Cut the pepper halves as directed.

ROASTING BELL PEPPERS

Preheat a broiler (grill). Cut the bell peppers lengthwise into quarters, then remove the stems, seeds, and ribs as directed above. Place the pepper quarters, cut side down, on a broiler pan and broil until the skins blister and blacken. Remove from the broiler, cover with aluminum foil, and let stand until the peppers soften and are cool enough to handle, about 10 minutes. Using your fingertips or a small knife, peel off the blackened skins. Then tear or cut the peppers as directed in the recipe.

Bread Crumbs Bread crumbs have many uses, including forming a crunchy golden topping on gratins or adding body or texture to a dish. To make bread crumbs, choose a good-quality, rustic-style loaf made of unbleached wheat flour, with a firm, coarse-textured crumb, usually sold in bakeries as "country-style," "rustic," or "peasant" bread. For fresh bread crumbs, cut away the crusts from the bread and break the bread into coarse chunks. Put them in a food processor fitted with the metal blade or in a blender and process to the desired consistency. For dried crumbs, spread the fresh crumbs on a baking sheet and bake in an oven set at its lowest temperature until they feel very dry, 30–60 minutes; do not let them brown. Store in a tightly covered container at room temperature. Dried bread crumbs, usually fine-textured, are also sold prepackaged in well-stocked markets.

Bulgur Grain made from wheat berries that have been steamed, dried, partially debranned, and cracked into coarse or fine particles that have a nutlike taste and chewy texture.

Butter, Unsalted For the recipes in this book, unsalted butter is preferred. Lacking salt, it allows the cook greater leeway in seasoning recipes to taste.

CLARIFYING BUTTER

Butter is often clarified—that is, its milk solids and water are removed—when it is to be used for cooking at high temperatures or as a sauce. To clarify butter, melt it in a small, heavy saucepan over very low heat; watch carefully to avoid burning. Remove from the heat and let sit briefly. Then,

using a spoon, skim off and discard the foam from the surface. Finally, carefully pour off the clear yellow oil and reserve, discarding, the milky solids and water left behind in the pan. Clarified butter can be refrigerated for up to 1 month or frozen for 2 months.

Celery Root Large, knobby root of a species of celery plant, with a crisp texture and fine flavor closely resembling the stalks. Also known as celeriac.

Cheese For the best selection, buy cheese from a well-stocked food store. The commonly available cheeses called for in this book include:

Cheddar Firm, smooth-textured whole-milk cheese, pale yellow-white to deep yellow-orange. Ranges in taste from mild and sweet when young to rich and sharply tangy when aged.

Feta White cheese made from sheep's or goat's milk, notable for its salty, sharp flavor and crumbly interior.

Goat cheese Most cheeses made from goat's milk are fresh and creamy, with a distinctive sharp tang; they are sold shaped into small rounds or logs.

Gorgonzola Italian creamy, blue-veined cheese. Other creamy blue cheeses may be substituted.

Gouda Firm, rich, yellowish Dutch cheese, with a flavor ranging from mild to strong. Similar to Edam.

Gruyère A type of Swiss cheese with a firm, smooth texture and a strong, tangy flavor.

Monterey jack Semisoft white cheese with a mild flavor and buttery texture.

Mozzarella Rindless white, mild Italian cheese traditionally made from water buffaloes' milk. Look for fresh mozzarella sold immersed in water.

Parmesan Hard, thick-crusted Italian cow's milk cheese with a sharp, salty, full flavor. The finest Italian variety is designated Parmigiano-Reggiano.

Ricotta Light, bland Italian cheese made from twice-cooked milk—traditionally sheep's milk, although cow's milk ricotta is now far more common. Produced from the whey left over from making other cheeses, typically mozzarella and provolone. Freshly made ricotta, available in Italian delicatessens, is particularly prized for its rich flavor and fluffy, creamy texture.

Chickpea Round, tan-colored member of the pea family, with a slightly crunchy texture and nutlike flavor. Also known as garbanzo or ceci beans.

Crème Fraîche French-style lightly soured and thickened fresh cream, generally used as a topping or garnish. Increasingly available in food markets, although a similar product may be prepared at home by stirring 2 teaspoons

well-drained sour cream into 1 cup (8 fl oz/250 ml) lightly whipped heavy (double) cream. Or, to make your own crème fraîche, stir 1 teaspoon cultured buttermilk into 1 cup (8 fl oz/250 ml) heavy (double) cream. Cover tightly and leave at warm room temperature until thickened, about 12 hours. Refrigerate until ready to serve. Will keep for up to 1 week.

Direct-Heat Cooking In grilling, refers to method of quickly cooking individual servings or relatively thin pieces of food by placing them on the grill rack directly above hot coals.

Eggplant A fruit vegetable, also known as aubergine, with tender, sweet, mildly earthy flesh. The shiny skins of eggplants vary in color from purple to red and from yellow to white, and their shapes range from small and oval to long and slender to large and pear shaped. The most common variety is large, purple, and globular; but slender, purple Asian eggplants—smaller, more tender, and with fewer seeds—are available with increasing frequency in food stores and vegetable markets.

Eggs Although eggs are sold in the United States in a range of standard sizes, large eggs are the most common and should be used for the recipes in this book. Some recipes contain raw eggs, which may be infected with salmonella or other harmful bacteria.

The risk of food poisoning is of most concern to small children, older people, pregnant women, or anyone with a compromised immune system. If you have health or safety concerns, do not consume raw eggs. Instead, seek out a pasteurized egg product to replace it.

Fennel Bulb Crisp, refreshing, mildly anise-flavored bulb vegetable, sometimes called by its Italian name, *finocchio*. A related variety is valued for its fine, feathery leaves and stems, which are used as a fresh or dried herb, and for its small, crescent-shaped seeds, dried and used as a spice.

Garlic Pungent bulb popular in cuisines worldwide as a flavoring ingredient, both raw and cooked. For the best flavor, purchase whole heads of dry garlic, separating individual cloves from the head as needed.

To peel a garlic clove, place on a clean work surface and cover with the side of a large chef's knife. Press down firmly on the side of the knife to crush the clove slightly; the dry skin will then slip off easily.

Ginger The rhizome of the tropical ginger plant, which yields a sweet, strong-flavored spice. Whole ginger rhizomes, commonly but mistakenly called roots, can be purchased fresh in food stores or vegetable markets.

Before fresh ginger is sliced or grated, the brown skin is peeled away. The ginger may then be sliced or chopped with a knife, or grated with the fine holes of a grater.

Indirect-Heat Cooking In grilling, refers to method of cooking larger items that would burn if direct-heat cooking were employed. Glowing coals are pushed to the perimeter of the grill's fire pan, and food is placed in center of grill rack and covered to cook more slowly in the radiant heat.

Leek Sweet, moderately flavored member of the onion family, long and cylindrical in shape with a white root end and dark green leaves. Select firm, unblemished leeks, small to medium in size. Grown in sandy soil, the leafy-topped, multi-layered vegetables require thorough cleaning.

TRIMMING LEEKS

Trim off the tough ends of the dark green leaves. Trim off the roots. If a recipe calls for leek whites only, trim off the dark green leaves where they meet the pale green part of the stem. Halve the leek lengthwise three-fourths of the way down to the root end.

Vigorously swish the leek in a basin or sink filled with cold water. Drain and rinse again; check to make sure that no dirt remains between the tightly packed pale portion of the leaves.

Lentils Small, disk-shaped legumes, prized for their rich, earthy flavor when cooked. Unlike most other dried legumes, lentils do not need to be soaked before they are cooked.

Mushrooms With their meaty textures and earthy flavors, mushrooms are used in many vegetarian dishes. Cultivated white and brown mushrooms are the most common. In their smallest form, with their caps still closed, they are often called button mushrooms. Chanterelles are subtly flavored wild mushrooms, usually pale yellow, trumpet-shaped, and 2–3 inches (5–7.5 cm) in diameter with flat, dark brown caps. Porcini, also known by the French term *cèpes*, are popular wild mushrooms with a rich, meaty flavor. Rare, honeycomb-textured morels are highly prized for their flavor and aroma, with the dark brown or black variety considered finer in taste and scent than paler ones. Many wild mushroom varieties are available both fresh or dried.

Mustard, Dijon Dijon mustard is made in Dijon, France, from brown mustard seeds (unless marked *blanc*) and white wine or wine vinegar. Pale in color, fairly hot and sharp tasting, true Dijon mustard and non-French blends labeled Dijon-style are widely available.

Herbs

Fresh and dried herbs alike can be used to bring bright, lively flavor to savory dishes. Those used in this book include:

Basil Sweet, spicy herb popular in Italian and French cooking.

Bay Leaves Leaves from the bay laurel tree that can be purchased fresh or dried. The French variety has a milder flavor than California bay leaves.

Chives Mild, sweet herb with a flavor similar to onion, to which it is related. Although chives are available dried, fresh chives possess the best flavor.

Cilantro Green, leafy herb resembling flat-leaf (Italian) parsley, with a sharp, aromatic, somewhat astringent flavor. Also known as fresh coriander or Chinese parsley.

Dill Fine, feathery leaves with a sweet, aromatic flavor. Use fresh or dried.

Marjoram Pungent, aromatic herb used dried or fresh to season vegetables.

Mint Refreshing herb available in many varieties, with spearmint the most common.

Oregano Aromatic, pungent, and spicy Mediterranean herb—also known as wild marjoram—used fresh or dried as a seasoning for all kinds of savory dishes.

Parsley This widely used fresh herb is available in two varieties: curly leaf and the popular, flat leaf that is also known as Italian parsley.

Rosemary Mediterranean herb, used either fresh or dried, with a strong aromatic flavor. It should be used sparingly, except when grilling.

Sage Pungent herb that can be used either fresh or dried. Sage complements many types vegetables.

Tarragon Fragrant, distinctively sweet herb used fresh or dried.

Thyme Fragrant, clean-tasting, small-leafed herb popular fresh or dried.

CHOPPING FRESH HERBS

Wash the herbs under cold running water and thoroughly shake dry. If the herb has leaves attached along woody stems, pull the leaves from the stems; otherwise hold the stems together. Gather up the leaves into a compact bunch. Using a knife, carefully cut across the bunch to chop the herbs to the desired fineness.

Nuts, Toasting Toasting brings out the full flavor and aroma of nuts. To toast any kind of nut, preheat the oven to 325°F (165°C). Spread the nuts in a single layer on a baking sheet and toast in the oven until they just begin to change color, 5–10 minutes for most nuts or about 3 minutes for pine nuts. Remove from the oven and let cool before using.

Oils Oils are used for cooking and/or to subtly enhance the flavor of recipes. Store all oils in airtight containers away from heat and light. Extra-virgin olive oil, extracted from olives on the first pressing without use of heat or chemicals, is prized for its pure, fruit taste and golden to pale green hue. Products labeled pure olive oil, less aromatic and flavorful, may be used for all-purpose cooking. Flavorless vegetable and seed oils such as safflower and corn oil are employed for their high cooking temperatures and bland flavor.

Okra Small, mild, slender green vegetable pods, about 1 1/2–3 inches (4–7.5 cm) in length, with crisp outer flesh and thick viscous juices when cooked.

Onions All manner of onions are used in vegetarian cooking as featured ingredients or to enhance the flavor of other vegetables. Green onions, also called spring onions or scallions, are harvested immature, leaves and all, before their bulbs have formed. Red onions are a mild, sweet variety of onion with purplish red skin and red-tinged white flesh. White-skinned, white-fleshed onions tend to be sweet and mild. Yellow onions are a common, white-fleshed, strong-flavored variety distinguished by their dry, yellowish brown skins. Small but pungent pearl onions about 3/4 inch (2 cm) in diameter, also known as pickling onions, are sometimes added whole as an ingredient in vegetable stews and braises.

Parsnip Root vegetable similar in shape and texture to the carrot, but with ivory flesh and an appealingly sweet flavor.

Polenta Italian term for specially ground coarse cornmeal and for the dish that results from its cooking. The latter may be enriched with butter, cream, cheese, or eggs. When cold, it has a consistency firm enough for it to be sliced and grilled or fried.

Potatoes Although potato varieties and the names that they go by vary from region to region, some common ones include:

New Potatoes Refers to any variety of potato harvested in early summer when small and immature, resulting in sweeter, more tender flesh best appreciated steamed, boiled, or roasted. Red-skinned new potatoes are the most common variety found in the market.

Red Potatoes Crisp, waxy, white-fleshed potato with thin red skin. Ideal for steaming, boiling, and roasting.

Russet Potatoes Large baking potatoes with thick brown skins that have a dry, mealy texture when cooked. Also known as Idaho potatoes.

White Potatoes Generally medium-sized potatoes with thin tan skins, whose texture when cooked—finer than baking potatoes but coarser than waxy yellow varieties—makes them a good all-purpose choice.

Yellow Potatoes Any of a variety of thin-skinned potatoes with yellow-tinged, waxy flesh well suited to steaming, boiling, roasting, or sautéing.

Rice, Arborio Popular Italian variety of rice with short, round grains high in starch content, which creates a creamy, saucelike consistency during cooking. Available in Italian delicatessens and well-stocked food stores.

Rutabaga Root vegetable resembling a large turnip, with sweet, pale yellow-orange flesh. Also known as swede or Swedish turnip.

Shallot Small member of the onion family with brown skin, white-to-purple flesh, and a flavor resembling a cross between sweet onion and garlic.

Spinach Choose smaller, more tender spinach leaves if possible. Be sure to wash thoroughly to eliminate all dirt and sand: Put the spinach leaves in a sink or large basin and fill with cold water to cover them thoroughly. Agitate the leaves in the water to remove their dirt, then lift the leaves out of the water and set aside. Drain the sink or basin thoroughly and rinse out all dirt and sand. Repeat the procedure until no grit remains.

Squashes Native to the Americas, squashes are divided into two main types: thin-skinned summer squashes, such as zucchini (courgettes) and pattypan, and hard, tough-skinned winter squashes, such as acorn, butternut, and pumpkin. The tender flesh of summer squashes cooks more quickly than the firm, sweet flesh of winter varieties.

PREPARING WINTER SQUASHES

Use a heavy, sharp kitchen knife to cut open the squash; if its skin is very hard, use a kitchen mallet to tap the knife carefully once it is securely wedged in the squash. Using a sharp-edged spoon, scrape out all seeds and fibers.

Tahini Smooth, rich paste ground from sesame seeds and used in Middle Eastern cooking to enrich the flavor and texture of both savory and sweet dishes. Jars and cans of tahini can be found in ethnic markets and well-stocked food stores.

Tomatillos The green tomatillo resembles, but is not related to, the tomato. Fresh tomatillos usually come encased in brown papery husks, which are peeled off before use. Canned tomatillos can be found in well-stocked and Latino markets.

Tomatoes During summer, when tomatoes are in season, use the best sun-ripened tomatoes you can find. At other times of the year, plum tomatoes, sometimes called Roma tomatoes, are likely to have the best flavor and texture; canned whole or crushed plum tomatoes are also good.

To peel fresh tomatoes, bring a saucepan of water to a boil. Using a small, sharp knife, cut out the core from the stem end of the tomato. Then cut a shallow X in the skin at the tomato's base. Submerge for about 20 seconds in the boiling water, then remove and cool in a bowl of cold water. Slip the skin from the tomato and discard. Cut the tomato in half and turn each half cut side down. Cut as directed in individual recipes. To seed a tomato, cut it in half crosswise; squeeze gently to force out the seed sacs.

Spices

Allspice Sweet spice of Caribbean origin with a flavor suggesting a blend of cinnamon, cloves, and nutmeg.

Cayenne Pepper Ground spice derived from dried cayenne chile peppers.

Chili Powder Commercial blend of spices featuring ground dried chile peppers along with such other seasonings as cumin, oregano, cloves, coriander, pepper, and salt. Best purchased in small quantities, as flavor diminishes rapidly after opening.

Cloves Rich and aromatic East African spice used whole or in its ground form to flavor both savory and sweet recipes.

Cumin Middle Eastern spice with a strong, dusky, aromatic flavor, popular in cuisines of its region of origin along with those of Latin America, India, and parts of Europe. Sold either ground or as whole, small, crescent-shaped seeds.

Curry Powder Generic term for blends of spices commonly used to flavor East Indian–style dishes. Most curry powders include coriander, cumin, ground chile, fenugreek, and turmeric; among other additions are cardamom, cinnamon, cloves, allspice, fennel seeds, and ginger.

Nutmeg Popular baking spice that is the hard pit of the fruit of the nutmeg tree. May be bought already ground or whole for fresher flavor. Whole nutmegs may be kept inside special nutmeg graters,

which include hinged flaps that conceal a storage compartment.

Freshly grate nutmegs as needed, steadying one end of grater on a work surface. Return the unused portion of whole nutmeg to the storage compartment.

Paprika Powdered spice derived from the dried paprika pepper; popular in several European cuisines and available in sweet, mild, and hot forms. Hungarian paprika has the best flavor, but Spanish paprika, which is mild, may also be used. Buy in small quantities from shops with a high turnover, to ensure a fresh, flavorful supply.

Pepper Pepper, the most common of all savory spices, is best purchased as whole peppercorns, to be ground in a pepper mill as needed or coarsely crushed. Pungent black peppercorns derive from slightly underripe pepper berries, whose hulls oxidize as they dry. Milder white peppercorns come from fully ripened berries, with the husks removed before drying.

Red Pepper Flakes Coarsely ground flakes of dried red chiles, including seeds, which add moderately hot flavor to the foods they season.

Saffron Intensely aromatic, golden orange spice made from the dried stigmas of a species of crocus flower; used to perfume and color many classic Mediterranean and East Indian dishes. Sold either as threads—the dried stigmas—or in powdered form. Look for products labeled "pure" saffron.

Turmeric Pungent, earthy-flavored ground spice that, like saffron, adds a vibrant yellow color to any dish.

Index

First published in the USA by Time-Life Custom Publishing.

Originally published as Williams-Sonoma Kitchen Library:
Grilling, Pasta (© 1992 Weldon Owen Inc.)
*Mexican Favorites, Pizza, Potatoes, Salads, Thanksgiving &
Christmas, Vegetables* (© 1993 Weldon Owen Inc.)
Beans & Rice, Stir-Fry (© 1994 Weldon Owen Inc.)
Stews (© 1995 Weldon Owen Inc.)
Cooking Basics, Vegetarian (© 1996 Weldon Owen Inc.)
*Breakfasts & Brunches, Healthy Cooking, Mediterranean Cooking,
Outdoor Cooking, Thanksgiving* (© 1997 Weldon Owen Inc.)
Casual Entertaining, Festive Entertaining, Risotto
(© 1998 Weldon Owen Inc.)

In collaboration with Williams-Sonoma Inc.
3250 Van Ness Avenue, San Francisco, CA 94109

Oxmoor
House.

OXMOOR HOUSE INC.

Oxmoor House books are distributed by Sunset Books
80 Willow Road, Menlo Park, CA 94025
Telephone: 650-321-3600 Fax 650-324-1532
Vice President/General Manager: Rich Smeby
National Accounts Manager/Special Sales: Brad Moses

Oxmoor House and Sunset Books are divisions of
Southern Progress Corporation

WILLIAMS-SONOMA
Founder and Vice-Chairman: Chuck Williams

Chief Executive Officer: John Owen
President and Chief Operating Officer: Terry Newell
Creative Director: Gaye Allen
Publisher: Hannah Rahill
Art Director: Nicky Collings
Associate Editor: Donita Boles
Editorial Assistant: Juli Vendzules
Production Director: Chris Hemesath
Co-edition and Reprint Coordinator: Todd Rechner
Color Manager: Teri Bell

Williams-Sonoma Vegetarian was conceived and
produced by Weldon Owen Inc.
814 Montgomery Street, San Francisco, CA 94133
Copyright © 2005 Weldon Owen Inc.
and Williams-Sonoma Inc.

First printed in 2005.
10 9 8 7 6 5 4 3 2 1

ISBN 0-8487-3057-7

Printed in China by SNP Leefung Printers Ltd.

CREDITS
Authors: Lora Brody: Pages 209, 222, 225, 260, 268, 304 (Cornmeal
Dumplings); John Phillip Carroll: Pages 17, 19, 21, 81, 188, 192,
193, 196, 197, 198, 203, 233, 251; Emalee Chapman: Pages 77, 78,
92, 96, 103, 120, 126, 128, 129, 130, 133, 137, 138, 141, 144, 150,
153, 155, 156, 163, 164, 168, 171, 173, 174, 181, 201, 286, 288, 289,
300 (Bèchamel Sauce), 301 (Caper Sauce), 302 (Tomato Sauce);
Lorenza De' Medici: Pages 167, 230, 234, 235, 238, 239, 305 (Pizza
Dough); Joyce Goldstein: Pages 16, 30, 35, 39, 59, 61, 66, 86, 134,
160, 166, 187, 226, 301 (Harissa Sauce), 305 (Pie Pastry); Kristine
Kidd: Pages: 38, 90, 95, 256, 259, 304 (Classic Risotto); Norman
Kolpas: Page 253; Jacqueline Mallorca: Pages 93, 145, 242, 255,
281, 283, 296; Susanna Palazuelos: Pages 14, 147, 213, 218, 278,
292, 303 (Tomato Salsa); Emanuela S. Prinetti: Page 31; Dianne
Rossen Worthington: Pages 26, 29, 98, 99, 101, 102, 107, 111, 112,
114, 115, 117, 118, 119, 122, 123, 139, 172, 177, 178, 180, 183, 184,
189, 190, 247, 271, 274, 297, 300 (All-Purpose Stir Fry Sauce), 301
(Pesto Sauce), 302 (Spicy Peanut Sauce, Chile Oil), 303 (Red
Pepper Aioli), 304 (Steamed White Rice); Joanne Weir: Pages 20,
22, 25, 32, 37, 40, 43, 44, 45, 46, 48, 49, 50, 53, 56, 60, 63, 64, 68, 69,
71, 72, 75, 76, 82, 85, 104, 108, 142, 159, 195, 202, 206, 210, 214,
215, 217, 221, 227, 236, 241, 244, 245, 248, 252, 261, 263, 264, 267,
272, 275, 282, 285, 291, 293, 294, 299, 300 (Vegetable Stock), 301
(Romesco Sauce), 302 (Balsamic and Red Wine Vinegar Dressing,
Garlic Mayonnaise), 303 (Tahini Mayonnaise, Tomatillo Salsa);
Chuck Williams: Pages 34, 65.

Photographers: Paul Moore (front cover), Allan Rosenberg (recipe
photography), and Chris Shorten (recipe photography for pages
93, 145, 243, 254, 279, 282, and 296).

ACKNOWLEDGEMENTS
Weldon Owen would like to thank Carrie Bradley, Ken
DellaPenta, Elizabet Der Nederlanden, George Dolese, Arin
Hailey, Karen Kemp, Norman Kolpas, Lisa Milestone, and Bonnie
Monte for all their expertise, assistance, and hard work.

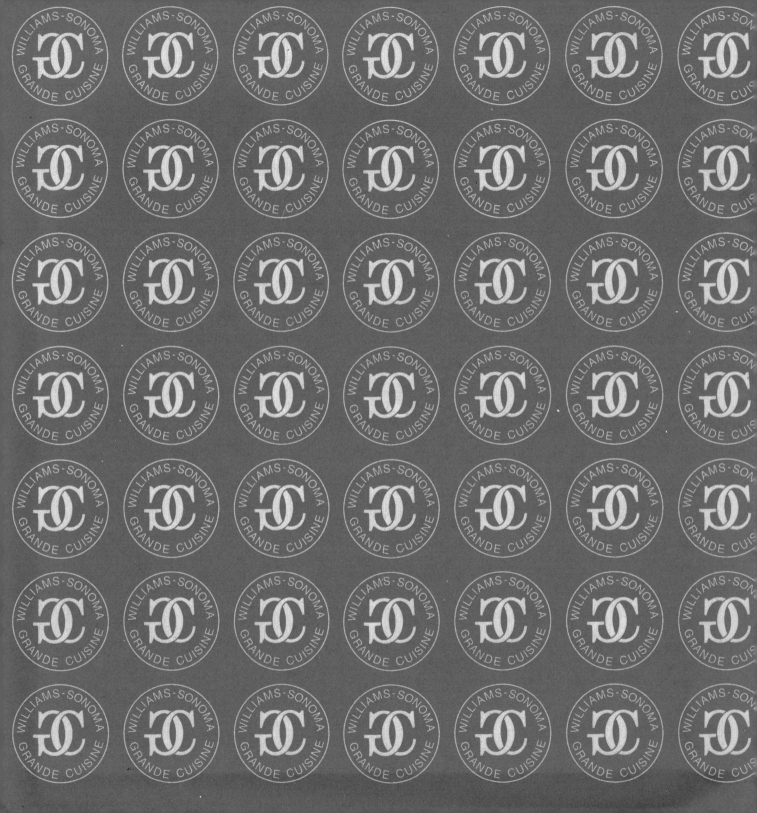